Devil's Music, Holy Rollei
and Hillbillies

Devil's Music, Holy Rollers and Hillbillies

How America Gave Birth to Rock and Roll

JAMES A. COSBY

McFarland & Company, Inc., Publishers
Jefferson, North Carolina

Library of Congress Cataloguing-in-Publication Data

Names: Cosby, James A.
Title: Devil's music, holy rollers and hillbillies : how America gave birth to rock and roll / James A. Cosby.
Description: Jefferson, North Carolina : McFarland & Company, 2016 | Includes bibliographical references and index.
Identifiers: LCCN 2016019908 | ISBN 9781476662299 (softcover : acid free paper) ♾
Subjects: LCSH: Popular music—Social aspects—United States—History—20th century. | Popular music—United States—1951–1960—History and criticism. | Rock music—United States—1951–1960—History and criticism.
Classification: LCC ML3917.U6 C67 2016 | DDC 781.660973—dc23
LC record available at https://lccn.loc.gov/2016019908

British Library cataloguing data are available

ISBN (print) 978-1-4766-6229-9
ISBN (ebook) 978-1-4766-2538-6

© 2016 James A. Cosby. All rights reserved

No part of this book may be reproduced or transmitted in any form or by any means, electronic or mechanical, including photocopying or recording, or by any information storage and retrieval system, without permission in writing from the publisher.

Front cover: (top to bottom) Bessie Smith, 1936 photograph by Carl Van Vechten (Library of Congress); Snake handlers at Pentecostal Church of God, Lejunior, Kentucky, September 15, 1946, photograph by Russell Lee (National Archives and Records Administration); Publicity photograph of Hank Williams (MGM Records)

Printed in the United States of America

McFarland & Company, Inc., Publishers
Box 611, Jefferson, North Carolina 28640
www.mcfarlandpub.com

To all of those African Americans who have
come through the Delta with song and spirit.
And also to the Kent Bangers.

Table of Contents

Acknowledgments

I would like to thank those who read drafts of this book and provided invaluable feedback: Emily Bilodeau, John Stone, Claire Good, Gerald Good, Cort Hodge and Dr. John McCafferty.

Preface

I was first introduced to the Beatles' catalog when I was about four or five years old. I could not believe how good they sounded or how much fun they were obviously having. I still believe that the Beatles, like all great artists, had tapped into something far bigger than the four of them.

I later came to find out that parents did not necessarily love this rock and roll stuff like I did. Some even hated it. In fact, it turns out that when rock and roll first came out, "the Establishment" seriously saw it as an evil—the Devil's music, even.

I eventually saw a glimpse of the "Devil" in rock myself. The rock and roll attitude and attendant lifestyle became synonymous with extreme rebellion and hedonism; as just one of so many examples, the lead singer of the rock band AC/DC, Bon Scott, was jokingly singing about a "Highway to Hell" (1979)—the title song of the first album I ever bought—which he and his friends were taking en route to good times and a huge party. A few months after that particular record was released, however, the thirty-three-year-old Scott suffered an alcohol-induced death.

In pondering this rock music stuff, I had to ask myself: When is rebellion positive, and when does it cross into self-destruction? When is structure and stability a good thing, and when is cutting loose required? In short, how does one reconcile "the Devil's music" with "I Want to Hold Your Hand"? For that matter, what *is* this rock and roll music?

Years later, I started to look back toward the origins of this amazing music that had come to mean so much to me. Where did it even come from? What was the first rock and roll song? What other songs existed right before the first rock record? How about Elvis—was he really a cultural thief? What is the evidence either way? How do I not know the answers to such basic questions?

As I began to dig into these questions, not only did I find some amazing answers, but I also found some more great questions. So who is Dewey Phillips? How does Ike Turner fit into this? And B.B. King? What is the truth of the near-mythic Elvis and the full-blown myth of Delta blues legend Robert Johnson? What is the relationship of the blues and rock? How did the blues come out of slavery? What is this fantastic connection between Pentecostalism and the formation of rock and roll? And Sister Rosetta Tharpe! Hillbillies and cowboys. Teens in the 1950s. Sex and nuclear Armageddon. Madison Avenue (and the true story of Marlboro cigarettes—it's relevant, trust me). U.B. Phillips. Jimmie Rodgers. And on and on.

A lot has been written about rock and roll, of course; there are maybe a dozen outstanding books that served just as the starting point and the foundation for this one, including *Dewey and Elvis, Shout Sister Shout, The Land Where the Blues Began, It Came from Memphis, Blues People, Mystery Train, Race, Rock and Elvis, Last Train to Memphis*, and others. I also took a couple of trips to rock's launching pad, Memphis and the Delta, to look around and get the feel of that region. I do not think that anyone has ever tied all of these amazing loose ends together, connected all of the dots, in a way that truly explains how rock and roll came to be or what it even is. It seemed to me that there is a whole slew of overlooked and misunderstood anecdotes each of which says a whole lot about the history of America, Western culture, and, well, the human condition.

As a long-time rock fan, a history buff, and a music writer, I was sure that if all of the above was completely new to me, it would likely be new to a lot of other people, too. This is essentially the book I wanted to read, and considering the incredible impact and popularity of rock and roll music, I hope and believe that others will be interested, too. It is a great history and one that everyone should fully understand.

Introduction: Rock in the Free World

"I do believe the music of the Beatles taught the young people of the Soviet Union that there is another life."[1]

—Mikhail Gorbachev

"By and large the literature of a democracy will never exhibit the order, regularity, skill, and art characteristic of aristocratic literature; formal qualities will be neglected or actually despised. The style will often be strange, incorrect, overburdened, and loose, and almost always strong and bold."[2]

—Alexis de Tocqueville

Today most are not old enough to remember just what a threat rock and roll was to America's traditional institutions and social mores when it broke loose in the mid–1950s. In fact, while rock music has since become a revered social institution in its own right, few of us even know how it actually came to be. Today rock is so accepted and ubiquitous, it almost seems to have just always been around, or perhaps as if the history of rock music begins with Elvis Presley, malt shops, and sock hops.

Currently even the pioneers of punk rock, those lovable fringe degenerates, the Ramones, for example, are a regular part of the soundtrack to otherwise wholesome family entertainment, such as major league baseball games. What used to be your grandfather's stuffy, luxury sedan, the Cadillac, is now sold to the heavy riffing of the heroin-using, occult-dabbling rockers known as Led Zeppelin. While rock and roll was first labeled "the Devil's music" (as had its predecessor, the blues), even the Vatican has since come around. A 2008 article in the papacy's official newspaper, *Osservatore Romano*, actually made positive references to rock's two biggest acts: Elvis Presley and the Beatles.[3]

From its beginning, rock music has inspired and given a voice to a youth movement that has since shaped much of current world culture. Rock came about at a time when America's institutions were largely failing to provide an outlet for the anxiety, fear, and confusion of life in a modern age that was changing much too fast. In mid-1950s America, conformity had become a prized national ideal, and many uncomfortable social topics were being avoided. The rock revolution presented pointed alternatives and outlets not only in music but in lifestyle and attitude. When the U.S. Supreme Court's 1954 decision to end segregation in *Brown v. Board of Education* was being rejected throughout the Southern states, for example, both performers and fans of rock music were coming together across racial lines like never before. When the topic of sex was scarcely acknowledged in public, rock and roll boldly pushed sexual boundaries on the most public stages imaginable. In short, rock music announced to "the Establishment" that the youth of America would not and, in fact, *could not* be controlled. Indeed, if the U.S. government of the late 1950s could have eradicated rock music, it would have.

So what happened? Is the ultimate, broad societal acceptance of rock and roll a victory of individual freedoms and expression, or a sign of a nation's steep moral decline? Did rock and roll upend American culture, or was America already unraveling? The purpose of this book is to get to the heart, soul, and spirit of the rock music, beyond what has yet been formulated. What exactly is rock and roll? Why did it happen? How did it happen? What does it really say about America? There is a wealth of overlooked and misunderstood anecdotes to unravel, myths to debunk, and dots to connect. For various reasons, I would submit that the bigger picture of the origins of rock and roll has often been reduced to a cleaner and tidier one that has not fully captured this phenomenon.

Yet how rock and roll came to be really is at the core of American history itself. Indeed, it was none other than Confucius who once said, "To understand the music people make … you will understand how they are governed."[4] Nothing better proves Confucius' point than the chronicle of America and rock music.

First, this book will spend two full chapters (chapters 2 and 3), and more, fully fleshing out the social, cultural, and even emotional context of rock's inception in early and mid-1950s America. These are mostly non-music chapters, but essential for setting this stage and obtaining a full appreciation of rock music.

The narrative will then jump back to the early African American music of the South, including the music first forged in the "peculiar institution" of slavery, so as to identify the seeds of rock and roll. From there, some key and often ignored cultural vignettes will help uncover and identify the spirit of rebellion, the freedom, and the sacred-secular tensions that have long defined not only rock and roll but also the American experience itself. These dynamics are then traced up through life in the Mississippi Delta and the blues and gospel music of the Jim Crow era, in addition to tracing a parallel track of hillbilly music. A *lot* is covered, but each piece is crucial.

The second half of this book focuses on the musical melting pot of Memphis circa 1950, the collision of race and musical styles, an extended examination of Presley's legacy, and finally concluding at the end of the first wave of rock and roll (circa 1960). Together these anecdotes will illustrate how those who have often been the most disenfranchised persons of a free and prosperous nation strove to find their voices, and themselves, and how they managed to make history in the process. It is an important history that needs to be better understood. Besides, any account of the Devil's music, holy rollers, and hillbillies cannot help but be thoroughly entertaining.

* * *

So what are some of these gaps in the history of rock and roll in America? Here are a few examples: Some are familiar with the decades-old myth of blues legend Robert Johnson, one of rock's greatest influences and long notorious for a supposed "deal with the Devil" that gave him legendary musical prowess. However, that supernatural myth has obscured the facts. Johnson was a very real black man who lived deep in the often brutal Mississippi Delta region during the first half of the twentieth century. The actual facts of Johnson's life have only begun to be extensively written about since the mid-2000s, and yet these facts still take a backseat to the myth.

In many ways the continued prevalence of that myth and a lack of knowledge of Johnson's life are symbolic of a lack of understanding of the black experience, as well as those social factors that informed the blues, and thus rock and roll. Johnson's and others' very personal experiences, struggles, and music, all illustrate the history of the most emotionally immediate and visceral music ever known: the blues. What will also be demonstrated is how all of this *directly* led to rock music.

Another example is Elvis Presley, arguably the biggest celebrity of all time. Presley's name, image, and music have all but saturated the globe. Yet somehow few know of his real life or of his rise to fame. In other words, few know how exactly Mr. Presley became *Elvis*. Was Presley a profoundly original artist? Did he invent rock and roll (and if not, who did)? Or was Presley simply a cultural thief, putting a profitable white face on black music and style? For that matter, was Presley *racist*, an old claim that continues to pop up today? Few know much about Presley aside from the now standard mocking of a former icon who badly lost his way in his later years, or the equally false deifications of Presley, too often done with little appreciation for his black influences or the social context of his life.

Even most life-long rock fans do not know the answers to the above questions. As a result, views of the Presley legacy have distorted history and, in many ways, served as a Rorschach test for America and observers of American culture. Here the facts and true significance of Presley's life will be put into their proper context.

As a final example, maybe the most overlooked, yet most fascinating, aspect of the rock music story lies in its spiritual core. It is widely understood that rock music came directly from the blues and from country music, yet rock is far more than a simple fusion of these genres. Rock and roll has been called a religion, and it most certainly has some spiritual components.[5]

It is surprising to learn how much impact Christian hymns and gospel music have had on rock, and these roots will be discussed. For example, Presley and Bob Dylan both recorded straight gospel albums, to say nothing of gospel crossover superstar Aretha Franklin, and gospel music provided the template for some of rock's biggest hits, such as the Beatles' "Let It Be" or U2's "Still Haven't Found What I'm Looking For." But what is *really* stunning is the impact of the so-called holy rollers of the Pentecostal church. The Pentecostal church is directly responsible for rock and roll achieving some of its greatest highs, though it has rarely been credited for doing so. And this makes it a great jumping-off point.

* * *

Consider that any short list of the mid–1950s pioneers of rock and roll who best exemplified the aggressive, and at times *unhinged*, approach to making this music, the most fun and most dangerous of performers, without question includes Elvis Presley, Jerry Lee Lewis, and Little Richard. Along with his talent, ambition, and, yes, skin color, Presley's brazen sexuality and swagger were enough to spark the worldwide rock and roll phenomenon. Lewis was nicknamed "The Killer" for a reason, and his wild live shows were essentially sexualized, proto-punk rock, with Lewis pounding out a beat on his piano, kicking his chair across the stage, and stomping on the piano keys with his feet, body, whatever. Richard bridged the spiritual ecstasy of the black church with the orgasmic highs of the secular world, put it all to music, and unleashed the most musical screams ever heard.

So, aside from being three of rock's most crucial pioneers, what else do these men have in common? Each was raised, and had his musical life formed, in the Pentecostal churches of the South. Thus the Pentecostal church is arguably at the heart and soul of this whole history.

The Pentecostals were given the pejorative nickname "holy rollers" due to parishioners being "slain in the Spirit," literally writhing and "rolling" in the church aisles, as well as "speaking in tongues" (*glossolalia*) and otherwise having wildly emotional services. All of this activity is fueled by an equally wild and emotional music, atypical religious instrumentation, and open-throated singing. In fact, the background of modern Pentecostalism (explored in depth later in this book), which effectively began in 1906 in Los Angeles, is oddly familiar: integration well before integration's wider social acceptance; practitioners speaking in a manner that made no sense to outsiders; and wildly emotive services fueled by equally frenetic music. The movement was so over the top, in fact, that observers truly thought its participants had gone mad.[6] (Ring any bells?)

There is one special performer most responsible for linking the "reeling and rocking" of the Pentecostal church to rock and roll: Sister Rosetta Tharpe. Tharpe is still largely unknown, though she was a very popular 1940s gospel/R&B crossover star. Viewing Tharpe's performances on YouTube today is a bit jarring. One video, a performance of "Up Above My Head," is black-and-white footage of a then-forty-seven-year-old black woman playing an electric guitar.[7]

The footage is actually from a television show broadcast in 1962, but the black-and-white stock and the conservative dress make it seem much older. Tharpe looks like she could be a younger grandmother in her conservative, ankle-length church dress. Everything about the footage is both confusing and electrifying at the same time. The set is made to look like a church, presumably in the South, and Tharpe is backed by some one hundred hand-clapping African American choir members in white robes. Tharpe is not simply singing the gospel—she is *rocking* the gospel. When she gets to her guitar solo, she effortlessly tears it up. Her singing is confident, joyous, and, as her biographer put it, both "fierce and smooth."[8] Tharpe is so enthralled that at one point she does a small windmill motion with her right hand, similar to the move that guitarist Pete Townsend of the Who later made his signature.

For whatever reason, it is rare enough to see a black woman on an electric guitar, but an anonymous black woman *shredding* one in a church back in the *olden days*? It almost comes across as a *Forrest Gump*–inspired special effect.

Tharpe's music did change somewhat after the onset of the rock revolution, but not her basic style. "Up Above My Head," for example, was first recorded in 1947. The guitar picking of the original version has a bit more of a country feel—Tharpe was in fact an extremely rare black performer on the Grand Ole Opry show itself in 1949—but it is the same bouncing tempos and guitar, and the same huge vocals. As will be seen, Tharpe is perhaps the linchpin to the whole rock and roll narrative.

Tharpe experienced considerable commercial success in the 1940s, but when the rock revolution came it was divided on generational grounds. Rock's troops were teenagers, and these troops were looking for one of their own to lead the way—not a forty-year-old with strong ties to the church (and perhaps not, at least initially, a woman or a black woman). Thus, sadly, Tharpe's name and music have largely faded and, even more oddly, her name scarcely resurfaced for decades. When Tharpe died in Philadelphia in 1973, her husband did not pay for a headstone. Thus Tharpe's grave remained unmarked until a benefit concert in 2008, when the Commonwealth of Pennsylvania proclaimed "Sister Rosetta Tharpe Day" and finally corrected the omission.[9] In 2007, Tharpe was the subject of an overdue biography by Gayle Wald, and, in 2013, PBS's *American Masters* documentary series produced a segment on Tharpe. Still, relatively few Americans have any idea who Tharpe is.

Having said all of that, those on whom Tharpe's music was *never* lost were those first giants of rock and roll. Just how crucial was the overlooked Tharpe? She was both Little Richard's and Johnny Cash's all-time favorite singer.[10] Richard has recalled that the defining moment of his life was the day as a child that he was introduced to his hero; before one of Tharpe's concerts, he sang for her, and Tharpe later brought Richard onstage to sing with her during the show.[11]

Tharpe also had devoted fans in deejay Dewey Phillips[12] and Sun Records founder Sam Phillips (no relation), along with the Sun rockabilly superstars, including Cash, Presley, Lewis, and Carl Perkins.[13] Tharpe's hit "Strange Things (Are Happening Every Day)" (1944) was the song Perkins learned the guitar on, as well as the all-time favorite of Perkins' father.[14] Referring to "Strange Things," Perkins said, "It was rockabilly, that was it—it was."[15] Lewis sang a Tharpe song as part of his first audition for Sam Phillips. After seeing Tharpe perform live in 1957, Lewis commented, "I said, 'Say, man, there's a woman that can sing some rock and roll.' I mean, she's singing religious music, but she is singing rock and roll. She's … shakin', man.… She jumps it. She's hitting that guitar, playing that guitar and she is *singing*. I said, 'Whoooo.' Sister Rosetta Tharpe."[16] Respected rockabilly performer Sleepy Labeef likewise swears that Lewis' piano style is directly patterned on Tharpe's guitar work.[17]

Both rock and Pentecostalism offered responses to restrictive, traditional practices: Pentecostalism was seen as an antidote to rigid, text-driven fundamentalist practices, while rock was bucking an oppressive life as a "square" stuck in a "rat race." Writing of Pentecostalism, Harvey Cox described the experience of the Holy Spirit, or "charismatic" experience, as "so total it shatters the cognitive packaging."[18] As one rock musician similarly described rock and roll's initial explosion in popularity, it was a "global psychic jailbreak."[19] Like rock music, Pentecostalism tapped into something: a *Holy* Spirit—or *human* spirit? Whatever it is, it runs deep. Together this rock–Pentecostal connection and the parallels between these two phenomena really speak to the sacred-secular tensions that run throughout America's history, and they are examined later in this book.

* * *

Rock music's first (and current) critics dismissed it as "primitive" and "jungle" music (a term often used as a racist dig), made by and for society's most vulgar members.[20] Yet rock's detractors have gotten it wrong—well, *mostly* wrong. As a general philosophy of life, it is true that rock and roll has not provided all of life's answers. Still, rock and roll has proven meaningful and profound in its own way. As partly evidenced by the Gorbachev quote that begins this introduction, it is hard to even measure the true, worldwide impact of rock music beyond record sales figures except to otherwise say that its impact has been enormous.

Primitive does mean "crude," but it also means "belonging to or characteristic of an early stage of development," a definition that more accurately speaks to the role that rock and roll played in the lives of 1950s American teenagers and others.[21] Facing a faster-paced and often impersonal work life, the "Red Scare," and the specter of nuclear Armageddon, many Americans found themselves unable to deal with the most *basic* and, yes, *primitive* feelings of fear, anxiety, or in lacking joy. And when such feelings are not dealt with somehow, one's quality of life suffers drastically, despite material prosperity, military superiority, or anything else.

And this is not just the view of some crazy 1950s rock and rollers, either. One illustration (*prior* to rock and roll's commercial explosion) came when U.S. president Dwight D. Eisenhower described precisely the above dynamic in his 1954 State of the Union address, noting "how far the advances of science have outraced our social consciousness, how much more we have developed scientifically than we are capable of handling emotionally and intellectually."[22] In other words, many Americans of the mid–1950s were incredibly anxious, afraid, and searching for meaning and direction in life, and no one really knew what to do about it. People were cut off from primal, core feelings, and they were emotionally disconnected from a sense of joy, spontaneity, creativity, and, in short, their *spirit*. People were jammed up with no apparent outlets.

Thankfully, in the American democracy, even the most disenfranchised and marginalized members of society may find their voice. The raw spontaneity and lack of limits in rock and roll would lead to certain significant problems, and they are addressed in this book as well, but early rock music allowed massive numbers of people to get in touch with basic emotions and to connect with one another on deep, personal levels. That is quite a feat.

Rock and roll's impact on the world continues to reverberate. Even the Vatican has had to give rock its due. The history of rock and roll has come to be a special piece of American history that has perhaps yet to be fully understood and appreciated. The rest of this book is an attempt to increase our understanding and appreciation of it.

1

"What Is Wrong with Us?"

Music is never created in a vacuum. The emotional, cultural, political and economic state of 1950s America was primed for a raw and rebellious musical format. The post-war years of top-down corporate structuring, the twin fears of communist infiltration and nuclear annihilation, and widespread comfort and affluence had all resulted in an enormous premium being placed on conformity. One can start with a look at the state of American popular music at that time to appreciate what this all meant.

Post-war radio in the U.S. was largely bland and homogenous. An efficient, corporate cookie-cutter programming model dominated the nation's radio industry. This meant that regional affiliates across the nation were all dominated by national network programs of the same top-40 songs and, in between those hits, commentary and news delivered by buttoned-up, overly polished, staid broadcasters. Local affiliates were limited to producing station breaks and local news reports. Worst of all, the songs topping the charts at the time included such painfully safe songs like Dinah Shore's "Buttons and Bows," Perry Como with "'A' You're Adorable" ("'c' is for cutie"), "The Woody Woodpecker Song," and, most infamous of all, Patti Page's "How Much Is That Little Doggie in the Window?" As music writer Robert Palmer summarized, "The heyday of Tin Pan Alley, when songwriters like Irving Berlin, George and Ira Gershwin, and Cole Porter had ruled the roost, was long gone; for the most part, fifties pop was treacle."[1]

Yet one could also ask: Why *not* play it safe? At this time, America was growing into its role as *the* world's leader. A faith in democracy, individual freedom, a superior military, technological know-how, and market capitalism had seen the nation not just survive the Great Depression and two world wars but also emerge as a so-called *superpower* enjoying success of historic proportions. America's diverse political, social and economic influences were reaching every corner of the world, making the country a beacon of hope and even a democratic role model for much of the rest of the planet. From 1940 to 1955, the personal income of Americans nearly tripled. By 1954, Americans were consuming one-third of the world's goods.[2]

Nonetheless, something wasn't right. As Eisenhower noted, underlying a sense of greatness was a deep and difficult-to-articulate uneasiness. There is at times a false notion that the peace and prosperity of the 1950s was upended by rock and roll delinquents, but the cracks in society were showing long before rock and roll came about. W.H. Auden touched on it in his Pulitzer Prize–winning poem, "The Age of Anxiety" (1947),[3] and, as detailed below, two other mainstream examples further clarify the nation's pre-rock troubles.

In August 1951, the editor of the *Cleveland Press*, Louis B. Seltzer, wrote a rather odd editorial discussing an emotional malaise and emptiness that he himself was experiencing, and he was sure he was not alone.[4] Seltzer could barely even articulate precisely what the emptiness was about, but he tapped into a collective national anxiety when he asked, "What is wrong with us?" Seltzer's piece spoke to an often vague, yet persistent, angst that had been dogging the modern age and that had hit even greater heights in the years following the atomic bombs being dropped on Hiroshima and Nagasaki. His article began as follows:

> Some people think it dates back to the first World War.... There are those who think science and the assembly line started it as we turn into the Twentieth Century.... We have everything. We abound with all the things that make us comfortable. We are, on the average, rich beyond the dreams of the kinds of old. Yet something is not there that should be—something we once had. The analysts whose job it is to examine our national behavior ... do not agree among themselves. About this, though, they do agree. Something has happened to us as a people—something serious.... Are we our own worst enemies? Should we fear what is happening among us more than what is happening elsewhere? No one seems to know what to do to about it. But everybody worries.[5]

After the article ran, Seltzer was inundated with a thousand calls and letters at his office, and the piece was reprinted in forty-one publications across the country, including *Time* magazine.[6]

A few months later, at the end of 1951, *Time* ran another article titled "People: The Younger Generation." That article was an effort to "paint a portrait" of a generation that had been born during the Great Depression, grown up during World War II, and was then coming to maturity in the Atomic Age. While the article noted underlying signs of hope, most of the conclusions (such as "they are grave and fatalistic" and "they expect disappointment") directly refuted the oft-idealized version of 1950s tranquility in the U.S. America's youth were indeed benefiting from immense economic prosperity, but they were also feeling disconnected from America's largely conservative institutions and lacking any clear social movement, direction, or purpose.[7]

As *Time* detailed, an increasing dominance of corporate culture, coupled with the New Deal tax structure and social security and pension plans, was all seen as squeezing out individual interests and autonomy in an "over-organized society."[8] Further, after seeing the brutally effective prosecution of alleged communists in Congress during the Red Scare, spontaneity and nonconformity had been made less desirable. America's youth were, *Time* said, defined by a "lack of conviction" for "fear of being tagged 'subversive,'" adding that "[t]oday's generation, either through fear, passivity or conviction, is ready to conform."[9]

And the young were already being sent off to fight another war, and a poorly understood one at that, in some place called Korea. The U.S. soldier was more than capable and still effective, *Time* said, but he also had "little enthusiasm for the military life, no enthusiasm for war," and, especially, he no longer trusted politicians. Thus *Time* concluded that the typical U.S. soldier in Korea lacked "flame": "He does not go in for heroics, or believe in them."[10] In other words, by 1951, the rugged, can't-lose heroism embodied by movie stars like John Wayne existed mostly on the silver screen.

The *Time* article further noted that church attendance among the young had increased, though the addition of social and sport activities was given as the main reason for this change. Clearly the youth of America had "an unquestioned spiritual need," and they "ha[d] a conscience," but the notion of God was as perplexing as it had ever been, or more so.[11]

Interestingly, the *Time* article made relatively short shrift of the nuclear issue. In a 4,500-word feature article, there were only two sentences devoted to the ultimate threat. This lack of examination suggests a nation that had scarcely begun to digest the full implications of "The Bomb." The fear was, perhaps, just too big. That fear would become even more real (and more surreal) as the Cold War years progressed.

Time diagnosed America's youth as having a lack of direction, purpose, and role models for what was being called "The Silent Generation":

> The fact of this world is war, uncertainty, the need for work, courage, sacrifice. Nobody likes that fact. But youth does not blame that fact on its parents dropping the ball. In real life, youth seems to know, people always drop the ball. Youth today has little cynicism, because it never hoped for much.[12]

America's traditional institutions were trying to provide a top-down societal structure and assurance for its youth, but too much was changing, too fast.

* * *

At that point in time, the twentieth century was not looking good for the human race. World War I had been called "The War to End All Wars,"[13] yet that conflict had introduced new levels of cruelty and destructive efficiency, and a staggering ten million people were killed in combat, while tens of millions more died of war-related illnesses.[14] Waves of soldiers were shredded by high-powered machine guns and artillery, thousands more were killed in trenches by newly developed poisonous gases, and more still were shell shocked into deep trauma.[15] Worse, World War II happened anyway. That war resulted in 70 million deaths, including the Holocaust, and ended with the introduction of nuclear weapons.[16]

On August 6 and August 9, 1945, the U.S. dropped atomic bombs on the Japanese cities of Hiroshima and Nagasaki, respectively. The bomb that fell on Hiroshima instantly killed 70,000 human beings. As the Japanese reported at Hiroshima at the time:

> The impact of the bomb was so terrific that practically all living things—human and animal—were literally seared to death by the tremendous heat and pressure set up by the blast. All the dead and injured were burned beyond recognition. Those outdoors were burned to death, while those indoors were killed by the indescribable pressure and heat.[17]

Over the next four months, an additional one hundred thousand Japanese died in and around Hiroshima from radiation burns and sickness.[18] The U.S. government itself soon acknowledged that this devastating secondary effect "left no doubt that man was faced with the necessity for coping with strange and unprecedented problems for which no solutions were available."[19]

Soon the inceptions of the Korean conflict and the Cold War showed that World War II was not going to be the war to end all wars, either. The existential dilemma of nuclear Armageddon—and the quite possibly doomed nature of mankind—cast a long, dark shadow over virtually every aspect of life.

As late as the latter half of the 1940s, the U.S. had little reason to believe that the Soviet Union could ever compete with it technologically, economically, or militarily. Top U.S. scientists used to tell a joke among themselves that the Russians had yet to develop so-called suitcase bombs—nuclear bombs small enough to be packaged in suitcases—because the Russians "had not been able to perfect a suitcase."[20] That joke officially stopped being funny on September 3, 1949, when the U.S. announced that the Soviets had indeed detonated "a nuclear device." Then-president Harry Truman had not even wanted to call the device a "bomb," somehow hoping to alleviate the nation's fears by continuing to understate Soviet capabilities.[21]

An arms race took off. U.S. defense spending went from negligible

Members of the 11th AB Division kneel on the ground as they watch the mushroom cloud of the atomic bomb test at Frenchman's Flat, Nevada (1951) (photograph by USASC, Library of Congress).

amounts in 1932 to over $400 billion a year by 1954, and a stockpile of 6,000 nuclear warheads by 1959.[22] In November 1952, the U.S. detonated its first hydrogen bomb, a device one *thousand* times stronger than the bomb that had vaporized Hiroshima.[23] The Soviets followed this up with their own H-bomb detonation in 1953. In response to all of this, the smartest man of the twentieth century, Albert Einstein, could only say, "I do not know how the Third World War will be fought, but I can tell you what they will use in the Fourth—rocks!"[24]

Even if the specter of nuclear annihilation could have somehow been minimized by rational thought (neither side *wanted* it to happen), statistical analysis (the chances of catastrophic error or successful espionage were, perhaps, *not likely*), or finger-crossing, the threat of nuclear Armageddon was real. Even further, on personal and emotional levels, the continued build-up of arms presented philosophical questions as disturbing as any that mankind had ever faced. This would not be a war with any real winner, nor would it be something out of human control like a plague or tsunami, nor was this an evil that could be eradicated by faith and hard work. This was man-made, and even the "good guys" had no satisfactory outcome.

As summarized by writer Robert Pattison in his 1987 book, *The Triumph of Vulgarity: Rock Music in the Mirror of Romanticism*:

> Not religion, nor reason, nor science can offer us any security, for the traditional certainty that there are aimless truths to guide us and protect is no more. We are on our own, the sole source of whatever meaning there is. Despite the enormous power we have developed, none of it is to any avail. On the contrary, it provides us with a frightening symbol for the "dreadful and total contingency of human existence: existentialism is the philosophy of the atomic age."[25]

Even the most powerful nation in the world had seemingly reached a philosophical dead end. Beginning in the 1950s, American institutions were manipulating world events with more power than ever—and yet somehow they were less capable of controlling their environment. It was all too much to process and reconcile, thus resulting in an "age of anxiety."[26]

* * *

The Silent Generation was hardly the first to raise such questions about war. Leo Tolstoy's *The Kingdom of God Is Within You* (1894),[27] for example, directly challenged what Tolstoy saw as modern Christianity's inability to reconcile church doctrine with its own basic texts, specifically Jesus' "Sermon on the Mount."[28] After all, wasn't that sermon an unambiguous call for nonviolence and *loving* thy enemy—not warring against or otherwise preparing to annihilate them and the world?

For many Americans, the United States' successes in the early 1950s represented its ongoing destiny and were directly attributable to constitutional guarantees of personal and religious freedoms, as well as a foundation of traditional Christian values. This contrasted with the oppressed and godless Soviet communists who had criminalized religious practice. One congressional response to the "Red Scare" was to add "under God" to the Pledge of Allegiance in 1954,[29] and the next year it ordered the phrase "In God We Trust" to be printed on all U.S. currency.[30]

The young Southern Baptist evangelical Billy Graham began his long-running ministry in the late 1940s. Graham was charismatic and accessible, and he also took a strong stand against segregation. By the early 1950s, Graham was connecting with packed arenas in the U.S. and around the world, filled with people starved for faith and connection to this bigger cause.[31] Yet if ultimately America was at least strongly informed by Christian values, where exactly was God in all of this? Was U.S. engagement in the Cold War arms race morally justifiable as self-defense? Or, looked at in a different way, would Jesus stockpile nukes? Still, to most Christian leaders in the U.S., the Cold War, just like World War II and the Korean War, was a "just" war in which the U.S. saw itself as merely protecting freedoms and high principles and, further, as a clear case of Christian ideals versus godlessness.[32] In any event, this was a time when clear direction was hard to come by for many.

* * *

Footage from 1950s news television, military instructional films, and public service announcements intended to deal with the fears of a nation further exposes the significant shortcomings of the traditional U.S. institutions of the day. Although earnest at the time, today the footage comes off at times as very dark, camp comedy, and at other times as the most surreal of bad dreams.

One stunning moment came on August 19, 1953, on a live national broadcast of the Sunday morning TV news show *Longines Chronoscope* (1951–1955).[33] The two interviewers, Edward Morgan and Bill Downs, discuss U.S. defense with interviewee Val Peterson, administrator of the Federal Civil Defense Administration and former governor of Nebraska. Peterson refers to a study indicating that 60 percent of Americans at the time clung to a belief that the U.S. military could stop Russian planes from dropping atomic bombs on the United States. In response to this, Peterson tells the TV audience, "Well, I'm sorry to have to tell you that … and the military will tell you, that as of today they cannot stop a successful Russian attack." At precisely this point, in real time, Morgan interjects, "That can be corroborated rather dramatically and we didn't plan it this way, Governor, but the floor manager has just handed me a bulletin saying that the Russians have just exploded a hydrogen bomb." There is seven seconds of dead silence on set, and then Downs simply drops his head.[34]

At the same time, U.S. schoolchildren were being shown instructional films such as one starring a not-so-reassuring cartoon turtle in a hardhat, while the not-so-helpful mantra "Drop and cover" is loudly repeated again and again over images of children scrambling for cover under their little wooden school desks.[35]

U.S. Army training films meant to reassure jittery American fighting men were equally ineffectual—even laughable. In one, specifically produced for soldiers about to embark on maneuvers conducted in concert with a live nuclear detonation, a narrator leads into a dramatization: "You wonder if everything is going to turn out all right, it fills your mind no matter what you were doing."[36] Two soldiers are then shown in the field, both presumably utterly overwhelmed with fear and confusion, seeking solace from an army chaplain. The chaplain, in a performance surprisingly stilted even by the standards of training videos, explains that "there is no need to be worried, as the army has taken all of the precautions and we'll be perfectly safe here." All that will happen, the chaplain tells the poor soldiers, is that there will be "a very, very bright light," a shock wave, a huge noise, and "a minor earthquake," and then they will see a "fireball as it ascends out into the heavens." "It's a wonderful sight to behold," the chaplain assures them. As the signature phrase of Alfred E. Neuman, the cartoon mascot of the popular satirical magazine *Mad*, went, "What, me worry?"[37]

* * *

Aside from the actual Soviet warheads, the very *idea* of communism had become another insidious fear that clouded the American consciousness. The problem, as 1948 presidential hopeful Thomas Dewey had put it, was that "you can't shoot an idea with a gun."[38] In the nuclear age, what previously might have been seen as a relatively modest threat of espionage was now being soberly viewed as a threat to the very viability of the nation. Worse, in the early 1950s, aside from its ability to annihilate America, Americans knew little of the Soviet Union except that it was a vast and incredibly secretive nation. As one observer noted, even the Russian *phonebook* was confidential.[39] This lack of hard information and understanding increased anxieties even further.

In 1949, Congress (spearheaded by a hard-charging and ambitious young congressman from California, Richard Nixon) tried former U.S. civil servant Alger Hiss for espionage, resulting in Hiss' conviction on related perjury charges.[40] Later that year, Julius Rosenberg, a civilian employee of the U.S. Army Signal Corps, was convicted of passing nuclear secrets from Los Alamos to the Soviets, and his wife Ethel was convicted as his accomplice.[41] The Rosenbergs were subsequently executed despite widespread protests due to questions regarding their guilt, as well as the appropriateness of the death penalty for Ethel. The Hiss and Rosenberg matters created unanswered questions for many and left public opinion divided: Was paranoia taking over, or was this all merely extreme measures for a new and extreme threat?

In 1948, Joseph McCarthy was a heavy-drinking and undistinguished Republicans from Wisconsin. In fact, in 1947 the Washington press corps voted McCarthy as the "worst senator" in Congress.[42] But then McCarthy appointed himself the head attack dog to take on the "Red Scare."[43]

McCarthy was so vicious and became so effective in his crusade that to even speak out against his cause was to risk being labeled unpatriotic or soft on communism, both labels being political career killers. In 1954, Congress passed the Communist Control Act, thereby criminalizing all Communist Party activity, with overwhelming bipartisan support.[44]

On the one hand, there was indeed communist infiltration of the U.S. government—and most now accept that Hiss and the Rosenbergs were in fact guilty.[45] On the other hand, most of McCarthy's targets were convicted based on innuendo and outright lies. McCarthy eventually put two war heroes in his crosshairs with charges of anti-Americanism: general of the army and eventual Nobel Peace Prize winner, George Marshall, and Robert Oppenheimer, the famed scientist and leader of the Manhattan Project that developed the Hiroshima and Nagasaki bombs.[46]

In late 1954, McCarthy's accusations finally began to fall flat. In the middle of a particularly vicious attempt to destroy the career of an army dentist, a fellow congressman finally asked McCarthy on live, national TV, "Have you no sense of decency, sir, at long last? Have you no sense of decency?"[47] McCarthy was censured by the U.S. Senate shortly thereafter. In 1955, McCarthy attempted to take the spotlight again, abruptly denouncing his four-year reign of terror as a "mistake." But McCarthy was done, and his speeches were ignored. He died in 1957, at the age of 48, from cirrhosis of the liver, generally understood to be a result of his alcoholism.[48]

Meanwhile, by 1951 the war in Korea, initially launched to stop the spread of communism, was already stalling. A lack of political will or support from a country tired of war; overconfidence, due in part to racism; and involvement of Chinese forces all turned the so-called police action into a quagmire.[49] The seemingly invincible U.S. military force of 1945 was now stockpiling what were essentially unusable nuclear weapons, and, on top of that, they had reached a rather embarrassing stalemate in Asia.[50]

2

Boom Time—and Cracks in the Foundation

The U.S. economy exploded in the 1950s. Individual freedom, technological advances, abundant natural resources, a switch from coal to oil, and the flexibility and know-how to facilitate corporate mergers and acquisitions all combined to bring unprecedented affluence. The nation's gross national product rose from $200 billion in 1940, to $300 billion in 1950, and to more than $500 billion by 1960.[1] U.S. might dominated the world economy.

World War II had decimated Europe's infrastructures and left millions dead, and post-war European nations were limited by class problems largely absent from the American economy. For example, while the Germans focused on high-end autos (Porsche, BMW, Mercedes), the U.S. auto industry, still following Henry Ford's vision, was able to mass-produce cars that could be purchased by the common laborer—also a historic feat. As historian David Halberstam wrote, "[H]ad Marx witnessed the industrial explosion of the Oil Century and the rising standard of living it produced among ordinary workers, he might have written differently."[2]

Still, American industrial success came at significant expense. Mass production and the more narrowed focus on the bottom line had consequences. The following six case studies are illustrative of a great nation—but also further set the stage for rock music's ascendancy.

Mass Production and Corporatization

Beginning in 1947, home builders Levitt & Sons developed a drastically streamlined concept for building small homes cheap enough for the middle-class veteran starting a young family.[3] Along with some federal help in the form of guarantees of mortgages and low-interest loans, the homes became affordable for the American middle class.

The Levitts bought some farmland in Long Island, New York, twenty miles from Manhattan, and "Levittown" virtually gave birth to suburbia as we know it. Using a reverse model of Henry Ford's assembly line, the Levitts broke homebuilding down into 27 basic steps, and each of 27 trained teams did just their one task, moving from lot to lot where the materials were already laid out. There was little craftsmanship required, and those pieces requiring special skill were assembled elsewhere and shipped in finished. At their peak, Levitt homes went up in eighteen minutes.[4] In Bill Levitt's vision, "The same man does the same thing every day, despite the psychologists. It is boring, it is bad, but the reward of the green stuff seems to alleviate the boredom of work."[5]

Critics of Levitt & Sons decried the soullessness of the work and the resulting cookie-cutter world of homogenous homes, as well as families now isolated into groups of "people whose age, income, dress, number of children, problems, habits, conversations, dress, possessions, perhaps even blood types are almost precisely like yours."[6] In fact, Levittown contractually barred African Americans at first, explaining that they were merely complying with the wishes of the consumers and the banks.[7] Suburban living was popular but also derided by many as being defined by sameness, a relative lack of social interaction, and lack of cultural venues.

Parallel dynamics were occurring in Detroit as the auto industry of the 1950s shifted away from a focus on technological breakthroughs toward seeking out new profits through marketing. New cars generally lasted for many years, so, to increase revenues, U.S. automakers had to create reasons for customers to purchase again. General Motors' top designer, Earl Harley, described the strategy as "dynamic obsolescence,"[8] meaning a new focus on ornamental features, often status indicators (such as increasing the size of the cars or adding the era-defining, futuristic tailfins), to alter the models every year.[9] As Harley explained, "General Motors is in business for only one reason. To make money. In order to do that we make cars. But if we could do that making garbage cans, we would make garbage cans."[10]

By the mid–1950s, General Motors was the biggest employer in the world, selling every other car bought in the United States. In 1955, GM had greater assets than Argentina.[11] By 1960, there were 74 million cars in the U.S. alone, for a population of 180 million people.[12]

With the family home and car easily attainable and automobile manufacturers' successful lobbying for the National Interstate and Defense Highways Act of 1956, middle-class, white America made a further dramatic shift to the suburban lifestyle. By 1950, for the first time, more Americans lived in rural and suburban areas than in the cities.[13] The downside, to some, was a homogenization and polarization of America. Where a generation before people had some interaction with most demographics daily, whether at the neighborhood store or on a streetcar to and from work, people were now segregated by housing tracts and isolated in pods.

Finally, similar mass-production methods were adopted for feeding and housing the mobile, middle-class masses. In 1940, in San Bernadino, California, brothers Dick and Maurice McDonald started a new kind of family drive-in restaurant that mass-produced fifteen-cent hamburgers. The McDonalds brought a new brand of hyper-efficiency to every aspect of the operation, from the clean and quick, one-pump ketchup-squirter to the realization that the on-the-go American public was okay with eating its dinner off of a paper wrapper instead of a plate, thus saving the restaurant enormous amounts of time and money on dishes and dishwashers.[14] Ray Kroc took over McDonald's in 1955 and then mastered the franchising of fast-food restaurants on a worldwide scale.[15]

Mass Marketing

Corporate America found a hugely profitable partner in modern advertising, further tapping into a consumer base flush with discretionary money, while magazines, TV and radio all needed ad revenues. However, the story of this teamwork also helps to illustrate a growing disillusionment with corporate America and how charges of immorality and hypocrisy would begin to undermine the moral legitimacy of the U.S. establishment. The story of Marlboro cigarettes is a classic case study.

In 1952, *Reader's Digest* published a series of articles titled "Cancer by the Carton," the first publicly reported link of smoking with cancer and other health issues.[16] In 1953, a medical report by Dr. Ernst L. Wynder provided further empirical evidence of the connection between cigarette smoking and cancer; other mainstream articles with the same conclusions soon followed. The result was an enormous decline in cigarette sales.[17]

Nonetheless, the tobacco industry launched what PRWatch.org has called "the costliest, longest-running and most successful PR 'crisis management' campaign in history."[18] The tobacco companies' public relations agencies declared in their own internal documents that the goal of their marketing campaign was "promoting cigarettes and protecting them from these and other attacks" by "creating doubt about the health charge without actually denying it, and advocating the public's right to smoke, without actually urging them to take up the practice."[19]

Prior to the *Reader's Digest* article, the vast majority of cigarettes on the market lacked filters, and filtered cigarettes were seen as a purely effeminate option comprising only a sliver of the tobacco market. After the surge of data on cancer, however, the industry was forced to embrace filtered cigarettes so that consumers could at least *feel* safer, if nothing else.[20] The brand that adapted quickest and most effectively was Marlboro.

In the 1920s, a sampling of some of Marlboro's ad slogans included "Mild as May" and "Fit for a King, Blended to the Queen's Tastes," and for a time Marlboro cigarettes even sported what was called a "beauty tip" so as not to smudge a woman's lipstick.[21] In the 1940s, the brand adopted a "classy woman" theme, and in 1950 there was a series of baby spots, with a baby appearing to speak to the smoker ("Gee, Mommy, you sure enjoy your Marlboros"),[22] as well as shots of women escaping with a Marlboro to exotic locations like the Taj Mahal.[23]

Marlboro cigarettes advertisement (1951) (author's collection).

Once cigarette filters became standard after the *Reader's Digest* article, there was no longer a need to limit the Marlboro market to women. In 1955, Marlboro began a "Tattooed Man" ad campaign featuring various manly men (e.g., a pilot, a sailor) with tattoos of an anchor on the hands holding cigarettes.[24] The most effective of those advertising characters was the ultimate American male figure, the ultra-rugged cowboy—manly, carefree, strong and independent—which became the iconic Marlboro Man. In 1955, the year the Tattooed Man campaign opened, Marlboro's sales increased over 3,000 percent, and they never looked back.[25] Despite decades more of science spelling out the highly addictive, carcinogenic and otherwise devastating health consequences of cigarettes and corporate cover-up,[26] in 1993, *Financial World* magazine had Marlboro ranked as the most valuable brand in the world, with a value of $39.5 billion.[27]

Some of the other social costs of the U.S. economy and corporatization, as well as their impact on individual workers and familial lifestyles, were portrayed in several popular books of the 1950s. David Reisman's *The Lonely Crowd* (1950) examined how corporate jobs took up more of people's lives, stifled individuality, and caused Americans to become more "other directed," meaning they were taking their moral cues based on what others were doing, (i.e., how much they were making or what they were consuming).[28] Sloan Wilson's protagonist in *The Man in the Grey Flannel Suit* (1955)[29] likewise saw his corporate job dominating his life to the exclusion of his family life. His psychological traumas from the war were ignored, and at home he and his wife relied on martinis to numb their pain. William H. Whyte's *The Organization Man* (1956)[30] spoke to individuals becoming absorbed by corporate culture and valuing conformity and risk aversion, which were becoming new American values.

Mass Media

Few things have impacted American culture and the American family more than television. In 1946, only 0.5 percent of U.S. households had a television set, by 1955, televisions were present in nearly two-thirds of U.S. homes, and by 1962, 90 percent of the country was tuned in.[31] Television became a social, informational and cultural centerpiece for American families. It was a medium that brought the rest of the world into one's living room, although it often brought distortions of it as well. Good and evil were always clear cut, whether it was Western heroes like *Gunsmoke*'s (1955–1975) Marshall Dillon corralling the bad guys every time and taming the Wild West, or lawyer Perry Mason routinely inducing criminals to conveniently confess in open court. Men ran the show and everyone was white (except for some house servants); in 1952 only 0.4 percent of TV roles were played by African Americans.[32]

The classic illustrations of American conformity equating to happiness in the 1950s are the TV family sitcoms, such as *Ozzie and Harriet* (1952–1963), *Father Knows Best* (1954–1960), and *Leave It to Beaver* (1957–1963). Each of these three sitcoms was based on nostalgic, although often unrealistic, views of Main Street family values, similar in theme to what Norman Rockwell had been doing with his paintings for the *Saturday Evening Post*: pure innocence, baseball, Boy Scouts, quaint small town living, and so forth. Television sitcoms fused those traditional values with the new and esteemed American value of conformity. The shows were made to be as comforting as possible, which meant easygoing entertainment but also ignoring the real problems of the times. Why make waves when a nation's economy is booming and the populace is living lives of leisure with new homes, cars, shopping malls, fast food, vacuum cleaners, refrigerators, electric clothes dryers, Polaroid cameras, and frozen dinners?

Ozzie and Harriet, whose cast was the real-world Nelson family, was a top-rated show when it first ran, carrying its popularity over from its beginnings on radio, while, tellingly, *Father Knows Best* and *Leave It to Beaver* were only moderately successful in the 1950s and did not see greater success until they ran as reruns in the 1970s and beyond. Those two shows, as TV historian Steven D. Sark wrote, "only began to gain mass popularity as that family model and the era it represented disappeared and the nation longed for both it and the stability it represented."[33]

All three shows' casts were strictly Anglo-Saxon and Protestant, despite the diversifying demographics of the U.S. at that time. The shows never mentioned McCarthyism or the threat of nuclear Armageddon. There was never any acknowledgment that divorce, serious illnesses (both physical and mental), family dysfunction, racism, sexuality, sexism, alcoholism, homosexuality, or drug addiction even existed. Moms and dads never raised their voices in anger. The three fathers never complained about work—in fact, no one even knew what Ozzie Nelson of *Ozzie and Harriet* and *Beaver* father Ward Cleaver did for a living! Few serious problems were ever dealt with head on, nor was any real emotional depth displayed; thus a plot might be "Will Ozzie play Ping-Pong in the father-and-son tournament with David or Ricky?"[34]

In other words, there were few, if any, outlets or models for dealing with angst, frustration, or dissent, much less for alternative ways of living. Careers in capitalism often meant selling "stuff" to people, whether they needed it or not (and sometimes even if it literally killed them), or maybe a job in the military industrial complex. Popular culture seemingly offered little in the way of expressing what many were really dealing with in their lives under their public surfaces.

Religion and Morality

One of the top-selling books of the 1950s was the Reverend Norman Vincent Peale's *The Power of Positive Thinking* (1952).[35] While Billy Graham represented the more mainstream religious status of America, an analysis of

Peale and his writings, as well as the complaints of his detractors, offers an ideal window into shifting national views of religion, individuality, and spirituality. In fact, Peale is not only an ideal starting point for many of the cultural debates of the 1950s but also a surprisingly key figure for understanding how the cultural debates would begin to unfold going forward, even up until the present.

The Power of Positive Thinking was a phenomenon, selling two-and-a-half million copies between 1952 and 1956, and sat on the *New York Times* best-seller list for a then-record 186 weeks.[36] Peale's popularity happened to occur at a time when Christianity in the U.S. was seeing a spike in church attendance but also seeing its legitimacy and relevancy beginning to be questioned more and more, particularly by the young.

Peale was a major American figure in the 1950s and 1960s. Billy Graham said of Peale and his wife, Ruth, "I don't know of anyone who had done more for the kingdom of God than Norman and Ruth Peale or have meant any more in my life for the encouragement they have given me."[37] President Ronald Reagan awarded Peale the Presidential Medal of Freedom, the highest honor a U.S. civilian can receive,[38] and President Bill Clinton lionized Peale upon his passing in 1993.[39]

Peale was also controversial, especially upon publicly declaring that Catholic John F. Kennedy should not serve as president due to what was seen as an inherent conflict between allegiance to the pope and an oath to the U.S. Constitution.[40] Peale also disparaged the popular child-rearing expert and author Dr. Benjamin Spock for encouraging a generation of parents to be overly lenient, and he later decried those youth who did not dutifully serve in the Vietnam War.[41]

Furthermore, Peale's belief that positive thinking and faith could lead to economic success for practitioners is seen as a precursor to the controversial "prosperity gospel," later popularized by Oral Roberts and others through the latter part of the twentieth century and into the current century.[42] He also linked "positive thinking" and biblical concepts to modern mental health, all of which has informed today's self-help and recovery movements. Peale was thus an important establishment and conservative icon; yet in other ways he is seen as an important progressive.

Peale's detractors, however, including many fellow Christians, asserted that there were at least three major flaws to Peale's approach: (1) he was overly simple; (2) he overemphasized materialism[43]; and (3) he encouraged a belief in *oneself* to the point of excluding a reliance on Christ.[44]

Taken in order, Peale's message was certainly simple. His goal was to make the scripture as relevant and as practicably useful as possible in a complex modern age, a society where worry seemed to have overtaken faith. As Peale colleague Dr. Smiley Blanton had put it, many were "[d]ammed up" with fear and anxiety, "making thousands sick."[45] Peale's template was to create a simple format such as "10 simple, workable rules," and statements like, "'I can do all things through Christ which strengtheneth me' (Phillipians 4:13). Repeat those words NOW."[46] Peale saw this as a way of adjusting one's own attitude; it was repetitive but self-affirming, and, as Peale saw it, it always brought one back to Christ.

Peale also did at least acknowledge the deeply-rooted and complex nature of psychological maladies (childhood issues, for example), and he encouraged more intensive one-on-one work with a professional.[47] Peale actually cofounded the American Foundation of Religion and Psychiatry with the Freud-trained psychiatrist, Blanton.[48] As the *New York Times* noted, Peale was "one of the first American clergymen to bring psychiatry practices into religion, preparing the way for thousands of professional, religious-based counselors."[49]

As to the second charge of materialism, detractors saw Peale as teaching that a belief in Christ was desirable because one result would be economic reward. That doctrine is rejected by many Christians, although others cite specific Bible passages suggesting that Christ wants to see his followers prosper and enjoy life in all ways, including financially.[50]

In *The Power of Positive Thinking*, Peale wrote that without a positive frame of mind, not only does personal growth become less likely, but new opportunities, including economic ones, will also be lost. However, he did *not* say that if one is obedient to God's word, God will give you money and money will equate to salvation. Peale instead wrote of a friend who had been overlooked for a long-expected promotion. Instead of turning sour at work and sabotaging his future there, Peale encouraged his friend to maintain a positive attitude. Eventually the position again became open and he was in place to accept the offer. Peale's reasoning was that a negative attitude may well have prevented his friend from having been offered the position the second time around.[51]

As to the final charge, Peale was denounced for writing that a belief in oneself is also a method of manifesting God in one's life. Peale believed in the existence of a soul and of a higher intelligence *accessed within*, specifically citing (as Tolstoy had) Luke 17:21 and similar tracts: "The Kingdom of God is within you."[52] Peale wrote, "Put yourself in God's hands. To that simply state, 'I am in God's hands.' Then believe you are NOW receiving all the power you need. Feel it flowing into you. Affirm that the kingdom of God is within you" (Luke 17:21).[53] Peale believed in a tangible and divine quality that existed within everyone. Made practical, Peale wrote, "In class, when the teacher calls on you, quickly pray before answering. Then believe the Lord will at that moment help your mind to deliver. When an examination is given, affirm in prayer that God is releasing your mind and that the right answers are given you."[54]

However, the notion of relying on one's own inner voice led to some of the strongest attacks on Peale, especially from more conservative Christians. Whether Peale cited scripture or not, many saw his writings as diametrically opposed to church teachings. As one observer noted, Peale's "emphasis on faith in oneself and one's fellow man as well as his emphasis on thinking one's way to success put off his fellow clergy and Christian friends who felt he diluted the Word of God too much and mixed too much humanism."[55]

Interestingly, toward the end of *The Power of Positive Thinking*, Peale specifically highlighted and praised the then young organization Alcoholics Anonymous (AA), which provided a groundbreaking self-help, 12-step program for those battling alcoholism. Alcoholics Anonymous has been a key player in the addiction recovery and self-help movements for decades since its original formation.[56] While grounded in certain Christian principles, as well as other religious and spiritual practices, AA is ultimately based on the notion of a personal God or "Higher Power." (Ironically, years later, a who's-who of overindulging rock and rollers would ultimately seek sobriety as well.[57]) Each individual member is ultimately left to define that power for him- or herself, or, as the AA literature puts it, "*as* I *understand Him*."[58]

Thus this approach comes back to individualistic and internalized notions of God—perhaps more similar to a Pentecostal approach. The more conservative view is that ultimately one cannot trust those inner impulses and feelings, and they are to be ignored. Instead, one is expected to look to a strict biblical interpretation to determine how to experience or respond to any given situation. So then what is this inner energy, voice or "spirit" ... or Holy Spirit? And what about a human spirit? What is the difference, exactly? These are central questions to consider for the remainder of this book.

Sex and Vice

In the 1930s, a professor of entomology and zoology, Alfred Kinsey, noticed an odd dearth of studies on human sexuality in America. Kinsey then conducted his own exhaustive research and interviews to explore what it seemed that, amazingly enough, no one had yet bothered to examine: the sexual lives of Americans.

Kinsey's first publication was *Sexual Behavior in the Human Male* (1948). That initial book was a wholly unexpected, runaway best-seller, something unheard of for a scientific report. Kinsey inarguably altered American views of sex. First, and most notably, Kinsey's work brought previously taboo sexual issues into the national conversation for the first time. Second, even though some of Kinsey's methods and conclusions were flawed and controversial, he did expose American males as being far more sexually active than most had previously believed, or wanted to believe, such as in the areas of adultery and masturbation, not to mention homosexual activity.[59]

As generally appreciative as the public and the media were of Kinsey's first volume on men, many were equally outraged by the second volume, *Sexual Behavior in the Human Female* (1953). To see American males as more sexual and generally living outside perceived social norms was one thing, but to say similar things about America's mothers, daughters and wives was too much. Now Kinsey's critics saw him as less of a scientist and closer to a pornographer, portraying women at their worst, most "animalistic" tendencies.[60] The National Council of Women called the book a "disservice to the nation that can only lead to immorality."[61]

Also in 1953, sex came to the forefront in a new men's magazine called *Playboy*. Founder and editor Hugh Hefner declared in the inaugural issue that *Playboy* was "a little diversion from the anxieties of the Atomic Age."[62] An exposed Marilyn Monroe graced the first cover, while inside were pictures of naked, large-breasted women; ads for high-end consumer products like hi-fi systems; and articles for the "sophisticated" bachelor.[63] Hefner's creation became wildly popular, achieving mainstream acceptance, in part bolstered by regular contributions from leading writers of the time, including Kurt Vonnegut, Joyce Carol Oates, John Updike, and Saul Bellow.[64] It would become one of the most recognized brands in the world.

Illicit drug use, specifically marijuana and the not-yet-criminalized LSD, was present in the mid–1950s, though not on the scale it soon would be. Prescription drug use also took off in the 1950s. In psychiatry, a "drug revolution" occurred as psychotropic drugs became central to the practice of psychiatry.[65] Tranquilizer use vastly increased as well, and at one point tranquilizers (especially the newly invented Valium) constituted one-third of all written prescriptions, most of which were given to women and often for the "anxious housewife."[66] Marijuana, underage alcohol consumption, and harder drugs were demonized, while the more "respectable" members of society indulged in a three-martini lunch, pep pills, and sedatives.[67]

Resistance

Not everyone was buying into the new norms. To more and more youth in particular, accepting careers in the military-industrial complex or being otherwise beholden to corporate America, including increasingly faster-paced, automated jobs in a "Rat Race," all to sell more stuff, was far from the American Dream.[68]

In literature, J.D. Salinger's protagonist in *Catcher in the Rye* (1951), Holden Caufield, was an alienated, restless anti-hero who saw the older generation as a lot of "phonies."[69] The so-called Beat Poets, particularly Alan Ginsburg, Jack Kerouac, and William S. Burroughs, explored the fringes and underbelly of society, and attacked social conformity and traditional literary conventions. The sarcastic and intentionally sophomoric *Mad* magazine had one of the largest subscription rates in the country.[70] In the movies, Marlon Brando and James Dean personified the new cool of detached, bad-boy rebels. A youth generation, labeled with the new term "teenagers," was starting to veer off the track laid in place for them.[71]

From the older generation's perspective, America's traditional institutions may not have had all of the answers, but they were far superior to anything that any other nation in history had ever come up with. Yet if the elder generation's best solution to their own problems was to stockpile nuclear warheads, continually wage war overseas, and work faster and faster to buy more superfluous material goods, while ignoring deeper, personal feelings and needs, why should the youth listen to them? Wasn't the only logical course for a new generation, even their *duty*, to try to find a new direction?

It turned out that one long-overlooked group of Americans, in particular, had already found a powerful voice in a world of alienation and oppression, and with no assistance or support from traditional institutions whatsoever: the black Delta bluesmen.

Since the turn of the twentieth century, the blues had developed around the Mississippi River basin, Memphis, Tennessee, and the mid–South, over several decades. It indeed became one of the most original, personal, and visceral musical genres the world has ever known. Also, poor whites of the Delta region were soon to find a connection with precisely these people with whom they were not supposed to have anything in common with at all. The music of both groups would combine to give a voice to a nation's and a world's troubles. A new attitude and some new "Southern Rebels," both black and white, were about to rise from obscurity to worldwide fame and influence.

3

The Oral Tradition

The blues originated in the Delta, though distinctive strains also developed elsewhere, including the Piedmont region in Georgia, Texas, and so on.[1] The Delta blues, though, were a powerful expression and record of people living in a unique time and place. The Delta blues were the cornerstone of the blues and then became the key foundation for rock and roll's ascendancy, not to mention the second critical movement: the British Invasion of the early 1960s. It follows, then, that in order to fully understand rock music, one must first fully understand the Delta blues and its social context. The rest of this chapter begins to examine the African American experience in the Delta so as to find the real roots of rock, not only on a musical level but also on personal and emotional levels. The Delta blues story is revisited later on, as well as the story of poor whites in the Delta, all on the road to the advent of rock and roll.

* * *

It has been said that, regarding racism, what the South was to the rest of the nation, the Delta was to the rest of the South.[2] Several factors made the racism there an especially brutal strain. First, the Delta had historically been effectively isolated from the rest of the nation, and it remained so through the first half of the twentieth century. Geographically, the region was set off by the Mississippi River itself and its vast, surrounding marshlands. Economically, the South had been held back by its agrarian economy, severe economic polarization, and some of the worst poverty in the nation.[3]

The Mississippi River Delta (technically an alluvian plain) is the low-lying area between the Yazoo and Mississippi rivers, between Vicksburg, Mississippi to the South, and Memphis, Tennessee to the north, an area of some 6,000 square miles.[4] The region boasts some of the most fertile farm soil in the world and has historically generated a high demand for low-wage farm labor.[5]

In the post–Civil War United States, the Delta region seemed to offer special promise for free African American farm laborers. In 1890, blacks were

60 percent of the population of Mississippi, and those African Americans comprised 10 percent of the total of all African Americans in the U.S.[6] The years immediately after the Civil War (1862–1865) and Reconstruction (1865–1877) had seen considerable progress, including black justices of the peace, black police officers (although they could only arrest blacks),[7] blacks in county positions, various black state representatives, a few black sheriffs, and even two black U.S. senators.[8]

Yet the integration of former slaves into a system of free market capitalism and a centuries-old racial caste system would be painfully slow and sometimes a seemingly impossible pursuit. Blacks faced a white-sabotaged educational system; they had no opportunity to vote, let alone establish political leadership; and any success in business remained entirely dependent on the benevolence of white people. Additionally, the combination of large numbers of African Americans and labor-reliant industry in the Delta meant that nowhere else was the threat of black autonomy and black empowerment greater. Immediately after the Civil War, one Southern news editor predicted that allowing black voting rights would be the end of the South as Southern whites knew it: "The whites must either abandon the territory, or there would be another civil war in the South—a war of the races ... a war of extermination."[9]

The world of slavery and the tragic failures of Reconstruction had evolved into peonage and sharecropping, or else the slightly better-paying but even more grueling and violent worlds of levee, turpentine, and lumber camps. Many black males, such as folk/blues legends Lead Belly (Huddie Ledbetter) and Son House, ended up in "prison farms," which were worse still.[10]

In 1935, sociologist Rupert Vance observed, "Nowhere but in the Mississippi Delta are antebellum conditions so nearly preserved."[11] Visiting anthropologist Hortense Powdermaker was stunned to see that the caste system in the Delta was even worse than she had expected:

> I had not known of such a society.... Tribal societies had their well-defined rules and customs and reciprocity. The Middle Ages, of which the South reminded me in some ways, had an established system of duties and responsibilities between lords and serfs. But the rules in which the sharecropping system was based were broken more often than followed.[12]

In sum, as writer James C. Cobb declared, the Delta was "The Most Southern Place on Earth."[13]

Perhaps worst of all, Delta blacks had no avenues of expression, no access to the media, no voice whatsoever either in Delta society or outside the Delta, and a devastatingly efficient legal system kept it that way. Ethnomusicologist, oral historian, and activist Alan Lomax, who worked for the Library of Con-

Picking cotton in Mileston, Mississippi (1939) (photograph by Marion Post Wolcott, Library of Congress).

gress and in the Delta, had noted that even renowned black folklorist Zora Neale Houston, whom Lomax had worked with in 1935, had previously "never elicited any account of oppression from anyone, nor did she discuss such matters." Lomax was confused by this omission until he experienced the Delta for himself, leading him to understand that even a simple act of free expression would certainly have been "too risky."[14]

For most blacks in the Delta in the 1930s and 1940s, there was no place for them in the economy except as sharecroppers. As Lomax wrote of Southern counties, each was "a small empire, with its own autonomous power," where the U.S. Constitution apparently did not reach.[15] Lomax encountered sheriffs making blunt threats and found out that "freedom of assembly" did not necessarily apply to a "nigger lover" looking to record black musicians.[16] Maintaining the white supremacist social order required silencing voices; thus the African Americans of the Delta were, as Lomax observed, effectively held "incommunicado."[17]

From this world came the murky and mythic story of the Delta bluesmen.

As late as the 1940s, future Delta blues legends such as Charley Patton, Son House, Robert Johnson, Muddy Waters, and Howlin' Wolf were unknowns beyond the black juke joints, porches, fields and street corners of the South. In 1941, and again in 1942, Alan Lomax traveled into the deep South and the Delta to act as what he called a "song hunter."[18] Lomax's mission had been to find and preserve the folk traditions of the otherwise unheard music of America's most isolated rural communities, as well as recording oral interviews. Lomax had made similar trips with his father, John, in 1933, throughout the South, and the elder Lomax's field recordings were hugely influential, most notably bringing black folk music legend Lead Belly to prominence.[19] On his 1940s trips, the younger Lomax was the first to record Muddy Waters, he made crucial recordings of Son House, and he recorded important interviews with both men.[20]

Alan Lomax had also set out on his trip in 1941 to find Robert Johnson in Mississippi, although he had not even been sure of Johnson's true name, let alone where he might be found.[21] The Delta blues story has since become synonymous with Johnson and his myth. Johnson was a revered bluesman, one of only three initial early influence inductees into the Rock and Roll Hall of Fame, and one of the most important musicians of the twentieth century.[22] Johnson's esteemed Delta blues contemporaries all readily agreed that Johnson was the greatest bluesman of them all, though he was not a commercial success in his day. Son House said of Johnson, "[T]hat boy could play more blues than air one of us. Folks would say he couldn't, but we know, as musicians, that he was the man. What little I know, I taught him, but he put his own sound in it, and sing with it, all night."[23]

It seems Johnson's story could hardly have been better scripted for dramatic effect: a poor black man from the poorest of regions, talk of a "deal with the Devil," dying young and under mysterious circumstances, leaving few traces of his life (including nary a photograph), no major live performances, and leaving behind just a handful of recordings of immense historical significance.

A young Johnson had learned the blues at the feet of House and another legendary musician, Willie Brown, though the older guitarists were never impressed with the young Johnson's musical skills. In House's words, they would "laugh and hurraw him about it, and he's [Johnson] would sull up and go off in a corner and pout."[24] But then Johnson left for a period of time (House was quoted as recalling the period to be maybe six months) before he came back completely transformed. House said that "Little Robert learnt to play quicker than anybody we ever saw around this section."[25]

The oft-repeated Faustian myth states that when Johnson went away, presumably a tortured soul (as reflected in his song "Love in Vain"), he came upon a literal "crossroads," supposedly outside Clarksdale, Mississippi (hence Johnson's song "Crossroads Blues"). There, at the crossroads, in the middle of the night and in the middle of nowhere, Johnson supposedly met a stranger who appeared as a large black man but who was in fact the Devil himself. The Devil offered Johnson the ability to play the blues like no other in exchange for his soul. Johnson took the deal, and, after having previously been by all accounts a mediocre musician, he suddenly became the greatest bluesman *ever*.

In the end, of course, Johnson paid the price. According to the myth, Johnson was chased down by the "hellhounds" of which he sings in "Hellhounds on My Trail." After living what some have since described as a phantom-like life around the Delta, and at only twenty-seven years old, Johnson died a violent death.[26] Witnesses had Johnson writhing on the ground at the end as if possessed, a victim of the "dark arts," or possibly a victim of poisoning.[27]

After recording a total of just 29 songs, and right before what was to have been his big public showcase, Johnson died, almost as if on cue. On the night of that concert, a now famous "From Spirituals to Swing" showcase at Carnegie Hall in December of 1938, host, producer and famed talent scout John Hammond announced to the crowd that Johnson had tragically died just the week before, and mere days after he had been approached for the concert. Surely this timing was no coincidence, especially in the context of the rest of the Johnson myth. Hammond played Johnson's music on a phonograph for the crowd.[28]

The details of Johnson's death had all been word of mouth. Son House recalled, "We never did get the straight of it. We first heard that he got stabbed to death. Next, a woman poisoned him, and then we heard something else. We never did get the straight of it."[29]

The first known photograph of this musical giant was not seen until a photo booth picture appeared in *Rolling Stone* magazine in 1986.[30] A second photo, a Memphis photography studio image, was released in 1989.[31] (A third photo was found in 2007 that has been claimed to be of Johnson, although the photo's authenticity is suspect.[32]) Johnson's death certificate was not discovered until 1968, and there are three separate grave markers around Mississippi, each allegedly the resting place of this Robert Johnson.[33]

These stories were repeated so many times that they eventually became unquestioned and treated as fact. It was not until the 2000s that more accurate assessments of Johnson's life were properly fleshed out and compiled at length. Yet, to this day, the myth still overshadows the rest.

Barry Lee Pearson and Bill McCulloch uncovered much of the lineage of the Johnson myth in their 2003 book, *Robert Johnson: Lost and Found.* It turns out that the myth can be traced back (at least in print) to an interview of House in 1966, conducted by Pete Welding for *Down Beat* magazine, and specifically a fourteen-word partial quote from House: "House suggested in all seriousness that Johnson, in his months away from home, had 'sold his soul to the devil in exchange for learning to play like that.'"[34]

As Pearson and McCulloch point out, that quote actually raises more questions than it answers. First, for some unknown reason, there is no transcript or recording of the House interview, which Welding had in ten other interviews with bluesmen. One question, then, is what was the context of that partial quote? Further, why did Welding qualify House's words by saying House "suggested" such a deal—did House mean this literally or not, and, if not, why not? Additionally, House had been interviewed a few months prior to the Welding interview and spoke at length about Johnson's rapid development as a guitarist without once mentioning a deal with the Devil, and he never referenced it again.[35]

Also, several years prior to such a myth being associated with Robert Johnson, the same idea of a "deal with the Devil" had already been associated with another bluesman—*Tommie* Johnson (no relation)—which begs the question as to whether the story could have conveniently been appropriated or whether there was a genuine confusion of the names and the myth simply stuck to Robert.[36] Those closest to Johnson, including Shines and a stepson, never bought the story at all. Others, including an ex-girlfriend, went along with the myth, although one had admittedly heard the story secondhand and all involved may have enjoyed the attention that came with speaking about Johnson's myth.[37] Indeed, several people who claimed to have been there when Johnson was poisoned or at his deathbed clearly were not.[38] There is simply a glaring lack of direct or even strong evidence to support this story.

Regardless, references to "the deal," even from noted authors—including the highly respected Greil Marcus book, *Mystery Train* (1975),[39] in which Marcus relies on the House quote—continued. The Johnson myth has since become a staple of pop culture. The story has been repeated in TV and cinema, including the film *Crossroads* (1986) and the popular Coen Brothers comedy, *O Brother, Where Art Thou?* (2000). These repeated references all began to create a faux-cumulative weight supporting the Johnson myth, while primary or other reliable sources remained nonexistent.

However, and particularly in light of the newer books, Johnson's story actually sounds pretty human. For a twentieth-century musician to be so influential and still so ephemeral, it could certainly seem that Johnson was from another time or another world. The reality of the matter, however, is that in the exceedingly isolated and impoverished Delta of the 1930s, black people, especially itinerant African American musicians (and, even further, ones who died young), did not necessarily leave paper trails. In fact, there are exactly *zero* known photos of Muddy Waters and Son House from similar timeframes in their lives. The two photos that have turned up of Johnson are, by Delta bluesman standards, actually quite a lot.

Pearson and McCulloch found that House's recollection, from decades after the fact, that Johnson's transformation had taken "six months" was probably inaccurate; the change likely took more than a year, and possibly more than two years.[40] It is still an amazing feat, of course, but not so supernatural.

It was discovered that Johnson had most likely died in a juke joint near Greenwood, Mississippi, a victim of poisoning at the hands of a jealous husband. Johnson's death may have indeed been excruciating—thus the account of Johnson writhing on the ground before he died. Again, while tragic, it is easily explained in mortal terms. Further, it turned out that Johnson had not in fact died a week before the Carnegie Hall show, but rather *four months* before the show. John Hammond intentionally exaggerated the time purely for dramatic effect—one of the first signs that a myth was forming.[41]

What *is* definitely true is that Johnson's music is enormously innovative, influential, and at times haunting, moving, and even beautiful. Johnson's catalog was a primary influence on Muddy Waters and numerous 1960s British superstars (such as the Rolling Stones, Led Zeppelin, and Eric Clapton), as well as American Bob Dylan and many others. Clapton called Johnson the most important of all of the blues musicians, which few would dispute.[42]

Johnson's voice is intense, and he wavers on notes, sometimes with intense anguish in his falsetto; yet he is always strong and tuneful. Vocally and emotionally, Johnson conveyed so much that it is often difficult to pin down precisely all that is being conveyed at any given moment, making some of Johnson's music both unsettling and moving. On some songs, like "Hellhounds on My Trail" and "Love in Vain," Johnson seems to walk right into a deep place of anguish, and then he stays right there to tell you all about it. Supernatural myth aside, it should be noted that Muddy Waters told Lomax that he was "afraid" of Johnson's "powers." It is not clear what exactly to make of this one quote or what "powers" Waters was referring to, or whether this perception was based on rumor or the myth. Whatever those powers were, Waters told of seeing Johnson perform once, but only "peaking" because Johnson was "a dangerous man."[43]

Looking at the songs most closely linked to the "myth" helps in its deconstruction, while a very different interpretation becomes more likely. In "Crossroads Blues," Johnson asks the Lord (and not the Devil) for salvation, but he is left behind, stranded by society and by God, and left on his own to figure out where to go next. "Crossroads" doesn't actually say anything about the Devil, and it is a psychological and existential dilemma that could quite clearly be connected to the dislocated state of Johnson and other black males in the Jim Crow Delta.

In "Love in Vain," Johnson expresses the emotional and psychological pains of heartbreak, maybe as well as anyone has ever expressed it. Of course, this is coming from a man who never had a proper family as a child, then as a young man tragically lost both his wife and his child, and who seemed unable to settle down in his twenties. Again, one need not look to the supernatural to find other possible inspirations for Johnson here.

In "Hellhounds on My Trail," Johnson sings of restlessness, even terror, and being on the run; yet he is unable to escape the hellhounds. It is one of his most moving and existential songs, and one that could clearly bolster said myth. But "Hellhounds" could also be a reference to all sorts of personal demons—not to mention a reference to the actual dogs that had hunted down black men on the run in the South for generations (not to mention that Johnson's biological father had been run off a plantation by white men!).

Johnson sings about a black man being out after nightfall, a serious situation in the South at the time, and one governed by a specific set of laws, the so-called sundown laws.[44] Johnny Shines, for example, noted that the itinerant black musician of the time, who by definition did not fit into the white power structure and thus was a *vagrant*, was as vulnerable as could be. If he were killed, there would be "nothing said about it."[45]

In addition, Pearson and McCulloch noted that Johnson recorded "Hellhounds" with Vocalion Records, and a producer on Johnson's session had a part in a previous blues recording with a similar and rare reference to "hellhounds."[46]

Lastly, "Me and the Devil Blues," the only song in which Johnson directly references the Devil, has Johnson talking with the Devil about his romantic relationship going bad and even committing domestic violence. Still, this song includes at least two references that are clearly comical, albeit dark humor, and that hardly fit any serious "myth" narrative. In *Escaping the Delta: Robert Johnson and the Invention of the Blues* (2004), Elijah Wald puts "Me and the Devil Blues" further into context. As Wald notes, in one verse Johnson gives the Devil a casual, lighthearted greeting. Next, Johnson requests that his body be buried by the highway so his spirit can catch a Greyhound bus, a new, expensive and high-class mode of transport in the 1930s, which is apparently important to Johnson in the afterlife.[47] This comic tone hardly suggests any evil subtext.

A case of selective history, and selective recording, must also be accounted for with regard to Johnson's body of work. Of the twenty-nine songs that Robert Johnson recorded in 1936 and 1937, only two directly reference the Devil, hell, or hell*hounds*, to be exact. "Preachin' Blues (Up Jumped the Devil)" doesn't actually mention the Devil, and the parenthetical addition in the title was likely tacked on later by the record label.[48] Indeed, references to the Devil were a bit of a blues fad in the 1930s and 1940s, generally serving as a comical reference and/or a mark of how "bad" a black man was. Peetie Wheatstraw, for example, was billing himself as the "The High Sheriff from Hell" at the same time.[49] For that matter, all bluesmen knew that in the eyes of white society and religious black society, they were in league with the Devil.

Further, bluesmen of the era were often encouraged to record their most extreme or edgy material, both to stand out and also to fit a marketing narrative that would help their music sell. Few things titillate more than a reference to the Devil.[50] As a traveling musician trying to make a living with the general public, Johnson would have known hundreds of songs across the spectrum of blues, pop, and country, so it is not even clear how these particular songs were selected for recording purposes.[51]

Of Robert Johnson's 29 recorded songs, 27 directly or indirectly reference *women*; thus there is much more evidence to suggest that Johnson was a womanizer as opposed to a Satanist. For that matter, more songs focus on traveling ("I'm a Steady Rollin' Man," "Travelling Riverside Blues," "Rambling on My Mind," "Hellhounds on My Trail," and "Walkin' Blues"), than on any "deal" or the Devil. Of course, those songs are never highlighted or grouped together to support any *myth*. Johnson's actual biography, as clear as can be determined, is laid out later in this book, along with a continuation of the rest of the Delta blues story.

* * *

"Hellhounds on My Trail," in particular, does bring to mind another piece of popular African American Delta folklore as recorded by Alan Lomax in his memoir, *The Land Where the Blues Began* (1993): the legend of Mister Greensnake. According to Lomax, "Greensnake" provides "[a] true picture of black destiny in the Delta as the blues began." It is also a story with "no end."[52] This African American folklore is rooted in the African folk tradition of the "trickster." The trickster character is usually a smaller animal (African Americans) that uses guile to outsmart the larger animal (slave owners), though some of these tales were adapted to illustrate the horrors of slavery.[53] The story of Greensnake is engaging, pure folk, and ultimately unnerving.

Mister Greensnake (the "Mister" signifying that he is white) is a boss looking to return a young African American boy to peonage, and he has demonic powers at his disposal to do so. The boy is trying to escape his apparent destiny, but Greensnake is "one of the fastest mens in the world. Been everywhere and knowed everything and do everything." The boy hides in a woman's closet, but Greensnake finds him. However, the boy uses some supernatural tricks he picked up from Greensnake and slips away again. The boy then transforms himself into a horse. When Greensnake offers the boy's father seventy-five thousand dollars for him, however, the father pleads, "Son, let your father go rich once in his life," and the boy agrees.[54]

Later, the boy escapes again by turning into a catfish, but Greensnake turns into an alligator. The boy turns into a hummingbird, and Greensnake into a bald eagle. Finally, the young boy turns into a pile of mustard seeds, but, alas, Greensnake transforms into "an old hen and a hundred chicks picking up them mustard seeds."[55]

The story of Mister Greensnake illustrates the physical scattering of African Americans, whether as itinerant musicians or as part of the Great Migration to the North (especially Chicago), beginning after World War I and continuing into the 1950s. The story also has powerful psychological implications. To connect this tale to Johnson, the story captures the feeling of being abandoned and of being trapped by wrongdoers and/or one's own personal demons, as well as the overwhelming psychological strains of such a life. One question, then, at the core of Johnson's story and the hellhounds: How to escape the inescapable?

Lomax also relates the sacred side of Delta music, including a story of some black Delta churchgoers dealing with intense pains and frustrations through their faith. Lomax wrote of one congregation singing, or wailing, some of the most stunning and emotional songs that he would ever hear:

> Oh, Jesus (Oh, Jesus), my rock
> In a weary land (Yes),
> Our shelter
> In a time of storm
> Please have mercy tonight. (Yes)
> Oh, Lord *(more high-pitched agony, shriller)*, Lord (Lord),
> Lord (lord), Lord Jesus *(scream)* (Howdy) *(woman shouts)*
> I know you heard me one Sunday morning
> When I was in sin.
> *(palms smacked together for emphasis, with agony. First strong responses from women, as shouting fervor begins)*[56]

This stark expression and release of deep pains was overwhelming. It was in fact too much for Lomax:

> I confess that I blacked out at times and did not attend to all that happened. Even playing back later to hear what had been recorded, I found I could not focus for long on this scene. It was too intense, too pain-filled. It had the emotional level and the sheer force of operative recitative, yet there was no make-believe. The agony was real. The impassioned coloratura of the ministers, the musical cries of the congregants, plainly came from the throats of tormented people.[57]

Lomax's recordings of the bluesmen and others onto acetate discs was the first time in their long history that they had a true outlet for their voices and a connection to the world outside of the Delta. As Lomax observed:

> The performers were heartened when they heard their own music and often spoke into the microphone as if the machine were a telephone, connected directly to the centers of power. One black sharecropper began, "Now listen here Mr. President, I want you to know they're not treating us right down here."[58]

So, beyond the mythology, what was the true significance of Johnson's "hellhounds" and of Greensnake? How and why were Delta African Americans being denied a voice, and what was being suppressed? And how does it all directly connect to the birth of rock and roll?

4

Being Black

In 1956, Kenneth A. Stampp published what became the new authoritative historical treatise on American slavery, *The Peculiar Institution* ("peculiar" meaning an institution unique to the South), and transformed understandings of slavery. Stampp's book put slavery and the perspective of the slaves into their proper context. Most of the previous efforts had, somehow, glossed over the true impact of slavery on African Americans on the most deep and personal levels, and in many ways they absolved or excused slave owners and their supporters. The message, it seemed, was that slavery was unfortunate, but it is over now, move on, and don't let it taint and overshadow an otherwise idyllic Southern society. According to historian Leon Litwack, "Dr. Stampp was among the first mainstream writers to devastate that comforting 'magnolia-blossom interpretation of the plantation'" that, somehow, had managed to minimize and gloss over the realities of the institution.[1] Thus, for *91* years after slavery, the "magnolia-blossom," Southern white interpretation of slavery had prevailed, despite slavery being one of modern times' greatest tragedies.

So how could this be? What was the real view of slavery by whites and by blacks prior to Stampp? What was the *real* state of black-white relations and mutual understandings of one another from 1865 to 1956? What reconciliation had taken place, or not?

The final word on slavery in most classrooms and universities across the country prior to *The Peculiar Institution* largely belonged to historian Ulrich Bonnell Phillips. Phillips' story provides valuable insight. As a history professor at the University of Michigan, and then Yale, in the 1920s and 1930s, Phillips published numerous papers on slavery, from the 1910s until his final book on the subject, *Life and Labor in the South*, released in 1929.[2] Phillips transformed the research methods for analyzing slavery, especially through his pioneering use and interpretations of slave owner diaries and journals. Even Phillips' critics acknowledge his substantial contributions to the study of slavery.[3]

Unfortunately, however, Phillips wrote of the institution in terms of economics and as a labor issue, with one typical work entitled, *American Negro Slavery: A Survey of the Supply, Employment and Control of Negro Labor as Determined by the Plantation Regime.*[4] Phillips concluded that due to the slavery-based economy's lack of flexibility, slavery was a doomed and inefficient labor model that only persisted as long as it did due to the high social status of owning slaves.

As to slaves themselves, Phillips, a Southern child of a family of slave-owning heritage, believed that the institution had served to lift Africans to a more civilized state.[5] Thus, for Phillips (and for many others, of course), slavery served to educate a primitive people so that they could transition to the superior ways of the West, especially by being "saved" through Christianity. Phillips genuinely believed that slaves "for the most part were by racial quality submissive rather than defiant, lighthearted instead of gloomy, ingratiated instead of sullen, and [their] very defects invited paternalism rather than of repression," not to mention that they were "easily frightened."[6] Phillips then focused on those acts illustrating the "kindness and benevolence of masters," which, in his mind, evidenced a "mild and permissive institution."[7]

Guided by such beliefs, it was easy to see slavery as not only benign but also a positive and effective institution for all involved, only allowing an unfairness in that there was no room for growth or "graduation" from slavery.[8] Phillips confidently declared that, all in all, treatment of African Americans by slave owners had been—no kidding—marked by "kindliness and patience."[9] To reiterate, this was not simply a random man on the street—this was America's leading scholarly voice on slavery.

Whatever academic excellence Phillips' works possessed, they were also marked by a complete failure to appreciate the severe physical, emotional, psychological and spiritual effects of slavery, much less those of the segregated, white supremacist Jim Crow South. Thus, writing from that South in 1929, Phillips saw an almost triumphant racial harmony in the South, as evidenced in his preface to *American Negro Slavery*:

> My sojourn in a National Army Camp in the South while this book has been going through the press reinforced my earlier conviction that Southern racial asperities are mainly superficial, and that the two great elements are fundamentally in accord. That the harmony is not a new thing is evinced by the very tone of the camp. The men of the two races are of course quartered separately; but it is a daily occurrence for white Georgian troops to go to the negro companies to seek out their accustomed friends and compare home news and experiences. The negroes themselves show the same easy-going, amiable serio-comic obedience and the same personal attachments to white men, as well as the same sturdy light-heartedness and the same love of laughter and of rhythm which distinguished their forebears.[10]

Thus it becomes clear that in 1956 there was a cavernous gap in perceptions and understandings of race in the South (and elsewhere). To now understand the Delta blues, at least a cursory understanding of slavery and its aftermath is necessary. What, then, was the true and personal black experience in the Delta of Johnson, House, Waters, King, and others, to which Phillips had been oblivious? Indeed, the roots and basic dynamics of the blues—the seeds, really—as well as its tensions with the sacred world and the white establishment, were formed under the extreme conditions of slavery. Thus the rest of this chapter provides a very condensed, but important, history of slavery, slave music, the Civil War, Reconstruction, and the launching of the blues near the turn of the twentieth century.

* * *

Colonists began using existing African slave trade routes in the mid–1600s. African tribes typically enslaved their defeated enemies,[11] and Europeans created an enormous market demand for those slaves, ultimately sending some 11 million Africans to the Americas. Transportation conditions, alone, were so inhumane that more than a million slaves died en route to their destination.[12]

In the American colonies, African slave labor was cheaper than other alternatives and Africans were more resilient to Western diseases than Native Americans. The moral justification for slavery was grounded in inherent notions of primitiveness, inferiority, and saving slaves through "civilizing" practices, especially Christianity. No other people looked less like the European immigrant colonists, given Africans' generally thicker lips, wiry hair, and dark skin that would "blatantly and permanently" identify one not merely as different but also as a slave or a slave ancestor.[13] The version of slavery that existed in North America would be far more devastating than other forms in history. The Greeks and others, for example, at least allowed for a human status of their slaves, though of a lower station, something that did not happen in the U.S.[14]

Religiously, Africans had generally seen themselves as being at the mercy of an array of gods. As Amiri Baraka wrote, theirs had been "a culture with complex concepts of predetermination and the subservience of the human being to a complex of gods." Their new world in America, however, was highly industrialized and commerce based, and it saw the "'ultimate happiness of mankind' as the sole purpose of the universe."[15]

Musically, too, the cultures seemed somewhat alien to one another. One culture focused on order and melody; the other embraced rhythm and fluidity. Even each culture's approach to a single note was distinctly different.

In the West, notes were addressed directly, while Africans addressed notes from different angles, "above or below," and, as Baraka further noted, "the timbre is veiled and paraphrased by constantly changing vibrato, tremolo and overtone effects. The timing and accentuation, finally, are not stated, but implied or suggested. The denying or withholding of all signposts."[16]Where Westerners had little appreciation of rhythm, the African neglect of harmony and melody and their use of polyphonic rhythmic effects were seen as evidence of primitiveness.[17] Further, Africans communicated by drums through a complex phonetic reproduction of words, which sounded to the European ear as little more than a primitive Morse code.[18]

African American innovation, rhythm and an ability to wring complex emotions out of even a single note would change everything. Some two hundred and fifty years later, the African approach would morph into jazz and the blues, foundations of the world's modern popular music. The once silenced voice of the slave would finally be heard, but it would be a long wait.

* * *

How to appreciate the day-to-day life of slaves in this "benign" and peculiar institution? First, these lives were notoriously hard to document.[19] Slaves were not allowed to read or write, and the usual societal avenues of expression were nonexistent.[20] As a result, the oral tradition of slaves was rarely documented until well after the events had occurred. As theologian James H. Cone observed, the experience of enslaved black Americans had been "to feel their way through the course of American slavery."[21]

A basic understanding of slavery can be gleaned from Kenneth Stampp's culling of the agricultural periodicals of the era that had effectively served as slave owner manuals, such as *Southern Cultivator, American Cotton Planter and Soil of the South*, and *Debow's Review*. From these, Stampp identified some of the universally accepted methods of successful slave ownership. For example, the first step was that slaves were to be "broke" through use of rigid discipline.[22] The goal was "unconditional submission," just like "a minor to his parent or a soldier to his general." Violence was a regular occurrence that "most" slaves experienced, and the threat was omnipresent.[23] Through rigid discipline a slave would learn to "obey implicitly" and "cheerfully and with alacrity."[24]

Also, from the time slaves were first marched off of ships in chains, slave owners instilled a stamp of "personal inferiority," and racial segregation ensured that blacks and whites would never become familiar with one another, as familiarity would lead to notions of equality.[25]

Other steps in the breaking process were to establish a continuous "principle of fear," or "awing" the slave with an overwhelming show of power. To do so, the plantation owners reasoned that "we have to draw the reign tighter and tighter day by day to be assured that we hold them in complete check."[26] Slave owners further cultivated a "habit of perfect dependence" by preventing slaves from becoming educated, and so on.[27]

Slave marriages were not recognized,[28] and a family unit was considered to be a mother and a child, often broken up at estate sales; a "father" of a slave was an "unknown" concept.[29] The father could not provide any physical protection for his wife and offspring, no matter how many abuses they endured.[30]

Despite the proclaimed subhuman status in every other aspect of Southern life, slave owners regularly had their way sexually with slave women. This practice, as one Southern judge of the time stated in a written opinion, was "too common, as we all know." Another Southern writer noted that it had "almost ceased to be a temptation to fail." Though hugely underreported, the 1860 census indicated that some 12 percent of slaves were mixed race or mulatto.[31]

While sex between white males and slave women was essentially winked at, it was accepted in Southern society that the Negro women were inherently lustful and the seducers of white males. At the same time, interracial sex between white *women* and slave *men* was—without question—rape, and an automatic and instant death sentence for the male slave.[32]

Finally, slaves constantly walked a line of appeasing white people while, internally, keeping a sense of self, dignity and resistance. "No massa, me no want to be free," was all a slave owner needed to hear to confirm what they already believed they knew of the contented slave.[33] Perhaps most challenging, psychologically, slaves had to find some sort of acceptance and to simply get by. As one song put it, "Got one mind for the boss to see; Got another mind for what I know is me."[34] A descendant of the "Happy Negro," of course, was all U.B. Phillips and others could see and well into the twentieth century.

Scientifically, no one was familiar at the time with the basic psychology of suppressed rage, post-traumatic stress disorder, the Holmes and Rahe stress scale, the effects of trauma and the resultant release of cortisol into the brain, and so on. One widely published physician of the 1850s, Dr. Samuel A. Cartwright, identified a condition he called "drapetomania," a scientific explanation as to why slaves escaped, why they did not take to their slave duties enthusiastically, or why were they otherwise lazy and lethargic.[35] The cure was, in the doctor's words, "whipping the devil out of them."[36] In reconciling notions of authority, the Devil, and Christian morality of the day, certain sacred-secular tensions start to come into focus.

Slaves and Religion

Bringing Christianity to slaves in the early 1700s had been a dangerous proposition. The stories of Jesus and Moses and the release of those in economic, social and political bondage were the antithesis of the goals of slave culture.[37] But the planters believed that they could impose a carefully crafted religious program that would actually strengthen the institution of slavery. At first, with only white ministers doing the preaching,[38] and using carefully censored Bibles,[39] planters believed that religion would help increase obedience and serve to sedate slaves, particularly the more pliable slave children.[40] Thus the white version of Christianity was heavy on ideals such as those expressed in Luke 12:47: "He that knoweth his master's will and doeth it not, shall be beaten with many stripes!" Few white theologians or clergy spoke out.[41]

Christianity did spread among slaves, although they did not necessarily accept a divine spirit that condoned slavery. One black minister of the day noted that most slaves *knew* that slavery was not God's will and "that oppression and slavery are inconsistent with the Christian religion; therefore they scoff at religion itself—mock their masters, and distrust both the goodness and justice of God."[42] From another slave narrative:

> Uncle Silas was near 'bout hundred, I reckon—too feeble to do no work, but always got strength enough to hobble to church when the slave service gonna be. Ol' preacher was Reverend Johnson—forget the rest of his name. He was a-preachin' and the slaves was sittin' there sleepin' and fannin' theyselves with oak branches, and Uncle Silas got up in the front row of the slave's pew and halted Reverend Johnson. "Is us slaves gonna be free in Heaven?" Uncle Silas asked. The preacher stopped and looked at Uncle Silas like he wanted to kill him, 'cause no one ain't supposed to say nothing except "Amen" while he was preaching. Waited a minute he did, lookin' hard at Uncle Silas standin' there, but he didn't give no answer. "Is God gonna free us slaves when we get to Heaven?" Uncle Silas yelled. Ol' white preacher pulled his handkerchief and wiped the sweat form his face. "Jesus says come unto me who are free from sin and I will give you salvation." "Gonna give us freedom 'long with salvation?" ask Uncle Silas. "The Lord gives and the Lord takes away, and he that is without sin is going to have life everlasting." Then he went ahead preachin', fast-like, without paying no attention to uncle Silas. But Uncle Silas wouldn't sit down; stood there the rest of the service, he did, and that was the last time he come to church.[43]

How could slaves find peace in a life of shackles and degradation, generation after generation, with no apparent basis for hope for the future? How could they accept such a fate as the will of God?

White Christians had much evidence that an unseen God was looking out for *their* interests, and a Manifest Destiny was, in their eyes, the result, just as it had been with the decimation of the Native American peoples. However, slaves had virtually no external assurances of God's existence. If God did exist, He did not seem to be offering the slave any hope for relief for *centuries*, or at least certainly not in the physical world. As slaves long sang in the fields, "Sometimes I feel like a motherless child."[44]

Slaves and Music

From the beginning of slavery, slaves embraced music. Music allowed slaves to express themselves religiously and spiritually to ease the burden of their labor and to manifest and affirm their own humanity. Planters made every effort to strip slaves of their African culture. The drum, for example, was banned outright to prevent slaves from using it to communicate across great distances in order to organize violent uprisings—the constant white fear. While it had been common to sing while working when living in West Africa, where most early slaves were from, references to African religions and spirituality were suppressed by whites. Still, slaves orally transmitted and incorporated African song traditions.[45]

Religiously, slaves took Christian hymns and added African lyrics, structure, and performance, as well as an immediate and heartfelt life experience. The result was something wholly original: the Negro spirituals.[46] Spirituals, the direct precursor of black gospels in the early 1800s, and, more indirectly, of the blues around the turn of the twentieth century, were further characterized by a certain physicality, such as handclaps and foot stomping. As one slave explained, "You see the Catholic preachers from France wouldn't let us shout, and the Lawd done said you gotta shout if you want to be saved. That's in the Bible ... you gotta shout and you gotta moan if you wants to be saved."[47]

At the same time, W.E.B. DuBois called the spirituals the "sorrow songs" because they were "the music of an unhappy people, of the children of disappointment; they tell of death and suffering and unvoiced longing toward a truer world, of misty wanderings and hidden ways."[48] But by working through their sorrows, spirituals allowed the slave to be "free in the midst of 'a powerful lot of tribulation.'"[49]

Many slaves applied their own perspective to the stories of the Bible and were thus able to deepen their faith in Jesus and lighten their loads at the same time. While Paul said, "Obey your master," slaves focused on the Old Testament and the Hebrews. Slaves saw themselves clearly as chosen people in songs like "To the Promised Land I'm Bound to Go," "Heav'n Shall-a Be My Home," and "We Are the People of God."[50]

Scripture provided decided underdogs as heroes, including Jesus, of course, as well as Moses, who leads slaves to freedom, and David, who slays a giant.[51] As to what slaves thought of the white perspective of the Bible, the last line in one spiritual explained, "But everybody talking 'bout Heaven/Ain't going there."[52] By relating to biblical figures and affirming the their own place in the world, slaves could reclaim the *self* that slavery could so easily strip away.

Jesus walked his lonesome valley
He had to walk it for himself,
Nobody else could walk it for him,
He had to walk it for himself.[53]

Black preachers eventually brought a new message: "You are created in God's image. You are not slaves, you are not 'niggers'; you are God's children."[54] Thus, many slaves found a path to a promised land beyond death, and that faith not only changed their instant reality but also brought a freedom where there was no such thing.

* * *

Not all slaves could accept Christianity in any form, of course. For some, centuries of slavery was either the clearest evidence of the absence of God or otherwise indicative of a nasty, evil entity. On the secular music side, slave work songs or field hollers, and slave recreational songs, were direct precursors to the blues. Work songs were used to synchronize tasks in rhythm, as well as allowing slaves to work out some of their frustrations with every step or thrust of a hoe. Music was thus integrated into a slave's day-to-day actions, and even the most mundane and physically draining of tasks could be transformed into something more life-affirming and cathartic. Some forms were called "moans" and "groans," which were deeply emoted versions of slave songs, combined with "humming and spontaneous melodic variation," probably derived from African vocal traditions.[55]

A singer in the fields repeated lines over and over until he or she could think up a new one—they had all day, every day, after all—often in AAA or AAAA patterns. The lead called out the first half of the line, and the rest responded. One work song was "Arwhoolie (Cornfield holler)":

Oh, etc.
I won't be here long.
Oh, etc.
Oh, dark gonna catch me here,
Dark gonna catch me here.
Oh, etc.

At other times, in different forms, secular music mocked the white man's religion:

> I don't want to ride no golden chariot
> I don't want no golden crown
> I want to stay down here and be
> Just as I am without one plea.[56]

When slaves did get free time, recreational music was characterized by improvised homemade string instruments, like the African-derived banjo, and drums, as well as dancing.[57]

* * *

In the film adaptation of former slave Solomon Northup's memoir, the Academy Award–winning film of the same name, *12 Years a Slave* (2014), Northup tells of his former free life in the North, with his family, until he is kidnapped into slavery in the South. Northup is shown being broken down and reduced to his core being, despite his personal strength and hopes of regaining his former life. In a later scene at a fellow slave's funeral, Northup finally gives in, partly to the hopelessness of his plight and the will of a brutal slave master. Yet Northrup is not quite hopeless. Really, he has surrendered to the Negro spirituals being sung all around him, and he finally joins in for the first time. Those songs, with their rhythms, melodies, soulfulness, and communal call-and-response, provide a very real salve, and even hope, in a world seemingly devoid of comfort. In those spirituals, the slaves found peace in a place so deep within that even slave masters could not take it away.

Capturing this moment of musical conversion, if you will, might be one of the great expressions of American history ever put on film. Along with the spiritual connection for Northup, one can also perhaps hear in that scene the blues, jazz, Mahalia Jackson, Little Richard, and, for that matter, the Beatles and so much of popular music since. It is an immense musical and spiritual legacy.

Emancipation and the Rise of the Blues

In the mid-nineteenth century, tensions increased between Northern and Southern states, primarily regarding slavery (and ancillary issues of states' rights, federal powers, and westward expansion). With the election of an anti-slavery president, Abraham Lincoln, in 1860, Southern states began to secede, and the Civil War broke out in the spring of 1861.[58]

Company E, 4th U.S. Colored Infantry, Fort Lincoln, District of Columbia (ca. 1863–1866) (photograph by William Morris Smith, Library of Congress).

On January 1, 1863, after more than two hundred years of slavery, Lincoln signed the Emancipation Proclamation, freeing the slaves in areas then in rebellion against the federal government. On April 9, 1865, Confederate general Robert E. Lee surrendered in Appomattox, Virginia, ending the South's drive for independence, followed toward the end of that same year by ratification of the Thirteenth Amendment, which ended slavery for good. Freed slaves rejoiced; at long last, a white man up north named Lincoln had done the almost unthinkable.

Nothing would ever be the same for African Americans; yet, for decades to come, nearly every milestone of racial progress and change in the Deep South would be met with violent resistance and retribution. On April 14, 1865, five days after Lee's surrender, Lincoln was shot in the back of the head by the well-known Southern actor and megalomaniac, John Wilkes Booth.[59] The reins of America, at its most critical juncture, were then handed over from one of history's highest-regarded presidents to one of its very lowest, Vice President Andrew Johnson.

The Civil War had been the nation's bloodiest up to that point, with 500,000 or more soldiers killed.[60] The South had tried to wear down the numerically and industrially superior North, and the North responded with ever more crushing advances and devastation, ultimately leaving the South in a physical and economic shambles.[61] The South was then left to rebuild its once thriving economy without its greatest capital asset: slave holdings.

Andrew Johnson was a former U.S. senator from Tennessee, as well as the sole Southern senator who had opposed cessation. Thus, where Lincoln had earned a measure of respect in the South with his stated agenda favoring quick reunification over retribution, the South saw Johnson as a traitor from the beginning. Johnson would subsequently manage to largely alienate the North as well, through various presidential acts that enabled the South to install white supremacist governments; "Black Codes," which formally denied blacks their civil rights, such as the right to vote; and anti-black generals. Instead of Reconstruction, the South saw and allowed all manner of physical violence and terrorist activity toward blacks, including a powerful and unchecked Ku Klux Klan.[62] Johnson became the first president to be impeached, and he avoided conviction in the Senate by a single vote short of the two-thirds requirement.[63]

In the first year after the war, 2,000 black men, women and children were killed in Louisiana alone in what one historian referred to as the systematic "culling of alpha males" that would not stay in their place.[64] There had been widespread looting by blacks immediately after the Civil War.[65] Northerners were more likely to see this as a by-product of the devastation of slavery on all aspects of black culture and psyche. As one Northern colonel said, "Slavery has made them what they are; if they are ignorant and stupid, don't expect much of them; and give them at least time to [improve] before judging them by the highest of standards."[66] Yet, because of their close proximity with African Americans for so many years, Southern whites believed that they understood such things in a way that Northerners did not,[67] and that slavery "had been a response to African's inferiority, and not its 'cause.'"[68]

Johnson issued a general amnesty in 1872, so that Southern state governments were scarcely different from what they had been in 1861,[69] and he revoked General Sherman's special field order that had granted freedmen forty acres and a mule, enough to start a small family farm. Despite modern estimates of unpaid slave earnings and reparations in the trillions in current dollars, freedmen were given nothing.[70] They were on their own in a hostile world.

Instead of redistributing plantation land to the poor whites and blacks, as Radical Republicans had argued for, the U.S. focused on massive railroad expansion. Heavy subsidies and land grants spurred a boom for wealthy landowners where the tracks would run, but overinvestment and a lack of immediate returns saw the bubble burst, leading to the Panic of 1873. The panic then became a depression, hitting the South particularly hard.[71]

There were also great successes, and a black middle class did begin to take shape. African Americans soon had their own doctors, lawyers, scientists, and authors, although the vast majority of jobs were still very low paying, such as maids and cooks.[72]

To secure the necessary Southern votes to retain the presidency in the disputed 1876 presidential election, Republicans withdrew federal troops and federal oversight, and they promised federal subsidies so that the New South could continue to rebuild without Northern or black influence in what became known as the Great Compromise of 1877.[73]

Crime (specifically black crime) increased in the South in the 1880s, including the number of rapes of white women by black men, but nothing that warranted the horrific levels of retaliation brought down on all blacks. Blacks were imprisoned and lynched for simply being a threat to the powers that be, and they were regularly convicted of crimes they did not commit.[74] Arthur Raper investigated nearly a century of lynchings and concluded that approximately one-third of all the victims were falsely accused.[75]

After some political progress, an economic collapse again hit poor whites hard, resulting in the Panic of 1893 and another depression.[76] After that, faced with reconciling the interests of rich whites, poor whites, and blacks, as historian John Hope Franklin wrote, demagogues "provided a solution of the class conflict among whites that offered no challenge to the political power and economic privileges of the industrialists and the planter class."[77] Between 1890 and 1900, more than 1,200 blacks were lynched, most in the Deep South.[78] Even a conservative, former governor of Alabama, William C. Oates, was left to wonder in 1901, "when the Negro is doing no harm, why [do] the people want to kill him and wipe him from the face of the earth?"[79]

By the turn of the century, it was widely accepted that race relations were worse than at any time since emancipation. Even longtime supporters in the North were losing faith in blacks as the movement toward equality seemed to stall out. Now the blame was being placed on African Americans for failing to assimilate.[80] The U.S. Supreme Court legitimized white supremacy and segregationist Jim Crow laws in *Plessy v. Ferguson* (1896), which upheld segregation in railroad cars, and other cases. Even the Northern bastion of liberal justice, the *New York Times*, weighed in with sympathy for the white South: "They have been forced to choose between a policy of manifest injustice toward the blacks and the horrors of Negro rule."[81] The white South was emboldened to even further entrench and formalize its racial caste system.

Finally, funds meant to educate blacks were diverted from Negro schoolchildren to white schools, since it was seen as unnecessary where blacks were going to be engaged in menial labor anyway. Educating African Americans only threatened to upend the system. Then-governor of Mississippi, J.K. Vardaman, proclaimed that the funds provided by the North for black schools in the South were "not money but dynamite; this education is ruining our Negroes. They're demanding equality."[82]

Even the highest-ranking members of the U.S. government in the South could unapologetically disfranchise as many black people as possible and publicly defend the extra-judicial lynching of blacks. In a 1900 speech on the Senate floor, a former governor and then senator from South Carolina, Benjamin Tillman, declared, "We of the South have never recognized the right of the negro to govern white men, and we never will. We have never believed him to be the equal of the white man, and we will not submit to his gratifying his lust on our wives and daughters without lynching him."[83]

In 1895, Booker T. Washington gave a speech recognizing the seemingly insurmountable obstacles of white supremacy. He advocated for blacks to redirect their efforts to carve out a niche foundation as solid working-class artisans (such as brick masons, carpenters, and blacksmiths), a pragmatic approach intended to recognize the realities of what the white powers were ready to tolerate.[84] Washington believed that blacks needed to start with more accessible jobs as a foundation for more complete participation as American citizens.[85] But even a call for pragmatism, applauded by whites in attendance, was seen by other blacks, including W.E.B. Dubois, as submissiveness and defeatism.[86]

Around the same time, the president of the United States, Theodore Roosevelt, entertained Booker T. Washington at the White House, something the *Richmond Dispatch* considered "a deliberate, threatening act" that undermined the very legitimacy of the Jim Crow South. Senator Tillman publicly opined, "The action of President Roosevelt in entertaining that nigger will necessitate our killing a thousand niggers in the South before they will learn their place again."[87] Roosevelt never publicly apologized for or defended his decision, though he did not invite another black person to the White House during his tenure as president.[88]

5

The Early Blues

> "The blues are about freedom. You know, there's liberation in reality and ... when they talk about these songs, they talk about being sad, the fact that you recognize that which pains you is a very freeing and liberating experience. It's just, it must be strange for other cultures where you spend most of your time trying to pretend like you don't have any of these problems, any of these, you know, situations. When I hear the blues, the blues make me smile."[1]
>
> —Branford Marsalis

Freedom for Southern blacks meant individual rights and physical liberty, but it often meant a more solitary existence as well. There was no social structure awaiting blacks leaving the plantations—no blacks in positions of true power or leadership, no political networks, no fathers as mentors, no friendly bankers, no employment apparatus, no Elks Lodge, no "good ol' boy" networks, no nepotism, and no unions to otherwise absorb the freedmen. This, along with many blacks' lack of respect for the white-imposed slave religion, meant that many free blacks chose to face an uncharted future truly on their own.

For black musicians, freedom often meant taking to the road and playing a new individualized and secular form of music wherever they could. As one writer explained, "With the disintegration of the closely-knit community came relaxed standards of conduct; the authority of the Church was partially undermined; the taboo on secular music became less effective."[2] The bluesman represented a new form of American individualism: not enslaved, free to wander, but not yet having a place in this new world. Giles Oakley wrote in *The Devil's Music: A History of the Blues*, "In this instability, this constant movement and rambling, the one thing which could not be suppressed, and may even have helped give them a sense of unity, was their music."[3]

Precisely how and when this evolving secular folk music came to be *the blues* is unknown. Sometime after the Civil War, in the Deep South, blacks combined the secular slave songs, the unadorned vocalizing and oral traditions brought from West Africa, and original folk music that had "reabsorbed"[4] songs from other popular forms, including traveling medicine shows (in which musicians drew crowds for so-called doctors hawking dubious "medicines"), black minstrels (popular musical stage shows in the second half of the 1800s, featuring African American–derived music, sometimes with black entertainers but also often racist and performed in blackface), and popular Tin Pan Alley songs (so named for the streets in New York where the professional song writers of the era worked). In particular, this music's defining characteristic was that it was "laden with emotional content" derived from the day-to-day lives and struggles of Delta blacks.[5] Finally, starting in 1894, the Sears and Roebuck catalog made well-built, inexpensive guitars available to the lower-income, rural areas of America.[6] Sometime in the 1890s, all of the above coalesced as the blues.

Prior to 1905, the blues were an isolated and purely rural form that had yet to reach a broader audience. At that time, classical European music was still considered far superior to the developing American musical traditions. African American musician and minstrel bandleader W.C. Handy's famous story began in 1903 while he was waiting for a train at a station in Tutwiler, Mississippi, 100 miles south of Memphis. Handy happened to catch a field hand playing the guitar, pressing a knife against the strings and bending them and playing "the weirdest music" Handy had ever heard. The song was about "goin' where the Southern cross the Dog" (a reference to a particular Mississippi railway crossing). Handy was familiar with "jump-ups," a rhythmic type of dance music closely related to the blues, but this was unlike anything he had heard. Handy was struck by the performance.[7]

The full significance of the blues did not occur to Handy until 1905, when he was playing a dance in Cleveland, Mississippi, with his polished band of professionals. During a break, a few locals were allowed to play some of the crowd's "native music." After playing, three young men with a battered guitar, a mandolin, and a worn-out bass took the stage. Said Handy:

> They struck up one of those over and over strains that seem to have no beginning and certainly no ending at all. The strumming attained a disturbing monotony, but on and on it went, a kind of stuff associated with cane rows and levee camps. Thump-thump-thump went their feet on the floor. Their eyes rolled. Their shoulders swayed. Through it all that little agonizing strain persisted. It was not really annoying or unpleasant. Perhaps "haunting" is the better word, but I commenced to wonder if anybody besides small town rounders and their running mates would go for it.[8]

Handy watched as "a rain of silver dollars began to fall around the outlandish, stomping feet.... They had the stuff people wanted. It touched a spot.

Their music wanted polishing, but it contained the essence."[9] Along with the flow of money, Handy was particularly struck by how the performers "pour[ed] their hearts out into song," and, as simple and unpolished as the music was, they did not "lack imagination."[10] Said Handy, "Those country boys back at Cleveland had taught me something could not possibly be gained from books, something that would, however, cause books to be written."[11]

Handy began composing blues numbers, and in 1909 he moved with his band to Memphis, which was already becoming the black entertainment capital of America. While he was not the first to publish blues, he did more to spread the reach of the blues than anyone else. Handy had great commercial success marrying the blues to European instrumentation and composing, recording and publishing blues numbers, including "Memphis Blues" (1912), and he became known as the "Father of the Blues."

Handy's early recordings were orchestral blues, which, to a modern listener, might sound more like Sousa marching songs, ragtime sounds, and very early jazz than the acoustic, rural-sounding, solo blues that might be expected. In fact, until the 1930s, the blues were popular on a national scale, and the biggest sellers were being written by professional songwriters in New York and Chicago. As one writer put it, the early American blues were really the delineation of "the sound of the raw African-American song being put into the recognizable form of a commercial context."[12]

The blues had first gained popularity as dance music, often played with fiddle, banjo, mandolin, harmonica, guitar, and piano. Guitars overtook the banjo in popularity in part because guitars offered the mobile, solo performer a bigger sound and percussive qualities, like a mini-orchestra.

In the mid–1920s, boogie rhythms (likely originating from lumber and turpentine camps) were introduced to the blues, in which "each beat is often subdivided into eighth-note triplets with the middle triplet omitted, creating a shuffle feel."[13] Up until the 1920s, there was little distinction between blues and "country music" played by Southern blacks and whites,[14] although a black performing style became more associated with "grainy vocal textures and emphasis on rhythmic momentum."[15]

The blues are best known for their capacity to convey the heaviest and deepest of emotions and life experiences. Harmonically, the blues became synonymous with a twelve-bar structure, which would also later serve as the template for jazz, country and rock music, and was typically played in 4/4 time. Like much African music, the blues often relied on syncopated rhythms, with accents placed on the weak beats and other unexpected points in the bar.[16]

Lyrical subject matter ran the gamut of rural, black, Southern life of the day: heartbreak, love, poverty, work, travel, rootlessness, restlessness, and death.

The solo blues singer usually followed an AAB pattern (where the first line is repeated in the second line before a new line concludes the stanza) and sometimes AABB. The repetitiveness of the lines often mirrored the repetitiveness of black lives and the challenges of hard labor, low pay, and no respect.

But the AAB structure was also used to convey the often tense and unpredictable nature of the post–Reconstruction, Southern black experience at the same time. In the AAB form, the repeated first line usually referred to an emotionally potent topic. From the first two lines of Alberta Hunter's "Broken-Hearted Blues" (1922):

> Say, I ain't never had but three men in my life.
> Lord, I ain't never had but three men in my life.

Especially with a deep and moving singer, the first two lines are gripping, but the listener is unsure of where the singer is going. The future is always tentative and uncertain. The repeated second line also has the effect of allowing the first line and the music to resonate and sink in deeper. Only with the third line does the listener understand the significance of the first two lines:

> 'Twas my Father, my brother and a man that wretched my life.[17]

The final crucial aspect of the blues is the "blue note." African Americans were not accustomed to the Western twelve-tone scale system, and they especially had difficulty with the third and seventh tones, which fell in between the adjacent tones that they did know.[18] They adapted those tones into their own style. As W.C. Handy noted, "[T]he Primitive Southern Negro as he sang was sure to bear down on the third and seventh tone of the scale, slurring between major and minor."[19] Slaves (and later bluesmen) flattened, or wavered, on those and other tones. Lomax called it "playful voicedness."[20]

The blues guitarist, and particularly the slide guitarists from the Delta, bent the note for emotive effect and to mimic nearly the full range of the human voice. The Delta bluesman could thus use this technique to reflect the call-and-response tradition, where, instead of a preacher and responding congregation, or a caller and field hands, it was the blues singer and his guitar, self-contained and self-sufficient.

Through manipulating nuances of pitch and tone through vibrato (a rapid fluctuation of the pitch) and melisma (singing several notes on the same syllable), a blues performer can convey a wide range of emotion with a single note. Generally, the flatter the pitch, the more intense the feeling. This allows blues songs to be grounded in particularly intense and deep emotions; even moans, shouts, and grunts can be crucial elements of music.

The blues has such varied syncopation that, along with the additional layers of improvisation, a single note can contain an entire spectrum of sounds and experiences, leading to a wide array of distinctive blues styles. Cover versions of blues songs are easily transformed into original works. It was, in fact, common practice for bluesmen to use the same "floating verses" interchangeably in different songs until around World War II.[21]

In the world of popular music, the 1920s saw the arrival of an "urban blues," or "vaudeville blues," dominated by black, professional women singers.[22] Ma Rainey, "Mother of the Blues," and Bessie Smith, in particular, were major stars. Both played the blues with a heavy vaudeville influence, often backed by horns, in black vaudeville theaters and minstrels around the country. Smith's 1925 single, "Crazy Blues," was the first vocal blues hit, Rainey had popular renditions of "See See Rider," "Bo-Weavil Blues," and others. Rainey and Smith were pop stars, but they also brought some sexuality into popular music with their bold, black slang expressions, such as references to jelly rolls and needing some sugar in one's bowl.[23] Those sounds would later be reabsorbed by the rural Delta and other Southern bluesmen of the 1920s, '30s, and '40s.

By 1929, the blues fell out of commercial favor, and many black female singers, such as Billie Holiday and Ethel Waters, moved forward in the more popular areas of jazz and pop. The blues were left to the itinerant blues musician and the more raw, rural blues of the South and of the Delta. This was an unruly life of barrelhouses, gambling dens, juke joints, street performances, and riding the rails, and it became the exclusive domain of men, often solo, accompanying themselves on guitar.

Bessie Smith (1936) (Library of Congress, Prints & Photographs Division, Carl Van Vechten Collection [reproduction number LC-USZ62-54231]).

* * *

Living quarters, store and "juke joint" for migratory laborers near Canal Point, Florida (1941) (photograph by Marion Post Wolcott, Library of Congress).

There is a persistent misconception that the blues are only about sadness and heartbreak. While certainly the blues often deal with sad or other emotionally heavy subject matter, sadness is only part of the story. Blues legend B.B. King explains, "It angers me how scholars associate the blues strictly with tragedy. As a little kid, the blues meant hope, excitement, pure emotion."[24] In fact, the blues are about expressing and *processing* deep emotions, including sadness. The blues are, as Branford Marsalis put it, a way to "recognize that which pains you," ultimately leading to a "freeing and liberating experience."[25]

The bluesman had a purpose in confronting deep, painful topics, even if (or especially if) situations were out of his control. In writer Howard Thurman's words, the blues are for those things that "disappointment can't do anything about."[26] This was the Delta, after all. The early bluesman was resigned to the fact that he only had so much control of his life; thus playing and feeling the blues was not wallowing in self-pity and grief, but rather an opportunity to feel and experience his way through an otherwise unavoidably difficult life, with little belief that things were going to change for the better. He was free, and free to roam, but incredibly limited and constantly vulnerable at the same time. After all, not only did the bluesman encounter social pressures and violence, but the fear of going to hell was stronger and more palpable in the evangelical churches of the Deep South than anywhere in the country. Alan Lomax related one terrifying such sermon, "Hell Is a Place," with its alarming warnings: "*There is a Hell!*"[27] As will be shown, that characteristic of the South, that tension, would inspire both great blues and great rock and roll.

The blues were about establishing meaning and identity largely without the outside reference points of white society or the white supremacist–endorsed Bible. Bluesmen sought what was real in what Howard Thurman, again, described as a "broken existence."[28] One early bluesman described the process for him: "If a man feel hurt within side and he sing a church song then he's asking for God's help.... If a man sing the blues it's more or less out of himself.... He's not askin' no one for help, and he's not really clingin' to no one. But he's expressin' how he feel."[29]

Unlike gospel music, the blues were not necessarily going to help the performer or listener deal with a Day of Reckoning or with his or her afterlife—at least not as the church saw it. Yet the bluesman was less concerned with heaven and more with dealing with the realities of the here-and-now, which was enough. A bluesman represented a different sort of spirituality. Thus James H. Cone noted, "By sharing trouble with each other, [Delta bluesmen] could move to another level of human existence, in spite of being a non-being in the community."[30]

To bluesmen, preachers often represented not only a less exciting (and possibly pointless) path in life but also an empty moral hypocrisy. Preachers were well off compared to their poverty-stricken parishioners, and some did not always embody the highest of Christian principles—the misdeeds of such men included using their status to engage in extra-religious relationships with female congregants.[31]

The freedom of emancipation had "meant that the church was no longer the only place for the 'new priests.'" In fact, aside from preachers, the *only* other job for African American males in the South that did not involve answering directly to a white man was that of the itinerant bluesman.[32]

The blues further embraced physical and sexual elements of music not present in either religious or white society. There had long been an inherent physicality to black life in the Delta, including all forms of abuse, deprivations, an utter lack of material comfort, and the unrelentingly physical nature of everyday work. Some poor whites experienced some of the above, but certainly in far less severe terms. The bluesmen also unapologetically embraced their sexuality and subverted respectable society's mores (at least those mores being presented publicly). This physical component is why theologian James Cone called the blues the "secular spirituals." Cone further explained:

> People who have not been oppressed physically cannot know the power inherent in bodily expressions of love. That is why white Western culture makes a sharp distinction between the spirit and the body, the divine and the human, the sacred and the secular. White oppressors do not know how to come to terms with the essential spiritual function of the human body. But for black people the body is sacred, and they know how to use it in the expression of love.[33]

In other words, white people have historically tended to be more uptight and stiff.

Since the church would rarely address sex, except in the context of procreation or sin, blues music filled a certain void in the life of many Southern African Americans, serving as a link in a mind-body-soul connection. To Cone, the blues "affirm the bodily expression of black soul, including its sexual manifestations. They are spirituals because they are impelled by the same search for the truth of black experience."[34]

Jitterbugging in a juke joint on a Saturday afternoon, Clarksdale, Mississippi (1939) (photograph by Marion Post Wolcott, Library of Congress).

Finally, where outspoken sexual aggressiveness had long gotten black men killed in the South, the bluesman could sing openly about whatever he wanted, whether in references like Big Bill Broonzy's "Rockin' Chair Blues" (1940) or partly humorous expressions, such as in Robert Johnson's "Terraplane Blues," in which Johnson uses a double entendre about checking a car's oil. The blues were a rare social avenue through which a black man in the Delta could truly express his manhood. Such references could certainly be crude, or at times even crass, but in general they reflected real life, they entertained, and they were also an expression of freedom and a reclaiming of both one's sexuality and one's self.

Jazz

The blues helped spawn jazz, and the two genres have always been heavily intertwined. First, ragtime came about in the 1890s in the piano parlors and brothels of St. Louis, popularized by Scott Joplin's ragged and syncopated piano rhythms (e.g., "The Entertainer," 1902).[35]

While W.C. Handy was cleaning up the blues in Memphis, the first strains of jazz emerged from the ragtime sound in the opening decade of the twentieth century in New Orleans, though with no clear "inventor." The name *jazz*, itself, is of unclear origins, possibly deriving from either one slang term meaning *spirited* or another meaning *sex*.[36] New Orleans brass bands approached the blues rhythm with a style that was "lazier and yet insistent: swinging."[37] The city of New Orleans saw regular interaction between Creoles (those of mixed black and white heritage) and African Americans. The Creoles brought European and parlor influences, brass instrumentation, and the sound of traditional French military marching bands, while the black influence provided a foundation of blues and deep African roots.[38] In jazz, the individual musician would let loose and improvise in a way never before seen in music. Jelly Roll Morton combined the blues with syncopated rhythms and expanded the reach of this early, Dixieland-style jazz.[39]

Yet jazz's individualized improvisations could still be done within an ensemble. For many, it personified the spirit of America. According to a 1925 *Survey* magazine article, "Jazz with its mocking disregard for formality is a leveler and makes for democracy."[40] Jazz was to become a worldwide sensation in the Roaring Twenties. Along with the artistic and intellectual movement of the Harlem Renaissance (e.g., writers Zora Neale Hurston and Langston Hughes), jazz announced not only the worthiness of African American musicians, such as Fats Waller and Duke Ellington, but also that African Americans could have enormous worldwide impact.

The establishment took notice of this new loosening of social norms. In 1921, the *Ladies Home Journal* ran a series of articles asking, "Does Jazz Put the Sin in Syncopation?" The magazine reported that "jazz disorganizes all regular laws and order; it stimulates to extreme deeds, to a breaking away from all rules and conventions; it is harmful and dangerous, and its influence is wholly bad."[41] In 1923 in Chicago, a group called the Illinois Vigilance Association announced the "downfall" of one thousand girls as a direct cause of jazz music.[42]

Louis Armstrong first broke the genre open, challenging how music was even approached. Armstrong's improvisational genius elevated the entire genre, and he became jazz's most important star. He was born in New Orleans in 1901, hailing from a poor neighborhood tough enough to be nicknamed "The Battlefield." Armstrong's father abandoned him at birth, and his mother regularly resorted to prostitution to make a living. Armstrong dropped out of school in the fifth grade to work. At twelve, he celebrated New Year's Eve in 1912 by firing his stepfather's pistol in the air, an act that landed him in the Colored Waifs' Home for Boys. There Armstrong took advantage of music lessons and further developed his passion for music.[43]

By the mid–1920s, Armstrong had his own band, the Hot Five (later known as the Hot Seven), with whom he made some of the most crucial recordings in jazz history, including "Potato Head Blues" and "West End Blues." Jazz became synonymous with the excitement—and hedonism—of the prosperous, "Roaring" 1920s. The youth of America, and in Europe, were cutting loose in Prohibition-era speakeasies with daring dances, including the Charleston and the cake walk, all set to jazz.

Armstrong helped jazz attain mainstream acceptance by reworking popular standards, such as "Ain't Misbehavin'" (1929) and "Star Dust" (1931). His radiant personality and humor further made him a lasting and irrepressible force, and he became one of the most popular entertainers in the world. Armstrong appeared with Bing Crosby in the 1936 film *Pennies from Heaven*, and he became the first African American with featured billing.[44] By the 1950s, Armstrong was a beloved icon and grand ambassador of jazz.[45]

The leaders of the great black, big band, jazz orchestras of the 1920s and 1930s, Duke Ellington, Count Basie, and Fletcher Henderson, became some of the biggest names in popular music. These bands brought further improvisational artistry to the form and popularized a swinging take on the traditional, black call and response.

In the 1930s, white musician Paul Whiteman popularized a tamer "symphonic jazz" that was more palatable to the mass white audience.[46] Whiteman became very wealthy, and the white press dubbed him the "King of Jazz."[47]

Big band leaders Benny Goodman and Glenn Miller, both white, also became giants of jazz in the 1930s and were hugely influential. In fact, Goodman was similarly crowned by the media as the "King of Swing" (and not Ellington or Basie).[48]

The early jazz players made integrated collaborations despite segregation, with Goodman's band being the most visible example. Goodman used his fame to promote the causes of black musicians at a time when even the premier New York jazz club of the 1920s and 1930s, Harlem's Cotton Club, only sat white patrons. Goodman brought African American stars Teddy Wilson and Lionel Hampton into his trios and quartets, though technically they were not actually in the band. Jazz showcased African American cultural achievement and increasingly put such dubious barriers into question.[49]

That jazz's biggest names were African American and Jewish players did not go unnoticed in certain corners. One prominent music critic warned of the effects of "Semitic purveyors of Broadway melodies." Additionally, automobile magnate, noted racist, and fierce anti–Semite Henry Ford wrote about jazz in his own newspaper, the *Dearborn Independent*, referring to the music of black jazz players as "[m]onkey talk, jungle squeals … camouflaged by a few feverish notes," and warning of "the abandoned sensuousness of sliding notes" from Jewish jazz players.[50]

At that time, jazz artists were not taking overt actions toward civil rights causes, nor would such attempts have been tolerated. By the 1950s, Armstrong, in fact, had been labeled by some other African Americans as overly subservient and even an "Uncle Tom."[51] Armstrong's relentless positivity and ear-to-ear smile was interpreted by some as being tantamount to the "Happy Negro" of the past. Realistically, though, the America of Armstrong's heyday (when even a Harlem club was segregated) was decades away from tolerating a black man using such immense popularity for political purposes. Armstrong did, however, become vocal in support of civil rights in the mid–1950s.[52]

One example of jazz's social impact came from Austin, Texas, in 1931. At that time Charles Black was a white, Austin born-and-raised sixteen-year-old. As Black later wrote, he and his friends had "literally never [seen] a black then in any but a servant's capacity." But when Black heard Armstrong play in an Austin hotel, he became "the first genius" Black had ever seen. "It is impossible," Black wrote, "to overstate the significance of a sixteen-year-old southern boy's seeing genius, for the first time, in a black." After completing law school, Black was inspired to join Thurgood Marshall's legal team in the march toward securing the *Brown v. Board of Education* (1954) school integration decision.[53]

Jazz historian Stanley Crouch summarized race and jazz as follows:

"Once the whites who played it and the listeners who loved it began to balk at the limitations imposed by segregation, jazz became a futuristic social force in which one was finally judged purely on the basis of one's individual ability. Jazz predicted the civil rights movement more than any other art in America."[54] Jazz did in fact allow black and white artists the individual freedom to express their own voices and artistry. But while jazz presented an enormous challenge to social norms and divisions, it did not yet quite crash those boundaries. There is also a distinction between the most artistically significant bands of the jazz era and what was popular, as "most of the top songs of the jazz era had their origins in Tin Pan Alley."[55] An act like Louis Armstrong's Hot Five, for example, was heard by relatively few music fans.

Musically, jazz helped inspire and shape rock and roll. According to the *Greenwood Encyclopedia of Rock History*, the "use of swing's horns playing riffs in a bluesy style, with vigorous sax solos and a driving rhythm," all directly led to rock and roll.[56] The fluidity and pulsing swing of jazz also ran through R&B and Western swing, and thus directly into rock's bloodstream, and most free-flowing piano or guitar solos are heavily indebted to jazz in one way or another. As Armstrong put it, "If it hadn't been for jazz, there wouldn't be no rock and roll."[57]

6

The Delta and the Devil—and Freedom

Fertile Land

At the turn of the twentieth century, the Mississippi Delta region was a place where the freedoms of post–Reconstruction America and the most severe oppression of African Americans clashed. It was a special environment for a special music.

In the 1880s and 1890s, African American journalist Ida B. Wells published controversial investigations regarding the true causes of lynchings in the Delta and the South. For example, in 1892, Wells published a pamphlet suggesting that white women and black men might sometimes have sexual relations because sometimes a white woman would be attracted to a black man. Upon publication, her Memphis office was burned down and she was run out of town.[1] However, Wells' findings on the real causes of lynchings were confirmed in later studies. One, a 1990 study by Beck and Tolnay, found that from 1882 to 1930, increased numbers of lynchings corresponded with times that white farmers faced tougher economies.[2]

Segregation formally took hold at the turn of the twentieth century, including the proliferation of small signs indicating "White" and "Colored," which appeared on everything from drinking fountains to theater entrances, and swimming pools to cemeteries.[3] In 1904, African American bishop Charles B. Galloway wrote that black Mississippians had begun "to feel friendless and hopeless."[4] In 1907, John Sharp Williams was elected to the U.S. Senate from Mississippi in part by explicitly opposing training schools for blacks, as they would put blacks "into competition with white mechanics and artisans."[5]

At that time, the plantation system was still at the center of Southern caste traditions, both literally and symbolically. The ingrained view of a landowning planter was that of a Southern gentleman at the highest levels of power and respectability, benevolently overlooking his fiefdom. That fading ideal of Southern life was always recalled with reverence, like the fictitious lead characters in *Gone With the Wind* recalling their beloved estate, "Tara." Southern historian David Cohn wrote that even though "most leading economic and political figures in the Delta pursued a variety of business and investment interests, most of them preferred to be identified as planters."[6] The working-class and poor whites of the South (i.e., the "hillbillies") did not have such options.

Noted Southern writer William Alexander Percy described the long-standing Southern aristocrat view of the three-part Southern class system (comprising white landowners, poor whites, and blacks) in his memoir, *Lanterns on the Levee: Recollections of a Planter's Son* (1941). Percy spoke for many in his statement about the poor white "hill-billies" who had "seep[ed] in" to the Delta "from the hills of Alabama and Mississippi":

> I can forgive them [poor whites] as the Lord forgives. But admire them, trust them, love them—never. Intellectually and spiritually they are inferior to the Negro, whom they hate. Suspecting secretly they are inferior to him, they must do something to him to prove to themselves their superiority. At their door must be laid the disgraceful riots and lynchings gloated over and exaggerated by Negrophiles the world over.[7]

The Southern caste system required constant monitoring and vigilant policing of "uppity niggras" and "nigger lovers," as Alan Lomax further documented.[8] Even peaceful demonstrations or discussions of racial equality were taken as threats to the Southern way of life and thus met with violence.[9] For example, in 1918, a long-practicing black Vicksburg physician, Dr. J.A. Miller, who was also a co-founder of Mississippi's first National Association for the Advancement of Colored People (NAACP) office, was jailed on charges of "sedition" before being taken from the jail by a mob, tarred and feathered, and then paraded around town before being put on train out of the state.[10] Successful farmers might see a new purchase of livestock poisoned,[11] and a black man painting his fence (or otherwise not "staying in his place") could find himself the victim of a lynching.[12]

Black women in the Delta worked for low wages either in white homes or on the farms, while black males were sharecroppers or workers in levee or turpentine camps. The reality of the Delta was that a black farmer's survival always required a special relationship with a white man,[13] whether for physical safety, protection in any transactions with third parties, or security in a courtroom. In short, not to be a pliant, obedient "good nigger"[14] was to be entirely on one's own.[15]

Whites continued to support black churches, largely for the moral legitimacy that such support afforded them, but also due to a perception that the churches reinforced the white status quo.[16] While black literacy rates rose from 5 percent in 1850 to 50 percent in 1900, the continued education of blacks remained a threat.[17] School funding ratios for expenditures by white students to black students were 5:1 in 1913, and up to 8:1 by 1941.[18] As late as 1940, the Mississippi state senate narrowly rejected the adoption of a textbook that would have excluded all references to voting, elections and democracy—this in a civics textbook specifically written for black children.[19]

The basic, hopelessly skewed rules regarding sexual relations remained intact through the first half of the twentieth century as well. A white man known to have mulatto offspring was not disgraced, whereas a white woman engaged in relations with a black man might be sent away by her family and labeled promiscuous, at the very least. A black male involved with a white woman, however, faced certain death; as Cobb put it, the only variable would be "the degree of horror" of that death. In the view of white society, such killings were heroic acts necessary to protect the purity of Southern white women. According to Cobb, fear of reprisal kept white men "in constant danger and in constant dread."[20] As such, any black men not at work from dusk to dawn, and thus with time to think and otherwise organize themselves, were a perceived threat and could be arrested for loitering.[21]

Since shortly after the end of the Civil War and into the twentieth century, Mississippi had instituted for-profit convict "lease" camps, with private landowners leasing convicts (mostly black) from the penal system. Convicts endured around-the-clock work,[22] clearing swamps, digging in gas-filled mines, and building railroads, while beatings, disease, and early death were all constants.[23] One writer noted that "[t]he fear of such a fate was in the backs of the minds of every black man in the South, always."[24]

Penal slavery was finally banished in 1906.[25] As late as 1957, however, the *New York Post* reported, "The state penitentiary system at Parchman is simply a cotton Plantation using convicts as labor."[26] One of the more prominent Parchman convicts was Delta bluesman Bukka White, the cousin and mentor of B.B. King, who memorialized his former residence in "Parchman Blues" (1940).[27]

* * *

African Americans serving in Europe during World War I were exposed to new horizons. First, the war brought African Americans into contact with Europeans for the first time, allowing them to meet white people who treated them as equals.[28] Never again did those African Americans have to accept

Southern protestations that racial equality was an impossible or unnatural state. The veterans returning from European tours were more emboldened than ever, and they were no longer willing to accept the status quo. Even in the North, some five hundred thousand newly migrating blacks[29] found themselves clashing with whites in bitter competition for industrial jobs.[30] The first year after the war, 1919, was the year of the Red Summer: an explosion of racial violence and rioting, much of it in the North, including Chicago and Washington, D.C., as well as some two dozen cities across Virginia, Nebraska, Texas, South Carolina, Arizona, Tennessee and Arkansas.[31] In Chicago, 23 were killed, 600 wounded, and thousands burned out of their homes.[32] The riots were largely massacres of black neighborhoods by whites, except that some blacks were responding with violence of their own.[33]

To a Southern white, an emboldened black vet was an "uppity nigra" and a danger to the Southern, Christian way of life. Thus post-war years were met with not only stronger Jim Crow laws but also a rebirth of the Ku Klux Klan, as well as public, extra-judicial lynchings of southern blacks.[34] In 1919, seventy blacks were lynched across the South, including many soldiers (some of them still in uniform).[35] Local police forces were always to blame either for encouraging mob rule or for willingly turning a blind eye. Each produced a lasting "shock effect" across black communities and on every black person in the region: *This could be you.*[36]

All manners of torture and mutilation were part of the show, particularly castration. Fingers and other body parts were common souvenirs. Anti-lynch laws were stymied by Southern congressman through the 1920s and into the 1930s.[37] By the 1920s, the KKK had a staggering four million members.[38] The NAACP took out a newspaper ad to note that the United States was "the only place in the world [where] they burn people alive."[39]

The conventional wisdom was that lynchings were necessary to protect Southern white women from savage black rapists and to maintain Southern order. As historian David Colburn put it, and dating to the influences of Sir Walter Scott, "Southern culture had been constructed around a set of mores and values which places white women at its center and in which the purity of their conduct and their manners represented the refinement of that culture. An attack on women not only represented a violation of the South's foremost taboo, but it also threatened to dismantle the very nature of southern society."[40] Yet rape was only an excuse for about 30 percent of the lynchings in the South. Indeed, two of the most notorious and devastating assaults on blacks—rioting in Tulsa, Oklahoma, in 1921, and the murders and razing of the all-black town of Rosewood, Florida, in 1923—both began with fraudulent allegations of a black man sexually assaulting a white woman.[41]

The Great Mississippi Flood hit in 1927. Pounding rains overwhelmed the banks and levees of the Mississippi River, killing 246 people and causing $400 million in damage. The federal government responded with the $325 million 1928 Flood Control Act.[42] This meant an infusion of job opportunities in levee camps and lumber camps. As Alan Lomax documented, however, instead of decent wages and autonomy, the result of this infusion was even worse working conditions. Camps even more isolated from outside eyes meant that blacks were "actually worked to death alongside the mules they drove." After all, a traditional aphorism in the Delta at the time was "Kill a nigger, hire another, kill a mule, you got to buy another one."[43]

In the farmlands of the Delta, plantations were self-sufficient communities, controlled entirely by the planter, with the larger ones even printing their own money, which may or may not have been accepted in the next town. Each planter treated a black sharecropper in his own way, and no one spoke up or interfered with another's personal dealings with blacks. Tenants got half the "profit," but the profit came after the tenant's living expenses, accrued over the year (i.e., "the "furnish," including tools, food and clothing), had been deducted. Tenants were not allowed to see the books, and complaining about discrepancies was dangerous. No Southern court would find in favor of a tenant.[44] Sharecropper families would often uproot themselves in the middle of the night to get a clean slate somewhere else, even if the overall terms were no better.[45]

Still, the white South had convinced itself that blacks were happy, and the realities (and perceptions of reality) for whites and blacks remained light years apart.[46] Even one of the more progressive Southern historians, David Cohn, wrote matter-of-factly in 1938, "[T]he present relatively untutored Negro of the Delta harbors no feelings of bitterness or revenge against the whites unless the disabilities under which he labors are too cruelly pressed upon him. If he is able to earn a living and seek happiness among his own people, he is content."[47] On the other hand, black Southern native Richard Wright wrote in *Black Boy* (1945):

> The white South said that it knew "niggers." ... Well, the white South had never known me—never known what I thought, what I felt. The white South said that I had a "place" in life. Well ... my deepest instincts had always made me reject the "place" to which the white South had assigned me. It had never occurred to me that I was in any way an inferior being. And no word that I have ever heard fall from the lips of southern white men ever made me really doubt the worth of my own humanity.[48]

Not unlike slavery, maintaining the Southern caste system required believing that it was the natural way of God, while, paradoxically, that system also required the most intrusive and violent coercion to enforce the so-called natural order. As soon as industrial jobs opened up in the North, beginning with the need for manufacturing jobs during World War I, hundreds of thousands of African Americans left Mississippi and the South in droves about as fast as they could, much to the surprise of most whites.[49]

* * *

When all political action, or even simply speaking up, is hammered down at every turn, and oppression is so complete that it seems that even God is against you, rebellion has to be seen in a new light. Since rebelling directly against the laws and religion of white society was futile, one view was that a true black outlaw needed to go further.

One famous story from the annals of the Delta passed on from the 1930s, from Natchez County, Mississippi, involved a black man known only as "Roy." Most condemned men—who were virtually always black—asked the attending preacher and God for forgiveness in their final minutes at the gallows. Roy, it was said, had refused to ask for forgiveness and before meeting his death had instead said that he "wuz goin' to hell an' bus' in de do' and break off de Devil's horns." Roy attained a form of folk hero status in the Delta, not so much because he had killed someone but because he did not ask for forgiveness in his moment of truth. In doing so, Roy refused to legitimize the white supremacist legal system and, more to the point, a white supremacist God. Roy rejected the white world in its entirety; even staring death in the face, he was going to take his chances in any afterlife. In this sense, Roy was free of white control.[50]

The essence of Roy's story is also represented in the most well-known black folk character of the Delta, "Stagolee" (also known as "Staggerlee," "Stag-o-Lee," or other variations). In fact, these two stories melded together over the years. Stagolee's story has been immortalized in innumerable blues songs and can in fact be traced back to a true story. In 1895, in a St. Louis saloon, black pimp "Stag" Lee Shelton got into a disagreement with William "Billy" Lyons. At some point, Lyons grabbed Stag Lee's Stetson hat. Lee told Lyons to give him back his hat, and when Lyons refused, Lee shot Lyons three times with his .44. With Lyons lying against the bar, Lee casually walked over, took his hat back, told the dying Lyons to never mess around with a man's hat, and walked outside. As in Mississippi John Hurt's 1928 blues song, "Stackolee," not only did the protagonist not go in for social niceties, but he also stood tall and unapologetically accepted his fate at the gallows.[51]

Stagolee came to personify the "bad nigger," the precise antithesis of the satisfied and compliant "nigra" that white society wanted.[52] In some versions, Stackolee scares the Devil himself before taking over Hell altogether.[53] Lloyd

Price's classic, hard-rocking 1959 track, "Staggerlee," was a hit, and it had to be censored to be played on *American Bandstand* (1952–1989). As rock writer Greil Marcus observed, the legend of Stagolee has carried on in spirit, as seen in "Muddy Waters' cool and elemental Rollin' Stone; Chuck Berry's Brown-Eyed Handsome Man" and "Mick Jagger's Midnight Rambler."[54] The head of the Black Panthers, Bobby Seale, used the legend as a recruiting tool in the 1960s. By the late 1980s, Stagolee could especially be found in the ultra-rebellious and often fatalistic spirit of gangsta rap.

A final real-life crime tale from the Delta is likewise telling. In 1934, near Cleveland, Mississippi, a white family comprising a father, a pregnant mother, and a young son suffered a horrific attack. The boy's head was battered, though he lived. The father died from a gunshot wound to the back of the head. The mother's head had been bashed in; an unborn fetus was ripped from her body.[55] The killer was a black man, James Coyner, who at the time was already being investigated for sending lurid letters to white women around the Midwest. When asked if he regretted the horrific murder, Coyner replied, "No, no more than if I had spilled a glass of milk. What's done is done, what's bothering me right now is that this jailhouse is cold."[56]

The threat of either a lynch mob or severe retaliation against all blacks in Cleveland was strong, and the governor of Mississippi sent in the National Guard to keep order. The Cleveland courthouse was converted to a fortress; machine guns were planted on the corners and rooftops, covering every way in and out of the courthouse, while an armed escort brought Coyner to trial. The spectacle sufficiently awed the crowd and dissuaded any thoughts of violence on the part of white observers.[57]

It was reported that blacks were not only present in large numbers outside the court house but also relaxed as they "talked, laughed and watched with keen interest and proud eyes the goings and comings of the guardsmen." Some sold drinks to the guardsmen. Others speculated on the weaponry: "Nigger if I had me a swamp-injin like dat I could sho raise me a ruckus."[58]

African Americans gathered outside the courthouse every day of the trial—normally a rare occurrence, given the high chance of racial retaliation. In fact, the black population of Cleveland could not even envision that it was the governor of Mississippi who had sent protection; they assumed that the troops must have come from Washington, D.C., to defend them. Many blacks gathered around the courthouse, partly infatuated with the outrageous outlaw Coyner, who could commit such a heinous act against whites—and with zero remorse. Blacks were also incredulous that such efforts were made to actually ensure a *trial*, and especially to protect the crowd itself.[59]

For many of the whites on hand (mostly poor whites), the message of the troops was different: blacks would be protected no matter what they did, and a centuries-old order was being destroyed. The fear, as it had been since emancipation, was that now blacks would become "uppity," and that was the worst outcome of all. "A white man ain't a-goin to be able to live in this country if we let niggers start getting biggity. Wish they'd lemme have him. I'd cut his black balls and th'ow 'em to the hawgs," said one. Said another, "That's what's ruinin' 'em and makin' fools out of niggers. Niggers air a braggin' on ever' plantation in this county that the governments a-pertectin' 'em and we gonna haf to kill a lot of the black bastards to knock some sense into their kinky heads."[60]

Coyner was hung at four in the morning to minimize trouble.[61]

The Delta Blues

Sociologist Charles S. Johnson described a 1930s and '40s Delta "underworld" where bluesmen, outcasts, so-called "bad niggers," renegades, gamblers, and prostitutes lived hard lives, though one payoff for these individuals was being free from the "regular" world under the thumb of a white man at all times.[62] Because of, and despite, these extreme living conditions, the Delta region produced bold experimentation and an expression of often turbulent stories, as well as some of the best and most influential music of modern times. Charley Patton, Son House, Muddy Waters, Robert Johnson, Willie Dixon, John Lee Hooker, Howlin' Wolf, B.B. King, and many others, rose out of the Delta to convey, in Baraka's words, "some of contemporary America's highest aspirations and darkest secrets with incomparable music."[63]

Robert Palmer described the Delta sound: "The Mississippi Delta's blues musicians sang with unmatched intensity in a gritty, melodically circumscribed, highly ornamented style that was closer to field hollers than it was to other blues."[64] Delta guitarists were deeply rooted in rural folk music, with a sparse but intense sound. They innovated with slide guitars, using the neck of a soda bottle to make the guitar "moan" and "speak," like another voice, as well as using guitar boogie patterns and bass patterns. Also, pop and vaudeville were more influential in the Delta than is generally appreciated.

The first great Delta bluesman was Charley Patton, "The Father of the Delta Blues." Patton was born in 1889 (d. 1934) in Bolton, Mississippi, one of twelve children, seven of whom died in infancy.[65] Patton left an abusive but staunchly Christian home to make a living as a performer. He was a protégé of a Henry Sloan, who introduced Patton to a very early form of blues,[66] and and he drew from nineteenth-century ballads, dance music of the time, as well as the up-tempo country blues, long enjoyed by both blacks and whites.[67] Patton stood 5'7" and weighed about 135 pounds, but he was an outsized personality with a powerful voice clearly heard several hundred feet from the stage in pre-electric amplification days.[68] He became a celebrity among blacks in the Delta and an immensely influential musical mentor.

Patton was also funny, with a vaudevillian flair and sometimes raunchy lyrics in songs like "Shake it & Break it (But Don't Let it Fall Mama)" (1929). He was a top-notch showman and a character, described as "rakish, raffish, easy to provoke, capable of downing massive quantities of food and liquor, a woman on each arm, [and a] flashy, expensive-looking guitar."[69] Some of the women on Patton's arm were spoken for, and at one point Patton survived a throat slashing, possibly from a jealous husband, that left him with a scar from ear to ear.[70]

Patton was a mesmerizing and technically excellent guitarist with a vast array of styles. Onstage, he could electrify by throwing his guitar in the air or playing between his legs. He used slide guitar techniques, with strong, syncopated rhythms and a driving beat. He also popped his bass strings, something funk guitarists would start doing in the 1970s. His voice was hoarse, whiskey-and-cigarette-scarred, and passionate.[71]

Patton sold well in the black South and he had several hits at the end of the 1920s and early 1930s, including "Pony Blues," "Screaming and Hollering the Blues," and "Boll Weevil Blues." The last song was tribute to the insect that drove white planters crazy, a quality blacks came to appreciate.[72] Further, Patton directly mentored and otherwise influenced future blues heroes, including Son House, Honeyboy Edwards, Willie Brown, John Lee Hooker, and a young Howlin' Wolf.[73]

Despite Patton's influence and popularity in the Delta, few whites ever heard him. His first recordings were lost when the record company folded, and his only other recordings were of poor quality and made when his voice was especially worn.[74] Patton's death went unnoticed outside the region.[75] His protégés' impact, however, is another story.

Son House was a legend in his own right, though he wasn't well known until a 1960s folk revival and the dawning of the British Invasion that he had heavily influenced. House was born March 21, 1902 (or thereabouts), near Clarksdale, Mississippi. House resented his sharecropper life, and he became a preacher until settling in as a top musician in the region in the 1930s. In 1928, he shot and killed a man under unclear circumstances; House claimed self-defense. He, too, served two years at Parchman until his family and a white plantation owner intervened and he was released.[76]

House's internal struggles once led him to say of the Devil and God, as well as his career choices, "the two just don't get along."[77] House recalled a time in his life when even watching someone play a guitar made him angry and uncomfortable.[78] House's intense style reflected that deeply felt conflict, and he sorted out some of his dilemma in "Preachin' Blues, Part I," in which he prepares to pray but instead the blues overtakes his spirit. House used a near religious fervor, and gospel and Negro spiritual influences, along with his distinctive slide guitar style, to help define the Delta blues.

One of House's disciples was Muddy Waters, who himself would, of course, eventually become a household name after migrating out of the Delta and making the Chicago "electric" blues famous, but back to him later. House also passed his blues sound and feel to Robert Johnson.

* * *

The true story of Robert Leroy Johnson, as best has been determined, begins with his birth in Hazelwood, Mississippi, likely on May 8, 1911. Johnson had a chaotic childhood. He was variously known as Robert Spencer, R.L. Spencer, Robert Dodds, and possibly other names.[79] Robert Johnson was the illegitimate child of Noah Johnson and Julia Major Dodds, while Julia Dodds already had ten children with her husband, Charles Dodds. However, in 1909, Charles had been chased out of Hazelhurst after a run-in with local white landowners. Julia then traveled around to various jobs in the fields, one by one sending the children to live with Charles (who had in turn taken on the surname Spencer). At about three years of age, Robert himself went to live with Charles. Julia, Charles, and the family would not be reunited for several more years.[80]

The teenage Johnson lived in Robinsonville, where he learned the blues from Patton, House, and House's partner Willie Brown. In 1930, at nineteen years of age, Johnson tried to start his own family—only to see his young wife, Virginia Travis, and their newborn both die in childbirth.[81]

Johnson went away for a year or two, possibly seeking his father, before returning to Robinsonville.[82] At one point, Johnson met up with another teacher, Isaiah "Ike" Zinnerman, in Martinsville.[83] Zinnerman was known to practice at night in graveyards, apparently because they were quiet places; however, this habit made him the subject of supernatural rumors of his own, which also could have rubbed off on Johnson.[84]

With Johnson's transformation into a top bluesman, he brought a whole new dynamic to blues rhythm, as well as a unique voice and songs that conveyed deep and complex emotions. Despite Johnson's modern reputation, songs like "When You Got a Good Friend" were surprisingly self-reflecting and sweet. As Johnson's former playing partner Johnny Shines described:

His guitar seemed to talk—repeat and say words with him like no one else in the world could. I said he had a talking guitar and many a person agreed with me. This sound affected most women in a way that I could never understand. One time in St. Louis we were playing one of the songs that Robert would like to play with someone once in a great while, "Come On in my Kitchen." He was playing very slow and passionately, and when we had quit, I noticed no one was saying anything. Then I realized they were crying—both men and women.[85]

Johnson was more diverse than just the limited songs he managed to record in 1936 and 1937. Delta musicians were often typecast as pure country hicks, though many Delta bluesmen, including Johnson, were usually meticulous in their appearance, very consciously leaving the backward stereotypes behind.[86]

Further, Johnson could and did play all of the pop hits of the day. To make a living playing the blues on street corners, as well as in juke joints, the dark, heavier blues alone were not going to cut it. Muddy Waters, for example, explained early on that his influences were as much Gene Autry and other mainstream fare, such as "Chattanooga Choo-Choo," as they were gut-bucket Delta blues.[87] Yet, while extremely talented, pop-style Delta bluesmen such as Leroy Carr, for example, did not fit the Delta stereotype and quickly faded from history.[88]

As a guitarist, Johnson was a crucial innovator credited with bringing the "boogie style" to the blues, in which he incorporated playing across the low-end bottom strings of his guitar, a new dynamic in rhythm at the time and now synonymous with the blues. When Rolling Stones guitarist Keith Richards first heard Johnson playing by himself, he asked who the "other guy" was playing with Johnson?[89]

Instead of floating verses, which both House and Patton had used extensively, Johnson created more personally themed songs. He was especially successful in combining real-world experiences with metaphor and blurring reality and myth. Thus "Crossroads Blues" is both a seemingly simple and literal tale of a black man at a crossroads, and an allusion to some deeper spiritual and psychological crisis (as opposed to a literal Satanic pact).

Johnson was constantly on the move, establishing few long-term, one-on-one relationships, although one peer, Honeyboy Edwards, recalled of Johnson, "He was an awful friendly guy. He talk with the public a whole lot—he played music in public and he liked to laugh and talk and drink.... He was a nice fellow.... You could get close to him. You could always talk to him."[90] But Johnson was also always on the next train, heading from the Delta through the Midwest and North to Detroit and Chicago. Shines recalled:

Say for instance, you had come from Memphis to Helena, and we'd play there all night probably and lay down to sleep the next morning and hear a train. You say, "Robert,

> I hear a train. Let's catch it." He wouldn't exchange no words with you. He's just ready to go. We'd go right back to Memphis if that's where the train's going. It didn't make him no difference. Just so he was going.[91]

Johnson sometimes specifically created songs that appealed to women for sympathy and a place to stay.[92] Johnson had a preference for those who might be more likely to take him in. As Shines put it, "Heaven help him, he was not discriminating. Probably a bit like Christ, he loved them all. He preferred older women in their thirties over the younger ones, because the older ones would pay his way."[93] This regularly led to trouble in the already unforgiving Delta environs. Shines recalled seeing Johnson chased by an ex-girlfriend with an ice pick, in addition to run-ins with their husbands and boyfriends, and that was what allegedly killed him.

Memphis: "Capital of the Mid-South"

The Delta region is vast and flat, resulting in relatively cheap land, though it is also highly fertile, making agriculture its most profitable use. As such, Memphis was the only large city to develop in the region. Memphis was especially well-placed to take advantage of the great transportation network of the 1800s: the Mississippi River and its tributaries. Plus, the city sits on the bluffs overlooking the Mississippi, so it doesn't flood, unlike most cities on the river. By 1850, Memphis was a prosperous hub for both "King Cotton" and slave trafficking.[94]

Later, the Memphis and Charleston railroad linked the East to the rapidly expanding West in 1857.[95] Memphis is so geographically centered, in fact, that at the beginning of the Civil War, Tennessee did not immediately secede along with the rest of the South. Those in Memphis' cotton industry were strongly tied to Northern markets and financial centers, although slave owners, heavily dependent on slave labor, ultimately won out.[96]

Being on the Mississippi River meant that everything came through Memphis, both good and bad. The swampy land and persistent flooding around Memphis were a breeding ground for mosquitoes and bacteria, giving Memphis a reputation as a tough place to live, along with repeated outbreaks of yellow fever and evacuations in the 1800s. At one point Memphis even lost its status as a city.[97] But there was also an influx of cultural influences, including fresh entertainment from the showboats and, later, jazz drifting up the Mississippi from New Orleans and down from St. Louis.[98]

Immediately after the Civil War, Memphis became the big city for newly emancipated slaves. African Americans traveled to Memphis from the brutal worlds of the cotton fields, levee camps, and lumber camps. If anyone needed a place of respite, a playground, or somewhere to blow off a whole lot of steam, it was the African Americans of the Delta.

By the turn of the century, Memphis was established as the un-official "Capital of the Mid-South,"[99] as well as the black entertainment capital of America. Memphis anchored black life as an entertainment mecca, an economic center, and a short-term waystation for blacks on their way out of the South forever.

Robert Church, who would soon become the first African American millionaire from the South, had bought up land along Beale Street and, in 1899, he built a 2,000-seat recreational center, a landscaped park and an arboretum. More black-owned and black-oriented businesses followed.[100] W.C. Handy continued to popularize the blues, and music clubs and bars flourished on Beale Street itself, the all-black entertainment district. Beale consisted of thriving clubs and theaters boasting an overabundance of top musicians, soon earning it the name "The Home of the Blues." At night, Beale Street filled with people: "A one block walk could mean a detour around the medicine show set up in a little hole in the wall, as much as stopping and listening to the wandering bluesmen playing for pennies and nickels." In the Roaring Twenties, the Palace and the Daisy hosted big vaudeville shows, Memphis jug bands played at the nearby park, and the red-light district thrived a block over on Gayoso Avenue.[101]

A prime example of the exciting but sometimes chaotic scene on Beale was the Lansky Brothers clothing store, which catered to a predominantly black, and flashy, clientele. Bluesman Sunnyland Slim summarized the feel: "All the best dressin' fellows in the world came from Memphis. It was the greatest town for pimps and hustlers. That's where a whole lot of people got killed, you know."[102]

A person could get just about anything they wanted in Memphis, from relaxation and church services to most any vice. By 1905, the city had 500 saloons for a population of 150,000. In many of the backrooms of those saloons, gambling and prostitution thrived. In 1905, Memphis was named "murder town" by one researcher, a reputation the city carried into the 1940s.[103]

In 1900, cocaine was so prevalent in Memphis that one official estimate was that 80 percent of black Memphians had tried the drug. In 1902, Coca Cola Bottling introduced cocaine into its popular soft drink, and a network of Columbian cocaine connections was established that remained even after the ingredient was removed from the drink in 1905.[104] In the late 1920s, a popular group known as the Memphis Jug Band was singing the "Cocaine Habit Blues."

Throughout the first half of the twentieth century, one man dominated Memphis politics: E.H. Crump. Crump first served as mayor of Memphis for two terms, from 1909 to 1915, and then held other offices, but it was always Crump calling the shots from behind the scenes through a highly corrupt (and highly effective) political apparatus. Crump even enlisted W.C. Handy to write a popular campaign jingle for him, "Mr. Crump," which was later adapted into the 1912 hit "Memphis Blues."[105]

During his reign, Crump maintained the strictest of racial segregation in Memphis, making interracial contact mostly nonexistent. As late as 1945, for example, the film *Brewster's Millions* was banned in Memphis because a black character was too chummy with the white characters in the film.[106] Crump further took care of those white business owners who profited from the vices in the black sections of town, ensuring their political and financial support, as well as support from those who partook of the vices. Thus, the rest of the white populace was happy to not have to deal with blacks except for doing the menial labor around the city. One could walk down a busy, all-white Main Street for blocks, but when one turned left onto Beale, it became strictly black. White Memphians were also largely oblivious to the music on Beale, and no radio stations played black-produced music in Memphis until the late 1940s.

In the 1920s and 1930s, national publications such as *Redbook* and *Collier's Weekly* exposed Memphis' blatant tolerance for organized crime and its huge profits.[107] During the Great Depression, the cotton economy faltered, and the profits from organized crime were in even greater demand. Memphis crime families built empires on prostitution, booze and cocaine. In a milestone of either forward or backward progress in civil rights, Memphis brothels became integrated in the 1920s. While white men had always had access to black prostitutes, for the first time black men could have relations with white prostitutes after 3:00 a.m.[108]

Crump controlled Memphis so thoroughly that after decades of working hand-in-hand with the city's organized crime interests, he later took full credit for cleaning up Memphis' vices in the 1940s. Many of those operations simply relocated across the river to West Memphis, Arkansas, at least until the political climate cooled off.[109] Crump long avoided the label of being among the worst of Southern racists, although once the concept of civil rights came to Memphis in the 1940s, he was heard to remark, "You have a bunch of niggers teaching social equality, teaching social hatred. I am not going to stand for it. I've dealt with niggers my whole life, and I know how to treat them."[110]

* * *

How the spirit of the Delta blues migrated from the fields to Memphis, and then to the world beyond, is figuratively and literally embodied in the life story of one B.B. King. King, also known as the "King of the Blues," was born in 1925 as Riley B. King, to Albert King and Nora Ella Farr, in Itta Bena, Mississippi. The family soon moved to a sharecropper's cabin on a Delta plantation just outside Indianola, Mississippi.

King lived in the shadow of slavery, growing up with stories from his great-grandfather about his life as a slave. As a child, King witnessed a lynching, and as a young man, he observed Nazi prisoners of war working in the fields being given breaks from the scorching sun, while African American laborers were not.[111]

King's father left when he was four, and they had little contact with one another for decades. King's mother was too poor to raise him herself, and she shuttled him back and forth from her home to that of his aunt. At six, King was milking cows before and after school, and by seven he was working in the cotton and corn fields.[112]

At nine years of age, King's mother became sick; little medical care was available for blacks at the time, and she soon died. King could not even be sure what she had died of. Suddenly alone, he later recalled, "I felt like the world might do anything bad to me at any time"[113]:

> Maybe I'd been a loner before Mama died. Maybe I was born with that temperament. But when Mama died, seems like I decided to become even more of a loner. I believe that's how I dealt with her death. I remember going over to Aunt Mima's and sitting on the floor with my ear against her Victrola. Something in the music kept pulling me in. The blues was bleeding the same blood as me. The blues didn't have to explain the mystery of pain that I felt; it was there in the songs and voices of singers like Lonnie Johnson and Blind Lemon Jefferson, in the cries of their guitars. I'd also listen to the spirituals of Sam McCrary of the Fairfield Four gospel quartet. For hours on end, I'd lose myself in the music until Aunt Mima would worry my mind wasn't right.[114]

King moved in with his maternal grandmother, but a couple of years later she contracted pneumonia and she died, as well.[115] The young King had an opportunity to move in with other relatives, but he instead chose to stay where the memories of his mother were. There was King, virtual orphan, fourteen-years-old, black and smack in the middle of Jim Crow, just coming out of the Depression, living by himself in a sharecropper shack, with no electricity or plumbing. Just King and his guitar. A few years later, he moved in with other family members.[116]

King went to school through the tenth grade; then he dropped out to work and make money. As a teen, King worked behind a mule for twelve-hour days.[117] He described the plantation he lived on as "a world unto itself," where plantation bosses were "absolute rulers" and sheriffs would not interfere with the planter-sharecropper relationship even if pursuing a suspected criminal. Said King, "It gave you a double feeling, you felt protected, but you also felt small, as if you couldn't fend in the world for yourself."[118] For example, to get his first guitar, King's boss had to buy it "for him" from out of his wages. Still, King developed lifelong friendships with two of the white plantation owners he worked for.[119]

Along with music, family trauma, racism, and music, women defined King's life story:

> To have a woman simply caress my cheek or stroke my forehead or hug me tight was a comfort and a thrill. I've been lost in the love of women my whole life, and I'm not complaining, not changing my attitude that I need women as much as I need water to drink and air to breathe. Without women, I'm lonely and unhappy and unable to cope. With women, seems like life makes sense and the stress goes away.[120]

In his autobiography, King recalled losing his virginity at *six* years old to a seven-year-old girl. King eventually fathered fifteen children in his life.[121] He even named his guitar "Lucille" after an incident at a bar in 1949, when two men got into a fight over a woman and knocked over a lantern in the process. A fire broke out and King ran back into the building for his guitar. He named his guitar as a reminder of the girl who was the subject of the fracas and to remind himself to never risk his life over either a woman or a guitar again.[122]

King's passion for music had first begun in church; later, when he saw T-Bone Walker playing the electric guitar, he felt "hope, excitement," and "pure emotion," and his fate was sealed.[123] Walker's jazz-inflected blues showed King "a modern bluesman whose blues were as blue as the bluest country blues with attitudes as slick as those big cities I yearned to see."[124]

King described the experience of handling his first guitar: "I couldn't keep my hands off of her. If I was feeling lonely, I'd pick up the guitar; feel like talking, pick up the guitar; if something's bugging me, just grab the guitar and play out the anger; happy, horny, mad or sad, the guitar was right there, a righteous pacifier and comforting companion."[125]

King told a story in concerts from his younger days in Indianola driving a tractor in the cotton fields and doing one long row at a time. At the end of each row, King would turn around and slowly crawl back down the next row. King spoke of one day seeing a gentleman whom he didn't know heading toward his girl's house. But King couldn't do anything about it because he was starting on a new row heading away from her place. King could only watch, not knowing what was going on until he finally returned to the end of the line and could sneak away. By the end of the story, King was on his knees pleading with his girl, and suddenly he was belting out his need for love. And that, for B.B. King, was the blues.[126]

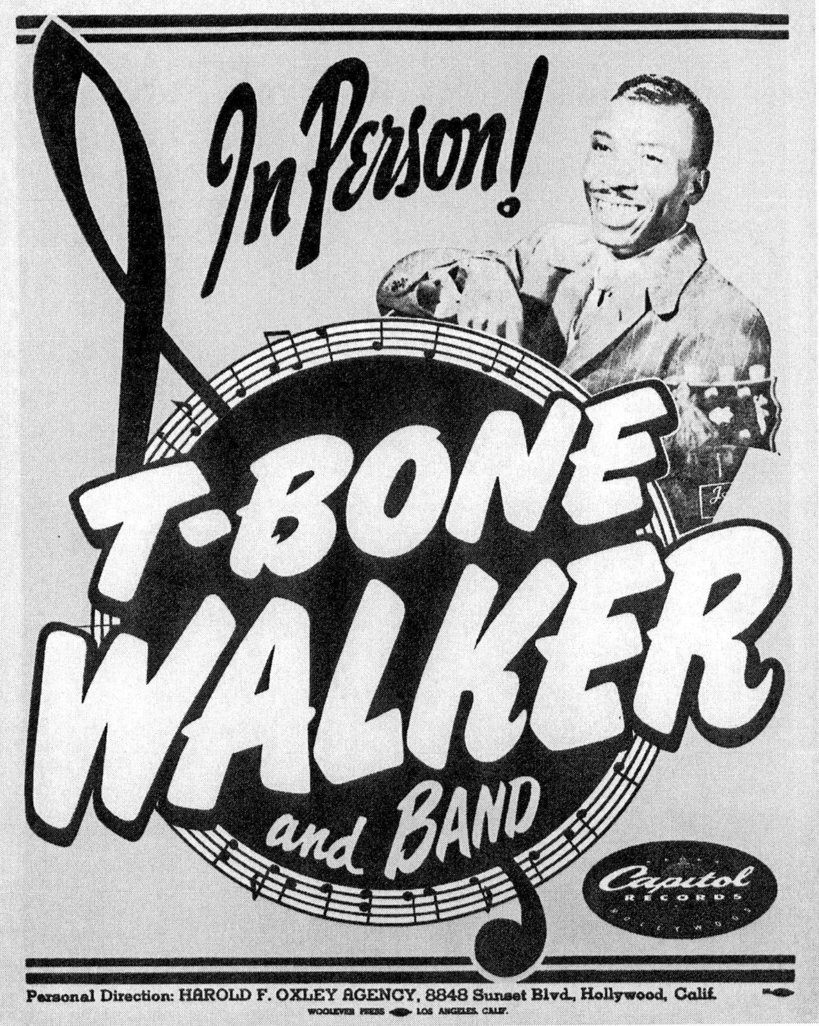

T-Bone Walker concert poster (1950) (author's collection).

Early on King made more money playing the guitar on a Saturday night than he was making working all week in the fields. Despite being scorned by religious locals for playing the secular blues—the "devil's music," as they called it—King gravitated toward the blues. This was partly pure pragmatism:

> I used to sit on the street corners after work. Usually I would sing gospel songs. But if I sang a gospel song, they'd pat me on the head, but never put anything in the hat. When a guy asked me to play something bluesy, often I never even knew what that was, but I would change "my lord" to "my baby"; then they would always give me a tip.[127]

In 1946, King was drawn to the bright lights and blues joints of Beale Street in Memphis. He began playing for peanuts at local talent shows, and he also deejayed across the river on the radio in West Memphis, Arkansas, and then at WDIA in Memphis. In 1948, King recorded tracks with Sam Phillips at Sun Records when it was still known as the Memphis Recording Studio. King helped set the tone in Memphis with Phillips, the now legendary producer then still bent on capturing the incredible but overlooked black musical talent coming out of the Delta and Memphis. King rubbed elbows with friends and contemporaries Elvis Presley, Howlin' Wolf, Ike Turner, Rufus Thomas and others, when all were still virtual unknowns on the local scene. King was soon christened the "Beale Street Blues Boy" or "Singing Black Boy," which was shortened to "B.B."[128]

King scored his first R&B number one hit in 1951 with "Three O'Clock Blues." Not only was he anointed the "King of the Blues," but his arrival in Memphis at the dawn of rock was crucial, for he helped define how the electric guitar would be played. The online reference guide Allmusic.com refers to King as "without a doubt the single most important electric guitarist of the last half century."[129] His style of precise string bends with vibrato with his left hand influenced numerous rock guitar players, including the Beatles' George Harrison, Eric Clapton, and so many others.[130]

In 1970, King scored a number one pop hit with "The Thrill Is Gone," and his career scarcely slowed on into the twenty-first century. He toured constantly and was often sought out for collaborations by everyone from arena rock stars U2 to R&B/pop star Christina Aguilera.[131] King went from his lonesome shack and guitar to audiences with presidents and a pope.[132] He would also happen to have a special (and even more direct) role in the very inception of rock music.

7

The American Hillbilly and Country Music

This book opened with two quotes, one of which was from eighteenth-century French political thinker, Alexis de Tocqueville. Tocqueville presciently predicted that the burgeoning American democracy would leave behind the old European models of class structure and Classicist ideals of order, reason, calm, and rigid class structures. Instead, as Tocqueville wrote, America would embrace a more spontaneous, "strange ... strong and bold" individualism.[1] Romanticism instead prevailed, from the Gothic works of Edgar Allan Poe to Edgar Rice Burroughs' primal tales of Tarzan to P.T. Barnum's transformation of the circus into a modern extravaganza. In the same way, popular music would not just come from those with classical training and folk music, minstrels, and vaudeville would all thrive as well.

In America, the promise was that anyone could celebrate their own story and their own voice, including (and especially) the common man. In Tocqueville's words, "[E]ach citizen of a democracy generally spends his time considering the interests of a very insignificant person, namely himself."[2] The distinction between individual autonomy and narcissism would be an ongoing conflict for individual Americans—and rock stars.

That these Romanticist qualities especially manifested themselves in the American South is not surprising. As writer Robert Pattison summarized:

> The ideal breeding ground for rock should be somewhere steeped in the ideas of nineteenth-century Romanticism, especially Romantic notions of the primitive. It should be an area that has history of translating Romantic ideas into action. It should be an area with a strong preference for the democratic ideas that abet the rise of vulgarity. It should be a locale remote from the intellectual mainstream of Western culture and therefore safe from the censorious scrutiny of an educated elite fussing about the popularization of Romantic ideas. All these conditions were met by the American South of 1954.
>
> The South was Romantic early on. [Southern commentator] W.J. Cash said the poor

Southern white, gorged on the leisure provided him by slavery, became "one of the most complete romantics."[3]

To further explain, pre–Civil War Southern society was especially impacted by Romanticism and especially by the nineteenth-century Scottish writer, Sir Walter Scott. Scott's novels *Ivanhoe*, *Rob Roy*, *Waverly*, and others, all reflected the strong Scots-Irish roots of the region. Scott's recurring themes were in fact the glorification of traditional Scottish ideals and the establishing of a heroic identity in the face of the powerful elites who looked down on them. Rob Roy, for example, was a real historical figure and a noted Highland outlaw, and Scott exaggerated his reputation as a Scottish Robin Hood.[4]

This was all utterly relevant to the rural American South of the late twentieth century. First, the Civil War was lost to the North, and for decades afterward the South lagged economically in an ever-modernizing world. A seemingly antiquated agrarian lifestyle and white supremacist government meant that outsiders often viewed the South as immoral, uneducated and backward. Through Scott's works, however, Southerners saw themselves as idealized Romanticists with strong traditional values in the face of oppression, including notions of chivalry, a glamorized view of war, the glorification of womanhood—and also racist.

To many non–Southerners, including Mark Twain, the Southern fascination with Scott's writings was a misguided attempt to hang on to a distorted and overly sentimentalized view of Southern chivalry. Twain satirized the same in his *A Connecticut Yankee in King Arthur's Court*, even coining the term "Sir Walter Scott disease."[5]

In the early twentieth century, for example, some white Southerners adapted the Scottish iconography of white hoods and burning crosses, symbols popularized by Scott and used by Thomas Dixon, Jr., in his books modeled on Scott's novels, including *The Clansman: An Historical Romance of the Ku Klux Klan*, as well as its popular film adaptation, *Birth of a Nation* (1915). Thus white hoods and burning crosses became central to the second movement of the Ku Klux Klan in the mid–1910s and the 1920s.[6]

Once slavery was abolished, this white Romanticist culture and so-called black primitivism seemed destined to collide with one another. All of the above, then, comprises some of the southern cultural context for the development of its dominant music—country music—as well as being the eventual breeding ground for rock and roll.

The Roots of Country

Country music's roots reach back to the American colonists and a mix of English ballads combined with elements of Scottish reels, Irish jigs, and square dances (i.e., "the poor man's version of the French 'cotillion' and 'quadrille'"), along with strong influence from black culture.[7] While an urban North focused more on modernism and change, rural America and the South embraced a slower pace and the maintenance of cultural traditions, including the music of their ancestors.

Rural Southerners did gradually change out the lyrics to old, love-themed ballads, like "The Lass of Lock Royal," in order to describe their own real-world experiences: work on the farm or on the railroads, tales of real-world tragedies and natural disasters, or stories of crimes such as bank robberies.[8] This music was secular in nature, though it became further infused with some of the religious themes and music of the Southern Protestant revival and camp meetings of the 1800s.[9]

The mid–1800s minstrels further provided a band model consisting of the African-derived banjo, the fiddle from Scotland, and a rhythm instrument, often a tambourine or bones (literally dried animal bones), while the Spanish guitar did not come to the white country bands until 1910.[10] The fiddle (a violin modified so that the fiddler could sing while playing) came to define early country music.[11]

Rural Americans and Southerners saw rural and agricultural life as a virtuous and independent way of living, and country songs were equated with that lifestyle. Common themes included the values of hard but honest work (e.g., "When the Work's All Done This Fall"), family and home life ("The Homestead on the Farm"), and Christian values ("What Would You Give in Exchange for Your Soul?").[12]

After the Civil War and into the twentieth century, however, the pressures of credit and market demands and industrialization would make that agricultural lifestyle increasingly difficult to sustain. Thus country music, like the blues, was born out of a daily struggle for survival and its own tensions. Many God-fearing, poor Southerners believed that getting to the Promised Land meant persevering through the drudgeries and tragedies of this world, including backbreaking work for little reward, hard lives with little medical care, and so on.[13] Traditional country songs like "Keep on the Sunny Side" and "Can the Circle Be Unbroken," both popularized by the Carter Family in the 1920s, represented rural Southern values of humility and faith, as well as helping to provide a spiritual center.

The South and country music also placed a premium on an idealized sense of the traditional rural "home," which included personal and familial bonds, a connection to nature, and a simpler, authentic life.[14] Curly Putnam's oft-covered "Green, Green Grass of Home" and the Carter Family's "My Home's Across the Blue Ridge Mountains" are representative country standards. As writer Cecelia Tichi explained, "Because the natural world is inherently ethical and moral, the farmer—and by implication the farm family—is equally ethical and moral, since he and his family embody the values of the natural world."[15]

Paradoxically, though, in the middle of a changing twentieth century, country music also embraced the freedoms embodied by America's open roads, rails, open spaces, and western expansion. In Laura Ingalls Wilder's famous *Little House* book series of the 1930s, she wrote of life on the nineteenth-century Western prairies, where cowboy songs were "not like lullabies" but "high, lonely, wailings, almost like howling of wolves."[16] That high lonesome style carried on to define the sound of country giants Jimmy Rodgers and Hank Williams.

In short, rural life has long existed with a certain tension with city life and its bright lights and higher-paying jobs.[17] For that matter, while families and small towns can nurture, they also sometimes stifle. As Tichi noted, these otherwise stabilizing institutions can also be "intolerant, blind to the virtues of its offspring, cruelly rejecting its native sons and daughters."[18] Thus sometimes small rural towns can push individuals *to* the open road.

Walt Whitman wrote in his classic American poem, "Song of the Open Road," of the need to get out on those roads to find oneself and become "loos'd

The Gulf Mobile & Northern "Rebel," with service between New Orleans, Louisiana, and Jackson, Tennessee (1935) (Harris & Ewing, Library of Congress).

of limits and imaginary lines, Going where I list, my own master total and absolute."[19] To Whitman, the American roads meant being "Forever alive, forever forward ... toward the best—toward something great."[20] Of course, the conundrum here is that without some sort of solid societal structure, healthy institutions, or perhaps some semblance of home, freedom can also lead to alienation, lack of direction, and loneliness. Often people are somewhere in between these extremes, finding their way. Early, rural country music fans strove to maintain conflicting traditional values and personal autonomy in the face of a changing modern world.

In sum, everyone has a deep need to explore the world around them, to individuate, and to find one's own self. And everyone needs a home. Country music, and not entirely unlike the blues, sought to help resolve that dilemma.

The Origins of the American Hillbilly

In America's southern and rural areas, there has long been a negative stereotype of a particular underclass of poor, fringe whites. This stereotype began to crystallize in the mid-nineteenth century, first around settlers of the Appalachian Mountain region, which generally includes parts of West Virginia, Virginia, Kentucky and Tennessee. These people were labeled with pejoratives such as "white trash," "corn crackers," or "rabbit twisters"; since the mid-1910s, they have often been known as "hillbillies."[21] The term "hillbilly," likely of Scottish origin, first referred to people in a couple of different rural, southern regions, and it was eventually picked up by joke book writers.[22] The name spread and became a catch-all term that included any poor, rural, southern whites, whether from Appalachia, the Ozark Mountains in Arkansas, or elsewhere. Most Americans would see the hillbilly stereotype as humorous, laced with truth and certainly as a largely denigrating term.[23]

One essayist from the mid-1800s described a lazy class of poor white people "condemned to a life of mere subsistence,"[24] while another saw a typical person of the region as one who "sits and plays the fiddle while neglecting his crops and household duties."[25] Into the twentieth century, America's perception of hillbillies continued as a "lazy, slovenly, degenerate people who endure wrenching but always comic poverty, embody[ing] an uncivilized state of raw physicality and sexuality, and possess[ing] an almost superhuman fecundity."[26]

These white folks were seen as so lowly that at times they were even thought to be of a "distinct" race or inferior gene pool, presumed to be the result of inbreeding, miscegenation, or poor diet.[27] They were further considered to be of a lower class even than black slaves and freed blacks. As one nineteenth-century planter put it, "They exhibited a natural stupidity or dullness of intellect that almost surpassed belief."[28]

The existence of such an underclass was also useful for both sides of the political aisle. Late nineteenth-century writers in New York City used the stereotype to further reinforce a social order with modern urbanites at the top.[29] The sad plight of this lower class was thus said to be the natural, logical result of a people not wholly embracing the inevitable march of modernism.[30]

For those in power in the South, the idleness of rural working-class whites further justified the need for rigid top-down hierarchies.[31] How could such a lazy lower class get anything done without strong, paternalistic leadership from above?[32] The hillbilly stereotype was a caricature of backward, rural degenerates, distilling moonshine in the woods, rebelling against federal authorities, and engaging in violent, decades-long, intra-family "feuds."[33]

Moonshining was a significant source of income in what had become an economically depressed region. Nineteenth-century mining mechanization had wiped out many of the already poor region's jobs, followed by the depletion of the area's mineral resources, and then similarly shortsighted and destructive logging practices.[34] As the practice of distilling alcohol was a traditional Scottish skill, moonshining filled an economic void of a poor but practical people.[35] In the late 1800s, in further response to federal officers and federal excise tax collection, moonshiners (many of them former Confederate soldiers) resisted federal law enforcement efforts.[36] Similar dynamics persisted with poor, rural, Southern whites and blacks through both Prohibition and the Great Depression in the 1920s and '30s.[37]

As for interfamilial feuds, they did occur in the region, especially right after the Civil War, when violence and guerrilla warfare were still common. The story of the real-life Hatfields and McCoys of West Virginia and Kentucky, who feuded in the late 1800s, captured the public imagination and became a lasting image. That feud saw a total of a dozen casualties over more than a decade, and the story became a part of the nation's folklore and came to define the region and the stereotype.[38]

* * *

While African Americans were sometimes elevated from the bottom social rung above their poor white neighbors (which in one sense was a positive outcome), this development also placed Southern blacks in direct competition with lower-class whites.[39] Following Reconstruction and into the twentieth century, poor whites, in particular, saw the elevation of blacks and their increasing political power as a direct threat to white supremacy, traditional morality, and their own economic prospects.[40] Further, it was a blow to the pride of an already battered class. After all, if African Americans were "subhuman," for example, and a black farmer was succeeding, what did that say about the poor white farmers left behind? As William Alexander Percy wrote, "Suspecting secretly they are inferior to him, they must do something to him to prove to themselves their superiority."[41] The answer for poor whites was to lash out with the only power they had: violence and fear.

Southern whites formed the first incarnation of the Ku Klux Klan in 1870, followed by the parallel terrorist groups of "white caps" and "night riders" in the decades afterward. That violent extremism was tacitly approved by the white power structure. In this way, and given the rigid social and economic hierarchy of the South, outrage from working-class whites was directed toward African Americans and away from the white elite.[42]

In the early twentieth century, the term "hillbilly" embodied rural Southern working-class values, both good and bad, but also with a parallel meaning that indicated traditional country music, or hillbilly music, and thus any practitioner or fan of that music. Hillbillies were decidedly blue collar, Romanticist, and vulgar, but they also possessed cultural pride and embraced their own traditions.

The Beginning of Modern Country Music

In the late nineteenth and early twentieth centuries, traditional old-time country music absorbed professionally written Tin Pan Alley compositions, along with music from the brass bands and singing clowns of traveling circuses, vaudeville, and medicine shows. In fact, country giants Uncle Dave Macon, Jimmie Rodgers, Roy Acuff, Gene Autry, and Hank Williams all got started in medicine shows.[43] Further, despite the fact that country music would become synonymous with the white South, the deeply complex relationships of white and black Southerners always allowed for the ongoing exchange of musical influences, both conscious and unconscious, in the fields, on the railroad crews, and anywhere else.

Vaudeville dominated American music prior to World War I. Music executives, based in New York City, assumed that there was no market for the raw, hillbilly sound, nor did they think much of that music anyway.[44] In the early 1920s, however, Texan fiddler Eck Robertson and Georgia fiddler

John Carson each released hillbilly records, marking the commercial birth of country music.[45]

In 1924, Chicago's WLS radio station launched "The National Barn Dance," the first radio show in the "barn dance" format.[46] This was quickly followed by others in Nashville, West Virginia, Kentucky, Louisiana, and elsewhere.[47] These shows featured comics, theatrical skits, and pop musicians, as well as country performers, though the shows quickly became more country music–oriented.[48]

The Barn Dance was the most important of the genre until the Grand Ole Opry supplanted it at the end of the 1930s. In 1925, Nashville's first radio station, WSM, originally began broadcasting the "WSM Barn Dance," and country music was well on its way to becoming a commercial and cultural force. Labels took to the South to record more string bands and cowboy-style artists.[49]

Given the concurrent blues craze of the 1920s (e.g., Ma Rainey, Bessie Smith), the recording industry believed that the market was ripe to exploit regional folk styles, especially by targeting different races with corresponding music, e.g., marketing blues and other "race" music to black people, and "hillbilly" music to whites.[50]

Vernon Dalhart was Texas-born and moved to New York to realize his dream of becoming an opera singer. When opera sales dropped off in the mid–1920s, Dalhart went hillbilly in 1924, and he recorded the seminal hillbilly event song, "The Wreck of the Old '97," and the flipside, "Prisoner's Song," the first million-selling hillbilly record.[51]

Two 1920s "string bands" (with fiddles and banjos), were crucial to the development of modern country music: the North Carolina Ramblers and the Skillet Lickers. Both were hard-living and hard-drinking bands (see, for instance, the Ramblers' "If the River Was Whiskey," while the Skillet Lickers name itself is a moonshine reference), but they also included serious and influential musicians. Further, both bands' fast and syncopated music marked the early roots of bluegrass.

The North Carolina Ramblers were more traditional country but with a heavy influence from minstrel and vaudeville. The Ramblers brought a tight professionalism to old-time music and saw significant success on a regional level ("Don't Let Your Deal Go Down" [1925] and "White House Blues" [1926], better known as "Cannonball Blues"). The group disbanded in 1930; the next year, after a heavy drinking binge, leader and banjoist Charlie Poole died of heart failure at thirty-nine years of age.[52]

The Skillet Lickers formed in 1926, in northern Georgia. This group was even more influential, with popular songs through the 1920s, like "Bully of the Town," "Pass Around the Bottle and We'll All Take a Drink" and "Soldier's Joy." The Skillet Lickers were a hillbilly supergroup with a changing lineup, led by chicken farmer, old-time fiddler and showman, "Gid" Tanner, as well as blind guitarist Riley Puckett. Featuring three fiddlers, the Skillet Lickers were as wild and raucous as the North Carolina Ramblers were tight and clean. They were talented and intense, and they incorporated humor into their songs and skits—often self-deprecating, long a common trait of hillbilly acts. One set of Skillet Licker comic sketches, "A Corn Licker Still in Georgia," for example, mocked the Southern establishment (here the police and preachers), who bemoaned hard drinking and hillbilly music while secretly craving both. The Skillet Lickers' music was also, however, rife with racial stereotyping (e.g., "Watermelon on the Vine"), typical of the casual racism of the times. Still, they helped to establish the eventual format and feel of the rock and roll band.[53]

* * *

Modern country music effectively began in August 1927, in Bristol, Virginia, on the border of Virginia and Tennessee. Music producer and talent scout Ralph Peer was looking to tap into the regional hillbilly market for Victor Records of New York. Peer decided to hold an open call for the Appalachian region, a known hotbed of country musicians. This was a poor, predominantly white, rural region, still largely removed from America's urban areas and black populations, and thus devoid of jazz and blues influences. In this way, Appalachia maintained a more direct and unbroken link to the traditional European music, leading to it being known as the cradle of "old-time" country music.

What would become modern country music's two most important acts responded to Peer's call. One act came from Appalachia and was seen as a living musical embodiment of old-time, Southern family values and traditions. The other was a more urbane, rambling, solo cowboy from Mississippi.

The Carter Family was a trio consisting of Alvin Pleasant (or A.P.) Carter on bass vocals and guitar, Sara Carter on lead vocals and autoharp, and Maybelle Carter on alto vocals and guitar. A.P. and Sara Dougherty had married in 1915, eventually having three children. The couple soon combined with Sara's cousin Maybelle, who had married A.P.'s brother, Ezra, to form the famous trio.[54]

A.P. Carter was born in 1891 at the foot of Clinch Mountain in Poor Valley, Virginia (now known as Maces Springs), the oldest of eight children in a family of tobacco farmers. A.P. had felt a strong connection with the older folk songs of his region since he was a young child. He also had a vision that one day "his name was going to mean something," and it soon became evident to him that it would come through pursuing the music he loved.[55] A.P. devoted his adult life to song-hunting trips around the region, later performing and recording the music he found.[56] The Carters modified and modernized the lyrics and music of old-time songs and incorporated them into their own original catalog.

Ralph Peer contracted for a cut of the publishing from all of his artists; thus, in order to increase his margins, he specifically looked for artists with original songs or old songs that had yet to be copyrighted. That approach fit perfectly with A.P. Carter's song-hunting habits.[57] Carter never hid the origins of the songs, though only he and Peer were listed on the credits.

On many of A.P.'s song-hunting trips he was accompanied by African American musician Lesley Riddles, in part because Riddles easily memorized the melodies. Further, Riddles' guitar style and blues licks became an important influence on Maybelle Carter's style.

The Carter Family further drew on gospel music, and they were especially moved by the unique energy of the sanctified sounds of the Pentecostals.[58] Vocally, the Carters developed the "close-harmony" style of country music vocals, with Sara and Maybelle the primary singers, Sara the lead, and A.P. jumping in with his baritone whenever he felt moved to do so.

Maybelle was a fine singer but an even better guitar player. Previously, the guitar had not played a prominent role in country, usually serving only as an accompaniment to the vocals, but that changed with Maybelle. She finger-picked blues licks and plucked a melody on the bass strings, which became known as the "Carter scratch."[59] As historian and musician Mike Seeger put it, Maybelle's style had a "fluid flowing, rhythmic sound, a way of playing the melody that was plain enough so that you could understand what it was, yet still brought you because it had rhythm and life to it." This style impacted American popular music for generations to come, including the music of Flatt and Scruggs, Joan Baez, Johnny Cash, Bob Dylan, and Jerry Garcia of the Grateful Dead, as well as various other musical styles.[60]

The Carter Family collectively wrote, adapted, or covered over 300 songs and a long line of classics, including "Wildwood Flower" (1928), "Will You Miss Me When I'm Gone?" (1928), and "Keep On the Sunny Side" (1928). In short, the body of work generally referred to as "Carter Family Songs" is at the foundation of much of country music as we know it. Also, along with Jimmie Rodgers and Woody Guthrie, the Carters later provided the soundtrack to the Great Depression for rural America, putting their faith and hope into songs like "No Depression in Heaven" (1936).

In 1932, Sara and A.P. separated, in part because Sara was already involved with A.P.'s cousin, Coy Bates. The Carters kept that discord under wraps, however, and they maintained a united familial image until the couple divorced in 1936.[61] The Carters' popularity really exploded in 1938, when they started broadcasting on a powerful, Mexican "pirate radio" station (Mexico not having been included in an agreement to limit radio transmissions in North America). As a result, the Carters' music reached households all over the rural U.S. In 1941, the Carter Family was on the brink of nationwide publicity when a cover story on them was slated for the December issue of *Life* magazine. Four days before that issue was to run, however, the Japanese bombed Pearl Harbor, postponing the Carters' and old-time country music's moments of national recognition.[62]

The Carter Family disbanded in 1943, although Maybelle and her daughters continued to tour and perform on the Opry as the Carter Sisters.[63] Daughter June Carter eventually married and recorded with "King of Country" and Sun Studio rockabilly star, Johnny Cash.[64]

* * *

Jimmie Rodgers, "The Father of Country Music," was born near Meridian, Mississippi, in 1897. Rodgers' mother, Eliza, died when Jimmie was five or six, leaving him to be raised by his father, Aaron. Aaron Rodgers was an extra gang foreman on the Mobile and Ohio Railroad, and his work took him all around the South to wherever repairs were needed.[65] As a result, from an early age, Jimmie Rodgers was exposed to a variety of life experiences and musical styles across the South—not only country and folk, but also early blues and jazz.

At fourteen, the young Rodgers took off on his own as a traveling musician. For more than a decade, Rodgers worked periodically on the railroads, thus earning the moniker "the Singing Brakeman." It was good work and a gritty and adventurous life. Only when Rodgers contracted tuberculosis in 1927 did he quit the railroads to focus solely on playing in minstrel shows and traveling.[66]

Rodgers eventually settled down in Texas, and he recorded over one hundred songs from 1927 to 1933. Rodgers' sound was rooted in the 12-bar blues on his guitar, along with the slide guitar style, as well as bringing in vaudeville, pop, blues and jazz influences. Rodgers, in fact, recorded "Blue Yodel No. 9 (Standin' on the Corner)" (1930) with an uncredited Louis Armstrong on trumpet.[67]

Vocally, where the black bluesmen would wring the emotion out of notes, Rodgers did, too, except that he also yodeled. While the Alpine-born vocal technique (with a vague lineage running through the South) and the Delta blues might seem as far as apart as could be, Rodgers combined these techniques to emote deeply, sometimes in a sorrowful manner, sometimes expressing joy.

Rodgers sang about his gritty life on the road ("My Rough and Ready Ways," 1930), about tragic lives ("Drunkard's Child," 1930), sometimes with humor ("I'm in the Jailhouse Now," 1928), and he especially loved to sing sentimental love songs ("My Carolina Sunshine Girl"). Rodgers was more urbane than the mountain-style music of Appalachia, but he was still a regular hillbilly with heart. The result was the "white man's blues" and hits like Rodgers' signature song and million-seller, "Blue Yodel No. 1," popularly known as "T for Texas" (1927), and many others, including "Waiting for a Train" (1928) and "Mule Skinner Blues" (1930).[68] Rodgers became an icon in the poorer regions of the South, as he sang from a variety of firsthand life experiences and was able to connect with listeners on a personal level. Particularly with the blues and jazz influences, Rodgers vastly broadened the definition of country music.

Rodgers did not let his worsening tuberculosis slow him down, he even sang the "TB Blues" in 1931, and he continued to record up until almost his very last day, earning him even more respect and admiration. Rodgers finally died on May 26, 1933; at the time he was a household name in the poorest regions of the South, though still virtually unknown to the rest of America.[69]

Jimmie Rodgers (ca. 1930) (author's collection).

Rodgers was the most influential of all country singers, and those major country stars who immediately followed him, Roy Acuff and Gene Autry, for example, copied his style to the point of sounding almost identical to him. Even across the racial divide, bluesmen Muddy Waters, Big Bill

Broonzy, and Howlin' Wolf all acknowledged Rodgers' strong impact on their own styles. Said Wolf, "I couldn't do no yodelin', so I turned to howlin'. And it's done me just fine."[70]

Rodgers' music also helped establish a more positive perception of the rural Southerner, moving toward the cowboy image and what would become known as "Western" music (e.g., "When the Cactus Is in Bloom," 1931). Before Rodgers, country music was the domain of the Appalachian and Southeastern states, but rural Southern culture had spread westward to the Southwestern states, e.g., Texas, Arkansas and Oklahoma, where the climate was also conducive to raising cotton.[71] Rodgers' success out of Mississippi and then Texas, with the blues, jazz, and cowboy influences, marked a clear shift of the music.[72] Thus the old-time, original "country" music, was distinguished from this new Southwestern music—that is, "Western." It would all eventually become known as "country and western."[73]

* * *

After World War I, the South remained hampered by a lack of an industrialized economy, worldwide condemnation of its white supremacist society and, further, an evangelical Protestantism that encouraged Bible literalism and resisted change. The Southern white establishment continued efforts to create a "New South," hoping to leave behind the worst of the Southern stereotypes. The South thus sought to embrace modernity, adding some manufacturing jobs, though the economic polarity of poor whites and blacks remained pronounced. Even moving into the middle of the twentieth century, both the hillbilly and the African American would still be outcasts.

Technological innovations of the post-war and Depression eras altered country and other genres as well. In 1931, Adolph Rickenbacker invented the electric guitar; in 1933, Laurens Hammond invented the Hammond organ; and in 1935, Bob Dunn of Milton Brown and His Brownies first recorded on an electrified guitar—a steel guitar.[74]

In late 1925, Nashville's WSM radio hired Indiana-born William D. Hay to re-create the barn dance success he had experienced in Chicago. WSM was owned by the National Life and Accident Insurance Company, which sold life insurance policies to the working-class people of the South, both white and black. National Life believed that old-time country music could be an ideal way to reach these demographics. On November 28, 1925, the *WSM Barn Dance* was first broadcast, featuring seventy-seven-year-old fiddler Uncle Jimmy, accompanied by his niece, Eva Thompson Jones, on piano. Although aired with low expectations, Uncle Jimmy drew a strong response.[75]

Hay brought on more and more local hillbilly and string bands, cultivating the show's down-home image. He gave the bands appropriate hillbilly names, so that even a band fronted by a distinguished medical doctor became Dr. Humphrey Bate and the Possum Hunters, followed by the likes of the Gully Jumpers and the Fruit Jar Drinkers.[76]

WSM's first big singing star was a local performer named Uncle Dave Macon. David Harrison Macon was a Nashville-area local, born in 1870, and a talented singer and banjoist, as well as a comic. Macon's enthusiasm, showmanship, and vast array of traditional styles set the tone for the show early on.[77]

Growing up, Macon's family ran a boarding house that catered to theater types performing in Nashville. As a small child, Macon thus learned music and show business from the vaudeville and circus people who came through.[78] Macon became a highly regarded regional performer, though in his 50s he finally became a top-selling artist of the 1920s with songs like "Keep My Skillet Good and Greasy" (1924), "Chewing Gum" (1924), and "Sail Away Ladies" (1927). In 1924, Macon and vaudeville fiddle partner Sid Harkreader recorded "Hillbilly Blues," bringing the term "hillbilly" into the world of commercial music for the first time and spurring Ralph Peer to officially name the genre.[79]

The *WSM Barn Dance* aired immediately after the *Musical Appreciation Hour*, a decidedly high-brow, classical music and opera show. One night in 1927, Hay was introducing African American harmonica star, DeFord Bailey, and his train song, "Pan American Blues." Goofing on the hillbilly persona of the show, Hay announced, "For the past hour we have been listening to music taken largely from grand opera, but from now on we will present 'The Grand Ole Opry.'" The name stuck.[80]

* * *

DeFord Bailey was not only an early Opry mainstay but also the sole regular African American performer in the show's history. Bailey was born in 1899, just east of Nashville in Smith County. His mother, Mary Reedy, died from an unknown illness when DeFord was one. Deford's father, a low-paid laborer, could not care for his son by himself, so he sent DeFord away to be raised by his aunt, Barbara Lou.[81]

Bailey was playing the autoharp, or harmonica, practically out of the crib. At three years of age, he contracted polio; while bedridden, he developed his feel for the harp. Bailey survived the polio, though it stunted his growth—he was only four feet ten inches tall as an adult, and his back remained slightly deformed.[82] His musical mentor was his former slave grandfather, Lewis Bailey, a champion fiddle player who played a style DeFord later called "black hillbilly." That genre was largely squeezed out of commercial markets once the record labels divided markets by race, though the impact of the songs was long lasting, including "Old Fox Chase," "She'll Be Coming Around the Mountain," and "John Henry."[83]

As a youth, Bailey was a houseboy for a prominent Nashville couple, Mr. and Mrs. J.C. Bradford. When the Bradfords recognized Bailey's musical talent, he was allowed to stop performing menial tasks around the home; instead, they gave him a coat and tie, and he began playing the harp for the Bradfords' house guests. As Bailey recalled, "I never did no more good work. My work was playing the harp."[84] He quickly developed a reputation around the Nashville area.[85]

At twenty-six, Bailey became one of the first performers for WSM, and he was one of the show's most popular and most regular performers through the 1920s and 1930s.[86] Bailey was at times mesmerizing, whether on a train song like "Pan American Blues," named for the awe-inspiring train that drove by his childhood home, or on old standards like "Fox Chase." His black hillbilly style pulled from a deep musical history, including the blues, as well as capturing the sounds and the feel of life on the farm.

At its inception, the Opry had set out to appeal to all fans of old-time music—that is, anyone who might buy insurance, regardless of race. Early radio audiences did not know Bailey was black, and the show tried to keep it that way, fearing such knowledge would hinder success among whites. Much to Hays' surprise, when Bailey's race did become generally known, he remained popular. Bailey was also one of the biggest draws when the Opry stars went on the road.[87]

The music industry did segregate along the hillbilly/race musical divides, of course, and the Opry quickly became synonymous with Southern *white* life and music. Bailey would remain the sole exception, mostly because he was extremely talented and an original cast member, but also no doubt due in some part to his diminutive, nonthreatening physical presence. He was at times even referred to as the Opry's "mascot."[88]

Bailey formed strong relationships with some of his fellow performers, including Roy Acuff and the Delmore Brothers.[89] Yet when Bailey and the other Opry stars went on tours around the South together, he was still subjected to all of the indignities of African American life under segregation. In public, Bailey could not socialize at all with his fellow white Opry performers or white fans, and he certainly could not be served at the same restaurants and hotels.[90] Put simply by Roy Acuff, Bailey's life was "rough."[91]

Bailey recalled that when he was out and about in the Southern towns he played in, he had to carry himself in a certain way or put himself in danger for simply being black and not working for a local white. The only entity powerful enough to protect Bailey from the white Southern police forces was the National Life and Accident Insurance Company. As Bailey put it, he had to behave "like a fine German Shepherd with a collar. You know somebody's behind it. They knew something happened to me, somebody would be checking on me." Bailey thus took to wearing a large "WSM" pin on his collar that "spoke for" him.[92]

Bailey was appreciative of the opportunity to perform on the Opry and the success he experienced, but he was also all too aware that he had to strongly subjugate himself in order to survive on the show. One white Opry performer, Harkreader, recalled that Bailey was "never out of place. You would never know he was here. He was very nice if someone talked to him. He never butted in." Another white performer, Herman Crook, also intending to compliment Bailey, said that "Deford never did get smart."[93]

Stylistically, Bailey knew that, as an African American on the Opry, he could not, as he put it years afterward, "get loose" or do anything bold, flashy, or otherwise outside of the box. He certainly knew not to do anything that could be construed as sexually suggestive, as white performers might.[94]

In 1939, the Opry moved to the larger Ryman Auditorium in Nashville. At this point, the Opry had become the preeminent institution for country music, a designation it has retained ever since. The power of radio and WSM's signal meant that everyone, white and black, across the South and Midwest could regularly hear the Opry. Thus not only did virtually all future white, Southern country music and rock and roll stars listen to the Opry, but so did future black blues and R&B stars of the South, including Ray Charles, Bobby "Blue" Bland, and Rufus Thomas.[95]

In 1940, NBC began broadcasting the Opry, and the corporate powers started forcing out the "old-timer" acts like Bailey in favor of slicker, more professional acts. At the same time, radio networks were having issues with the song-licensing service ASCAP (Bailey's service), leading to a boycott and the formation of rival BMI. In the boycott aftermath, and for not entirely clear reasons, Bailey was let go, although some white artists in the same boat as Bailey were kept. The foremost Opry historian Charles Wolfe called Bailey's dismissal "essentially a mystery" and "one of the great tragedies in American music."[96]

Bailey was already running a shoeshine stand in Nashville to supplement his modest pay from the Opry, so he opened a string of such stands and devoted himself to that. Over the years, Bailey came back to play the Opry four more times.[97]

* * *

Tennessean Roy Acuff became Nashville's first star with two songs already recorded by the Carter Family: "The Great Speckled Bird" (1936) and "Wabash Cannonball" (1936). Acuff became a national superstar in the 1940s, with hits such as "The Precious Jewel" (1940), "The Wreck on the Highway" (1942), and "Beneath That Lonely Mound of Clay" (1946). Acuff's popular and emotional solo performances marked a shift in country away from the string band format. Acuff also filled the void left by Jimmie Rodgers and would himself be widely regarded as the King of Country Music until his death in 1992.[98]

Additionally, Acuff altered the music business when he partnered with songwriter Fred Rose in 1942 to form the hugely profitable Acuff-Rose publishing company.[99] Acuff-Rose spawned more music business industry activity in Nashville, and, combined with the importance of the Opry and some major Nashville artists, Nashville became the capital of country music.[100]

Alabama's Delmore Brothers were also stars of the early Opry. The pair excelled in harmonies, and they were among the first to incorporate black boogie music in hits like "Brown's Ferry Blues" (1933) and "Blues Stay Away from Me" (1949). The result was an influential, proto-rock style.

* * *

In 1934, the hillbilly stereotype was further popularized and solidified in American pop culture with the inauguration of three different cartoons: Paul Webb's "The Mountain Boys" in *Esquire* magazine, Billy DeBeck's character Snuffy Smith in his "Barney Google" comic strip, and Al Capp's "Li'l Abner" (and after World War II, the long-running Ma and Pa Kettle film series).[101] All relied on a successful mixture of "ridicule and empathy."[102] So-called hillbillies have often taken on the name with a certain pride, as a self-deprecating but proud take on their culture, thus blurring the pejorative/prideful meaning of the word (and which has largely carried on as "redneck" in current pop culture). The hillbilly label, in fact, was one pejorative that tended to stick around even in more polite society, precisely because its use was mixed with humor.[103] By the late 1930s, however, the music industry began to shift away from the hillbilly label and image and more toward a cowboy identity and the "country" or "country and western" label.

Texas singer-songwriter Gene Autry had a hit with "Silver Haired Daddy of Mine" (1931) when it was included in the 1935 film *Tumbling Tumbleweeds*. In the era of big musicals, Autry was Hollywood's first "singing cowboy," followed by Roy Rogers, Tex Ritter, Johnny Bond, Jimmy Wakely, and others.[104] This marked a further shift toward the Western style and greater association of country music with the cowboy.[105] Many of the songs of the singing movie cowboys were written by Tin Pan Alley songwriters, while those songs subsequently influenced the sound of future country music performers. Through the 1930s and by the end of the 1940s, Hollywood's non-singing film cowboys, such as John Wayne and Gary Cooper, helped to solidify the rugged, independent cowboy image, especially in northern cities, and Southerners and "hillbillies" were likewise influenced.

* * *

In the pre-war years, four country sub-genres emerged that would each have strong influences on rock: western swing, honky tonk, bluegrass, and folk music. Western swing effectively began with singer-guitarist Milton Brown and fiddler Bob Wills bringing big band jazz orchestration into the country music fold in 1930. The pair split in 1932, with Brown forming the Musical Brownies, one of the first groups with amplified steel guitars and rhythm sections based in ragtime influences.[106] Wills became hugely successful fronting the Texas Playboys (though based in Oklahoma), combining a country string section and a jazz horn section.

As a child in Kosse, Texas, Wills learned traditional country songs and cowboy hollers from his dad and his grandfather, in addition to learning

Bob Wills and His Texas Playboys (ca. 1946–1947) (used by permission of the University of Missouri–Kansas City Libraries, Dr. Kenneth J. LaBudde Department of Special Collections).

black jigs and blues from black playmates, as well as style and showmanship from black performers.[107] Wills' group had pre-war hits with "Steel Guitar Rag" (1936) and "New San Antonio Rose" (1940), their greatest hit and recorded with an 18-piece band, as well as some of the first nationwide hits of country music in "Time Changes Everything" (1940), "Smoke on the Water" (1944), and "New Spanish Two Step" (1946).

Ernest Tubb's "Walking the Floor Over You" (1941) appeared in the film *Fighting Buckeroos* (1941), making Tubbs a star and helping to launch honky tonk. The name "honky tonk" was derived from the hard-partying Southern bars of the same name, and the songs reflected a blue-collar lifestyle and edgier themes such as hard drinking, carousing, and loneliness. This sub-genre would take off after the war, largely due to Hank Williams, with both Tubbs and Williams serving to further shed the more clownish aspects of the hillbilly stereotype.[108]

The third important sub-genre came from the Southeast and Kentucky. Mandolinist Bill Monroe took hillbilly music and incorporated an instrumental, jazz-derived virtuosity and a souped-up tempo to create bluegrass. This genre took its name from Monroe's band, the Bluegrass Boys, which in turn was named for his home state of Kentucky, "The Bluegrass State". In the post-war years, that faster picking and driving guitar became another key component to the rock story. Still, country remained a regional and rural phenomenon; *Billboard* magazine only began listing a "hillbilly" chart in 1944.[109]

A fourth and final strain of country music—folk music—came out of the Carter Family songbook, adding traditional American folk and some left-wing politics. Woodie Guthrie arose during the Great Depression and the calamity of the Dust Bowl in his home state of Oklahoma. In the process, Guthrie became America's first great singer-songwriter.[110] Guthrie began with his *Dust Bowl Ballads* (1935; first recorded in 1940), "Pretty Boy Floyd" (1939), and "This Land Is Your Land" (1940; first recorded in 1944), providing an earnest and solemn, acoustic guitar–based challenge to poverty, fascism and racism.

In the 1940s, Guthrie took the folk sound to New York City and helped establish a countercultural movement in Greenwich Village. That scene became the launching pad of politicized rock and eventually major 1960s folk rock figures such as Bob Dylan, Richie Havens and Joni Mitchell.

At the same time, Pete Seeger's Almanac Singers recorded "We Shall Overcome," and other important works, some with communist overtones. Folk separated from traditional country in that it became the genre of urban intellectuals and leftists, while the rest, including the so-called hillbillies, took country in its own direction.[111]

8

A Prelude and a Melting Pot

After World War II, numerous sub-genres of the blues, gospel, and country set the stage for rock and roll. In the glow of victory and prosperity immediately after World War II, the big radio stations and record labels were dominated by the stylings of the previously mentioned Perry Comos, Dinah Shores, and queries as to the price of dogs in windows. A booming U.S. economy and music industry, along with cheaper recording technology, helped smaller record labels and studios spring up across the country, including King in Cincinnati; Duke/Peacock in Houston; Chance, Vee Jay and Chess in Chicago; Modern, Specialty and Imperial in Los Angeles; Sun in Memphis; and Atlantic and Savoy in New York.[1] Those labels captured a new, fringe sound, a more emotionally relevant music that the big labels were otherwise ignoring.[2] If one looked a little further down the charts at that time, signs of change and all of the building blocks of rock and roll were present.

Most crucial in this development was a strong, insistent beat, originally borrowed from gospel music, with its handclaps and foot stomping. In the 1940s, the harder beat in the blues was referred to as a verb, as in "to rock."

Some of the first songs to "rock," in fact, rocked about as hard as any songs since. In 1934, John and Alan Lomax recorded an old African American ring shout, "Good Lord (Run Old Jeremiah)," performed by Joe Washington Brown & Group, in a small, rural church in Louisiana. In the recording, the dancers stomp out the beat on the floorboards as they shuffle around in a circle. The vocals are nearly indecipherable, but they are Christian inspired. It also is undoubtedly rawer and has a more slamming beat than any hardcore punk, gangsta rap, or death metal recorded since.[3] "Uplifting" is not the word for it, though it is a strong expression of faith. "Visceral" would be an understatement. It is a song performed by people who *had* to find relief in their lives, and one can hear (and feel) them achieving catharsis.

Other early examples of the "big beat" include "The Back Beat Boogie"

(1939), by Harry James and his orchestra, and, in the 1940s, hillbilly bands were using a "slap bass" technique on the stand-up bass for a similar effect, with Hank Williams' group being a prime example.

* * *

The other crucial development of the 1930s and '40s was the emergence of a network of black-owned clubs, theaters, and juke joints throughout the South and in many Northern cities, the "chitlin' circuit". As black acts were excluded from the nicer, white-owned clubs of the South, venues arose in the black entertainment districts in the various cities. Thus "numbers rackets, dice parlors, dance halls, and bootleg liquor and prostitution rings financed the artistic development of breakthrough performers."[4] Black luminaries such as B.B. King, Joe Turner, Wynonie Harris, T-Bone Walker, Little Richard, James Brown, and Ray Charles, all spent time on the circuit.[5] There, black artists had freedom to explore new sounds.

Along with the new, more pronounced beat and the new venues, the mid–1940s brought a higher-energy, more urban, and brasher strain of the blues, combined with the loose rhythms of big band swing: the jump blues. The jump blues vocalist was the strong, central figure, usually backed by a horn section, a piano, a bass, a drum, an electric guitar for rhythm, and a driving beat. The vocalist sang over the shuffling boogie-woogie rhythms.

The jump blues was particularly popular with black, former Southerners already familiar with blues music who had migrated to the big cities of the North; the new music served as a bridge of sorts for blacks thankfully leaving behind the miseries of their rural, Jim Crow past. Juke boxes (named for the juke joints they often occupied) provided an important commercial outlet that did not need to worry about radio censors, something that would also help rock and roll sales into the 1950s.[6]

Crucial jump blues practitioners included Big Joe Turner, Big Bill Broonzy, Roy Brown, and Wynonie Harris. The first jump blues superstar was Louis Jordan, a saxophonist, singer and bandleader who migrated from Brinkley, Arkansas, to New York City. Jordan and his combo, the Tympanny Five, dominated the "race" charts throughout the 1940s with hits like "Choo Choo Ch'boogie," "Caldonia," and "Saturday Night Fish Fry," the latter two being prototypical rock and roll songs. Jordan's music was confident, sophisticated, urban, and filled with his "jive talk" asides and carefree lyrics, typified in "Let the Good Times Roll." As one writer puts it, it was "body music rather than head or heart music."[7] Jordan crossed the jump blues over into the pop (i.e., "white") top ten on several occasions. His music and style also provided a crucial influence for his Decca label mates Ray Charles and Bill Haley, who both come into the picture shortly afterward.[8]

Through the 1940s, the jump blues morphed into rhythm and blues, or R&B, with many artists' careers, like Jordan's, effectively spanning both genres. Rhythm and blues began as a more gospel-flavored, fervid version of the blues, with smaller combos and the insistent backbeat. All black music was still labeled as "race" records until 1949, when a *Billboard* music writer, future music mogul Jerry Wexler, coined the new R&B term.[9] That change reflected

Louis Jordan in New York (1946) (photograph by William P. Gottlieb, William P. William P. Gottlieb Collection, Library of Congress).

a slowly shifting culture as well as increasing the potential for crossover and commercial success for African Americans.

At a time when any overt references to sexuality were taboo on the big labels and their white rosters, jump blues and R&B often had raunchier and innuendo-laden lyrics. Standout songs in that category were Wynonie Harris' "I Like My Baby's Pudding" (1950) and Billy Ward and the Dominos' early doo wop hit, "Sixty Minute Man" (1951), along with "party records" like Roy Brown's "Good Rockin' Tonight" (1947), Wynonie Harris' hit cover of the same song the next year, and Amos Milburn's "Chicken Shack Boogie" (1948). At the same time, the genre was pulling in more soul and, at times, transcendence from the church, with Lloyd Price's "Lawdy Miss Clawdy" (1952) being the prime example (a song that would be a permanent staple in Elvis Presley's live sets, in addition to being covered by the Beatles and other musicians).

Thus the music was challenging social mores but also growing in popularity at the same time. In 1949, New Orleans' Fats Domino had a huge hit with "The Fat Man," and bluesman John Lee Hooker sold a million copies of "I'm in the Mood." In sum, blues and early R&B were growing fast and still transforming.

* * *

Around the same time, on the south side of Chicago, migrants from the Delta and other Southern bluesmen, such as Big Bill Broonzy, John Lee Hooker, Muddy Waters, Howlin' Wolf, and others, were updating the country blues of the Delta and electrifying the sound with electric guitars and amps. The electric amps in part served to overcome the noisier city streets and clubs, but it was also part of a new vision of the blues: the electric blues.[10]

Muddy Waters was born McKinley Morganfield in 1915 in Rolling Fork, Mississippi. Growing up poor in the Delta, young Morganfield dropped out of school after the third grade to work for less than a dollar a day and to care for his grandmother.[11] Things did not get a whole lot better as an adult. At one point, Waters, his wife, and his uncle's family farm was only clearing between $100 and $300 a year total, after paying the furnish. Waters once said that his only other non-sharecropping options coming out of the Delta were to be either a preacher or a baseball player.[12] The blues, however, would treat him well.

Recording with Alan Lomax in 1942, and again in 1943, confirmed for Waters what he already knew: he was a special talent. That experience provided the impetus for Waters to get out of Mississippi for good in 1943, and his heading to Chicago.[13] Waters bought his first electric guitar in 1944 in

Chicago, where he fronted legendary lineups, including harmonica player Little Walter and others, and later performed songs by bass player and prolific songwriter, Willie Dixon.[14] Waters married the grittiness and the heart of the Delta with a bold, street-smart swagger from Chicago's South Side ("I Can't Be Satisfied," 1948; "Got My Mojo Working," 1957). As the Rock and Roll Hall of Fame described him, "Waters was a fierce singer and slashing slide guitarist whose uncut blues bore the stamp of his mentors, Robert Johnson and Son House."[15] Waters' band was tight and powerful, while an often macho self-confidence announced a new, first-class citizenship in the North.

Dixon penned numerous classics, including "Hoochie Coochie Man," "I Just Want to Make Love to You," "I'm Ready," and "Rollin' Stone" (from which the Rolling Stones would take their name—to say nothing of the influence of "I Can't Be Satisfied" on the Stones' own signature song, "(I Can't Get No) Satisfaction," 1965). Dixon's compositions became a foundation for 1960s rock music, being covered by the biggest rock acts, including Bob Dylan, Jimi Hendrix, Led Zeppelin, Queen, and the Grateful Dead.

Chicago's top electric bluesmen recorded at Chess Records, a now famed studio founded by the Chess brothers, Phil and Leonard, in 1950 (it was called Aristocrat Records from 1947 to 1950[16]). Chess also had an important early connection with Sun Studio in Memphis, releasing some of that studio's first classic recordings before Sun Records formed and started its handling releases in 1952. Chess became home to crucial pre-rock blues and R&B, as well as early rock giants, including Waters, Dixon, Howlin' Wolf, Buddy Guy, Bo Diddley and Chuck Berry.

* * *

Similar to the rebranding of race records, in 1949, *Billboard* magazine stopped using the demeaning "hillbilly" label to refer to what we now call country music, instead using the term "folk and blues." That name was quickly replaced with either "country," or "country and western," which at that point was comprised of traditional country, cowboy music, and western swing.[17]

In those post-war years, country music was redefined by the Alabama-born Hank Williams. Williams was born in Mount Olive, Alabama, in 1923. As a child, Williams contracted spina bifida, which caused lifelong back pain. After serving in World War I, Hank's father, Lon, ended up in a veterans' hospital for seven years, from the time Hank was six until he was thirteen. One reason for the hospital stay was a brain aneurysm, likely suffered in a barroom brawl in Europe, although psychiatric care was also part of his stay. Hank's mother, Lillie, kept the family afloat during the Great Depression.

Lon and Lillie had little love for one another; Lon was a hard drinker and Lillie regularly disparaged him in front of Hank.[18]

Williams first learned guitar as a child from an African American street musician named Rufus Payne, also known as "Tee Tot" (the name a play on his definitely *not* being a teetotaler). Williams had said that he paid Tee Tot "15 cents or whatever I could get a hold of for a lesson."[19] Payne taught Williams the guitar basics, especially the blues and the importance of rhythm, both of which became crucial aspects of Williams' country style.[20]

Williams later mastered the forlorn, "high lonesome" style of singing with "a plain-spoken vulnerability," exemplified in hits like "Lost Highway" and "Cold, Cold Heart."[21] Williams was a prolific and classic songwriter, and songs like "Your Cheatin' Heart" and "Hey, Good Lookin'" become country standards with enormous impact across popular music and, later, rock music. Williams brought rhythm to country in "Move It On Over" (1947), "Honky-tonking" (1948), and "Howlin' at the Moon" (1951), helping to develop the honky tonk sub-genre.

Honky tonk musicians had previously been shunned by the country music establishment, and vice versa, but Hank Williams lifted the genre artistically to where it could no longer be ignored.[22] Williams thus helped turn the lowly hillbilly into an independent, everyman hero.

Those who knew Williams spoke of a good heart and a likeable, funny guy, but also someone carrying a lot of loneliness and sadness. One rather odd story, but one that seems to shed some light on Williams' life, comes from Opry comic mainstay, Minnie Pearl. Pearl recalled that one night after Williams received a drunken beating at a club, he had been taken to his mother's house, and his mother had looked at her son and said, "First, we get you sewed up; then we go get him." Hank then told Pearl, "Minnie, there ain't nobody in the world I'd rather have alongside me in a fight than my mama with a broken beer bottle in her hand."[23]

Hank Williams (ca. 1950) (New York World-Telegram & Sun Collection, Library of Congress).

Williams' anti-establishment

streak helped define honky tonk, although he and his honky tonk colleagues did not necessarily rail against affluence. As David Halberstram wrote, they railed against their own "poverty and the problems caused by their poverty, their women problems and their whiskey problems."[24] Williams wasn't political, although he sang of class in songs like "Mansion on the Hill" and "Wealth Won't Save Your Soul." He wasn't overtly religious, but he exhibited an unmistakable faith in songs like "I Saw the Light." Williams got what his fans got—that they had little control over their lives—and all he could do was help people find some temporary relief, some truth, and some good times in his music.

By 1951, Williams' drinking and painkillers for his bad back, however, had led to failing health; he lost weight off his already thin frame and started missing shows. The Grand Ole Opry would not even book Williams because of his drinking, until finally relenting in 1949.[25] Williams eventually succumbed to heart failure and an early death, in 1953, at only twenty-nine years of age.[26]

The country music establishment had shunned Williams while he was alive, but it embraced him in death, and appreciation of Williams (and his celebrity) soared. Williams' music was an edgier kind of country that would directly feed into the harder sound of early rockabilly artists, particularly with Elvis Presley, Johnny Cash, and Jerry Lee Lewis.

Another big post-war country music star was Kentuckian Red Foley. Foley was a versatile singer who, in addition to singing traditional country and being the first performer to record in Nashville, incorporated boogie, blues, and bluegrass into his repertoire. Foley had the first million-selling gospel hit in Thomas Dorsey's "Peace in the Valley" (1951), which also crossed over into the African American market. Two more crucial players were Texan honky tonk legend Ernest Tubb ("Walking the Floor Over You," 1942) and Canadian-born Opry regular Hank Snow ("I'm Moving On," 1950).

Bob Wills and his Texas Playboys continued to refine their sound and style after the war and enjoyed substantial commercial success, fusing the smooth, driving rhythm of swing music with country. Wills was also among the first to include not only an electric guitar in his band but also drums at a time when country music traditionalists were still rejecting their big beat (the Grand Ole Opry even banned drums from its stage until the late 1940s[27]).

Also in the late 1940s, Wills and the Playboys relocated to California, where they hosted huge dances up and down the West Coast, drawing in tens of thousands of fans and broadcasting their own radio show that surpassed listenership for traditional big band jazz of the time.[28]

In 1948, Bluegrass Boys guitarist/vocalist Lester Flatt and banjo player

Earl Scruggs left Bill Monroe to become Flatt and Scruggs and the Foggy-bottom Boys.[29] Flatt and Scruggs gave bluegrass its greatest worldwide profile, most recognizably with the double-time hit, "Foggy Mountain Breakdown" (1949) and, later on, the beloved theme song for *The Beverly Hillbillies* (1962–1971), "The Ballad of Jed Clampett" (1963). While lacking the big beat and blues feel, Flatt and Scruggs were supreme instrumentalists and brought a speed and excitement that would further define rock guitar.

Also crucial to guitar history, in 1950, for the first time, Leo Fender's company began to mass-produce affordable, solid-body electric guitars, where each string could be clearly and distinctly heard, as well as advancing the electric bass and gradually making the stand-up bass obsolete.[30] Finally, Les Paul ("Tennessee Waltz," 1950, and "Mockin' Bird Hill," 1953) channeled a strong influence from legendary French jazz guitarist Django Reinhardt and scored pop hits with his singing wife, Mary Ford. Paul was also a master technician, revolutionizing the solid-body electric guitar (and later inventing the classic rock and roll guitar, the Gibson Les Paul) and pioneering many studio effects and electronic effects devices.[31]

9

The Church and Rock

In the 1940s, Sister Rosetta Tharpe (as mentioned in chapter 1) pushed the gospel genre in new directions and to new audiences. Other 1940s gospel groups, such as the Blind Boys of Mississippi, Clara Ward, and the Soul Stirrers, were also popular and influential. Mahalia Jackson, however, was the preeminent star and is generally accepted as the greatest gospel singer ever.

Jackson, the daughter of a Baptist minister in New Orleans, started her career in 1929, when she met famed gospel composer Thomas Dorsey, and by the mid–1940s she was gospel's first superstar. Jackson brought blues phrasing and other secular influences to gospel, and she had some influence from the Pentecostal church she grew up right next to. Her voice brought new levels of emotional scope and depth to popular music. Jackson's stature was such that she was asked to sing at John F. Kennedy's presidential inauguration in 1961 and was the natural, handpicked choice of the Reverend Martin Luther King, Jr., to sing at the March on Washington when King gave his "I Have a Dream" speech in 1963. Jackson became a civil rights figure in her own right, and her version of "We Shall Overcome" was the movement's unofficial theme song.

Jackson had first broken into the public consciousness with Reverend W. Herbert Brewster's "Move On Up a Little Higher" (1947), followed by many other hits, including her rendition of "Amazing Grace" (1947) and her signature song "Take My Hand, Precious Lord" (1956). Jackson brought gospel music to concert halls across the world and avoided crossing into secular music, despite having plenty of financial incentives to do so (although she was selling millions of records anyway). Still, some criticized Jackson for watering down gospel in the process of attaining mainstream success. Jackson influenced rock vocalists and virtually all of R&B and soul music to come; she was another "Early Influence" inductee into the Rock and Roll Hall of Fame in 1997.[1]

This brings the story back to Sister Rosetta Tharpe and the "reeling and rocking" of the Pentecostal church. Tharpe represents that point where the deepest corners of the Holy and human spirits seem to overlap one another. It is also where the black church directly connected with the secular worlds of the Sun Records stars and Little Richard.

Tharpe was born in 1915 in Cotton Plant, Arkansas, to devout parents and members of the Church of God in Christ (COGIC), a Memphis-based, Pentecostal Christian denomination. Tharpe's mother was Katie Bell Nubin, better known as "Mother Bell," a traveling evangelist and musician. Tharpe's parents split when Rosetta was young and she lived the evangelical life, traveling with her mother and rarely seeing her father.[2]

Tharpe recalled her first musical experiences in COGIC: "I started playing music at the age of three years old. [My mother] sat me on her knee, and I would play an organ 'This Far By Faith' or 'Nearer My God to Thee.' I heard angels singing."[3] Tharpe was a prodigy, mastering the guitar by the age of six and performing alongside Mother Bell on the road at holiness conventions.[4] Pentecostal services were marked by handclapping, swaying, a sense of humor, and prayers "in the Spirit"—that is, *glossolalia*, or "speaking in tongues."[5] Glossolalia is nearly indescribable if one has not heard it firsthand except to say that it often occurs in a trance-like state and is a stream-of-consciousness verbalization of sounds, though none of the verbiage is recognizable as any known language. It is often accompanied by music, a "polyphony of tones," and atypical church instrumentation, including the electric guitar, drum, trumpet, tambourine, and so forth.[6]

Many mainstream Protestant churches banned dancing and avoided any music that caused listeners to lose control of their bodies. Pentecostals' entire purpose, however, was to play that music that most let them feel the Holy Spirit within, and running through, their bodies. This was all to help them "shout" their faith, and they drew elements from not only hymns and slave spirituals, but also the blues.[7] The point was to let loose and sing full-throated to the Lord, from a place deeper or beyond the physical or the intellectual self.

The Pentecostal denomination mostly caught on in poor regions of the South to start with, and it came to be known as a very odd, poor black and hillbilly religion. It has since grown far beyond the Deep South and currently has an enormous, worldwide following.[8] To the Pentecostal, charismatic experiences facilitate something beyond a rote, theoretical understanding of the Holy Spirit or salvation in an afterlife. Instead, each individual parishioner has the opportunity to experience a deep and personal connection with God, and to truly *feel* that connection.

While white and black churches influenced secular music in the South and elsewhere, and vice versa, Pentecostalism's impact on rock is such that it demands more in-depth analysis. Further, its own historic trajectory not only mirrors rock, but it also happens to be a fascinating piece of American history itself.

The term "Pentecostal" refers to the holy day commemorating the descent of the Holy Ghost upon the disciples of Jesus Christ. The tenets of Pentecostalism are taken from the biblical book the Acts of the Apostles, which refers to the earliest practices of the church, where it was said to be necessary for Christians to be baptized in the Holy Spirit:

> When the day of Pentecost had come, they were all together in one place. And suddenly a sound came from heaven like the rush of a mighty wind, and it filled all the house where they were sitting. And there appeared to them tongues as of fire, distributed and resting on each of them.[9]

The outpouring of spirit that came out in wild and seemingly nonsensical language was said to be beyond any known tongue: it was a universal language that united peoples from all nations. "The day of the Pentecost" was also said to mark the beginning of the End Times. Those who experienced the phenomenon of speaking in tongues were spiritually baptized and would experience "prophecy" and "dream dreams" before being shown "the wonders of Heaven," while for the rest, "blood, and fire, and vapour of smoke."[10]

For many years the Catholic Church's official interpretation of all such spiritual gifts, or *charismata* (i.e., the abilities to speak in tongues and prophesy), was that they were in the exclusive realm of the prophets and no longer relevant phenomena, and practitioners could simply ignore the text.[11] Even during the Reformation and the embrace of individual spiritual experiences, Protestant churches firmly opposed such "religious enthusiasm." Martin Luther and John Calvin had explicitly denounced glossolalia as something whose purpose, both as a sign to the Jews of the End Days (referred to by Peter in Acts 2:17) and as a way to preach to foreign nations, had passed.[12]

Still, spiritual gifts remained a part of various Christian practices, usually in Easter ceremonies. A Pentecostal revival in the mid–1800s brought those practices back in the Northeast U.S.,[13] and another "holiness" revival in the late nineteenth century brought the charismatic phenomenon across the world, including India, Korea and Wales.[14]

* * *

The modern Pentecostal movement came about around the turn of the twentieth century. Kansan Charles Fox Parham was a former Methodist preacher who started a healing ministry in 1898. He spearheaded the Pentecostalism movement in the U.S. with an emphasis on glossolalia, as well as bringing the sense of urgency that came with a belief that the End Days were near.[15] Parham's beliefs, however, were also rooted in a racist Anglo-Israelism, wherein all Anglo-Saxon Protestant nations, particularly the United States and Britain, were said to be descendants of the "lost tribes" of Israel.[16]

Parham did not believe in either the co-mingling of the races or the ecstatic manifestations of the black churches.[17] Said Parham, "Sick at my stomach ... to see white people imitating unintelligent, crude negroism of the Southland, and laying it on the Holy Ghost."[18] At times Parham did preach to mixed-race audiences, but he was also a KKK sympathizer.[19] Parham was eventually disgraced by unsubstantiated allegations of homosexual acts, as well as financial irregularities among his backers.[20]

In 1898, Parham was teaching at a Bible school in Houston, Texas, where he was heard by an African American Holiness preacher, William Joseph Seymour.[21] Seymour had been allowed to listen to Parham's white-only sermons through an open window.[22] Seymour was the son of freed slaves from Louisiana,[23] and he had taught himself to read, though he had no formal theological training. Yet Seymour was inspired to relocate to Los Angeles in 1905 to try to start his own Pentecostal congregation.[24]

In L.A., Seymour's belief in spiritual baptism got him kicked out of one church, leading him to start the Apostolic Faith Mission in April of 1906.[25] His first congregants were servants and poor blacks; these members were quickly joined by poor and disenfranchised white domestic servants, janitors and day workers.[26] The Azusa Street revivals were racially integrated and included women in the church leadership, both characteristics being well ahead of their times. The group saw itself as a new way of living, beyond racial and socioeconomic differences, through a unity in Christ.[27]

Seymour's congregation met at people's homes, or wherever they could, before establishing themselves in a church on Azusa Street. The denomination was a new strain of Christianity baptized in the Holy Spirit.[28]

Seymour was widely respected and seen as humble, even letting rivals speak to his congregation.[29] Azusa Street eschewed handbills and posters and relied on word-of-mouth, so that only those who were truly compelled would come. The only collection was a small box by the front door, which helped pay the rent.[30] Seymour's meetings had no organized format, and members spontaneously spoke out, sang, spoke in tongues and were otherwise "slain in Spirit."[31] As Cox put it, they were "[n]o longer praying *for* a revival; they *were* the revival."[32]

Outsiders, however, were not exactly impressed. Typical early headlines included "Whites and Blacks Mix in a Religious Frenzy" and "Holy Kickers Carry On Mad Orgies."[33] In September 1906, one local reporter described the happenings as follows:

> [D]isgraceful intermingling of the races ... they cry and make howling noises all day and into the night. They run, jump, shake all over, shout to the top of their voice, spin around in circles, fall out on the sawdust-blanketed floor jerking, kicking and rolling all over it. Some of them pass out and do not move for hours as though they were dead. These people appear to be mad, mentally deranged or under a spell. They claim to be filled with the spirit. They have a one-eyed, illiterate, Negro as their preacher who stays on his knees much of the time with his head hidden between the wooden milk crates. He doesn't talk very much but at times he can be heard shouting, "Repent," and he's supposed to be running the thing.[34]

Few outside the denomination understood or respected the group, as would largely be the case for Pentecostals in the decades to follow.[35]

Near the end of the first decade of the twentieth century, when the End Days had still not occurred, many practitioners lost their fire and their faith.[36] Internal divisions between Parham, Seymour, and others, splintered the movement. In the 1910s, the modern Pentecostals also began to fracture in part due to a chasm between Oneness Pentecostalism and Trinitarians. Ironically, the splintering caused the movement to branch off across the country and the world, helping it grow instead of falling apart.[37] By the end of the 1910s, Pentecostalism was in parts of Europe, South America and various parts of the U.S, including the Pacific Northwest and the South. It was arguably the greatest expansion of Christianity in history.[38]

African American Elder Mason had attended a mixed-race service on Azusa Street in 1907; he then took the Pentecostal movement to Memphis under the name Church of God in Christ (COGIC).[39] The first COGIC congregation was integrated, despite being in the Jim Crow South, although Pentecostalism became formally segregated by the late 1910s and officially remained so until 1965 (and effectively so well after that).[40]

Again, it was working-class blacks and whites who were most drawn to Pentecostal denominations. In the South, wealthier blacks belonged to denominations like Presbyterianism, which was thought to be more dignified. Despite their wild services, though, the Pentecostals lived clean, with no alcohol or tobacco, no gambling, and no social dancing. Pentecostal women favored modest dress: no makeup or jewelry, in part to avoid stereotypes of black women as "Jezebels and temptresses."[41] Crucial to spiritual liberation was the church music. Mason took a particularly liberal stand on a definition of sacred music, as detailed in one account:

> A shouting session could last the better part of an hour, its duration limited only by the energy of the congregation; often a member fainted or, if touched by the Holy Spirit, commenced ecstatic tongue-speaking and holy dancing. As Pastor Roberts preached, beginning with Scripture but then launching into an improvisational riff, the congregation buoyed him with their own shouted responses: "Yes, Sir." "Say it." "Praise the Lord." "Amen to that."[42]

Healing "laying on of hands" ceremony in the Pentecostal Church of God, Lejunior, Harlan County, Kentucky (1946) (photograph by Russell Lee, Department of the Interior, Solid Fuels Administration for War).

Black Pentecostals let go of their past and liberated themselves through charismata. Their children didn't attend the movies or theater, but they used to "laugh at the slow music the Baptist kids had to sit through."[43]

In the mid–1920s, Katie Bell Nubin and her daughter Rosetta relocated to Chicago, where Rosetta grew up. In 1934, a nineteen-year-old Rosetta married a COGIC preacher named Thomas Thorpe (from which "Tharpe" is a misspelling), though the marriage was short lived. In 1938 the couple separated, and Rosetta moved to New York City.[44]

Rosetta had strong blues and jazz influences, as well as an independent streak, and she pushed the sacred-secular line for her entire career. Also in 1938, Tharpe had her first hits with bouncing up-tempo takes on gospel standards, "This Train" and "Rock Me," backed by jazz orchestras, including Thomas Dorsey's. Tharpe also performed with mainstream superstars, including Cab Calloway and Benny Goodman, and in secular venues, such as concert halls and even nightclubs, including the Cotton Club, as opposed to solely in church glorifying God. Tharpe's "swinging" take on gospel offended much of her church fan base, but it attracted droves of new secular fans.[45] Tharpe was a key performer in John Hammond's renowned Spirituals to Swing Concert, where black gospel was first brought to mainstream white audiences.

Tharpe's style confounded the press as well, who didn't know how to classify her (they would have a similar problem with Elvis Presley a decade later), variously describing her as a "swingcopated manipulator of loud blue tones," a "Swinger of spirituals," or a "Hymn swinging evangelist."[46]

In 1944, Tharpe began recording with boogie-woogie pianist Sammy Price, and their first record, "Strange Things Happening Every Day," was one of the rare gospel numbers to crack Billboard's "race" records top ten, a feat Tharpe would repeat several more times in her career. In 1946, Tharpe teamed up with the more restrained but talented contralto, Marie Knight, a perfect complement to the exuberant Tharpe. The pair were reputed to be lovers as well.[47] More success followed, including "Up Above My Head." Despite not being a household name today, Tharpe's success was such that when she married Russell Harrison in 1951, she and her promoters put on a wedding/concert/publicity stunt at Griffiths Field in Washington, D.C., home of the Washington Senators baseball team. Twenty thousand paying fans attended, despite a trolley strike.[48]

In 1952, Tharpe and the white country star Red Foley teamed up for a duet—which was apparently an unprecedented, mixed-gender, interracial collaboration.[49] Tharpe and Foley were already mutual fans of each other's work. Both were versatile performers whose music crossed genre barriers, with Foley having already garnered many black admirers, especially for his 1951 cover of "Peace in the Valley." Plus, both were Decca recording artists, and Decca was certainly motivated to capitalize by trying to connect the pair's otherwise separated demographics.[50]

The song selected for the duet was "Have a Little Talk with Jesus." Given that interracial marriage was still a criminal act at this time throughout the South, including Tennessee, where they recorded, this was no small risk.[51] The pair got along and the studio atmosphere in Nashville was friendly, though the song was a light, if pragmatic, choice.[52] In this recording, Tharpe and Foley sing as a duet, but when they are singing together they sing directly to the listener about Jesus, and they have personal conversations with Jesus, as opposed to with one another. It is a historic performance by two important performers, though the song choice all but assured that there would be little chemistry between the two.

Tharpe and Knight recorded some straight secular music in the early

Sister Rosetta Tharpe (1940s) (author's collection).

1950s, marking the end of Tharpe's gospel career. She mounted a brief comeback in the 1960s and, with an important tour in England, more directly influenced some of the British Invasion players. Tharpe seemed to be forgotten, but her influence was powerful.

10

Memphis, Sun, and the Dawn of Rock

Post–World War II Memphis saw the arrival of a new economic force. After years of experiencing an influx of African Americans from the Delta and the Deep South, Memphis had become home to a new black middle class. By 1950, 40 percent of Memphis was black, including three million African Americans living in the greater Memphis region. Of those, half were in families considered middle class. Memphis radio stations had never before had reason to see the Africa American demographic as worth targeting; thus no station was geared toward black interests or even playing music by black performers.[1]

In 1947, two white Memphis businessmen, Bert Ferguson and John Pepper, launched a low-power, 250-watt, country radio station: WDIA. Because the signal was so weak, WDIA was drowned out at peak listening hours until they received an upgrade a few years later. Until then, WOIA was limited to daytime broadcasting.[2]

At first, Ferguson and Pepper struggled to establish a foothold. In 1948, the pair made the seemingly bold decision to try tapping into the dormant African American market. Not only was the entire country format scrapped in favor of black performers and the blues, R&B and gospel, but WDIA also hired all black deejays, making it the first such operation in the country. The station's first hire was Nat D. Williams, already a prominent Memphis emcee, high school teacher, writer, and editor for the cities' major black newspaper, *Memphis World*. Most of white Memphis was outraged to hear black Memphis coming through their radios, and demands were made for WDIA to pull the show. Ferguson and Pepper ignored the complaints, and Williams' show, "Tan Town Jamboree," became an enormous success. Williams engaged listeners in a folksy manner and entertained, but he also educated, helping WDIA breach racial issues on a regular basis with shows like *Brown America Speaks*.[3]

Rufus Thomas was another Memphis institution. Thomas began as an emcee for the Palace Theater Amateur Night on Beale Street in the 1940s, as well as being a WDIA deejay, a natural comedian, and a recording artist. Thomas later recorded soul and funk hits, "Walking the Dog," "Do the Funky Chicken," and "(Do the) Push and Pull." Along with Williams, Thomas became a draw for WDIA with his naturally funky style and humor.

WDIA billed itself as "The Mother Station of the South," and it monopolized Memphis' black market by the following year, 1949. For the first time, news was being broadcast that directly impacted African American interests, advertisements were tailored toward blacks, and "black" music was made readily available to the masses. Beyond 5:00 p.m., as WDIA's signal was not strong enough to compete with the bigger stations, they shut down at night. Nonetheless, by the end of the year, WDIA was the top-rated station in town.[4] Soon, 70 percent of black Memphis was tuning into WDIA at some point during the day.[5]

Also in 1949, B.B. King was deejaying in West Memphis, getting his name out and paying the bills by grabbing every gig he could get on Beale Street. King walked into WDIA studios on Union Street in Memphis and asked Williams for a slot. At Williams' request, King came up with a jingle on the spot for Peptikon, a "blood-building" medicine of sorts (with 12 percent alcohol), and he was hired.[6] King became WDIA's top deejay before moving on to become a full-time performer and the eventual "King of the Blues."

Even under white ownership, WDIA was a sea change from anything else King had experienced. King recalled that working at WDIA was the first time in his life that he "didn't have to say 'yes, sir' or 'yes, ma'am,' simply because a person was white."[7]

Along with virtually all of Memphis' black listeners, many of the Memphis region's white youth discovered WDIA, including the future Sun rockabilly stars, such as Elvis Presley and Carl Perkins.

In 1948, another Memphis radio station, WHBQ, was struggling badly as it watched WDIA's transformation.[8] WHBQ was being squeezed out of the top ratings by the other traditional stations. They did have a stronger signal than WDIA, however, and could broadcast at night; thus the station owners decided to try to capture WDIA's enormous black listening audience after 5:00 p.m.[9]

Choosing the man to deejay the new radio show was easy enough. Dewey Phillips was originally from Crump, Tennessee, and had been drawn to Memphis by the rich music in its parks, on its street corners, and especially on Beale Street. After seeing combat in World War II, he took a job running the record department at Grant's department store, not far from Beale Street, where the white Phillips focused primarily on selling black records.[10] In fact, the first half of the 2009 Tony Award–winning musical *Memphis* is based on Phillips' fascinating real life. Still, in part because the lead character in the musical's name was changed to Huey Calhoun, many do not know that there is an actual nonfiction basis for the show. Phillips' name and role in rock history have been vastly overlooked.

Phillips' job at Grant's store was to play music, talk to the customers, and draw people into his racks of records. His obvious passion for black music and overwhelming personality and sense of humor were a huge hit. So good was Phillips that Grant's gave him a microphone, increasing his drawing range and power.[11] Dewey thus had all of the trappings of a successful deejay—except a radio signal.

Grant's put Phillips on straight commission, meaning that he needed to even further ingratiate himself with his black customers and Memphis' black community. In the late 1940s and early '50s, Memphis was still utterly segregated, but Phillips was immediately accepted by the black community.[12] On Beale Street, virtually no white people mingled except for the occasional white business owner. It was an unwritten code that, as B.B. King put it, "we believed Beale Street was ours."[13] Phillips was about the only exception.

Rufus Thomas said of Phillips, "[H]e was the only white person who could go anywhere in the black neighborhood anytime he wanted to go and be accepted."[14] To Thomas, Phillips "had no color." B.B. King, who had known Phillips as far back as 1948, agreed that he "didn't think of him [Phillips] as being black or white." To King, Phillips "was always a lot of fun," and he had a feel for the blues that was "unusual" for a white guy.[15] Whether he had a financial incentive in his dealings or not, the black community knew he was authentic and accepted him.[16]

Phillips began his radio show, called "Red, Hot and Blue," in 1949. With a nearly out-of-control, stream-of-consciousness delivery, a wild sense of humor, and music that covered seemingly every range of the spectrum, the show was literally and figuratively all over the place. And it worked. Phillips' liberal use of amphetamines also enhanced his persona, although that and alcohol would contribute to later erratic behavior, hampering his career in the mid- and late 1950s and leading to an early death in 1968.[17]

WHBQ was only the second station, after WDIA, to bring the Delta blues and R&B to the airwaves. After Phillips' debut, WHBQ received a handful of postcards asking for specific R&B songs; the next day saw several dozen requests, then several hundred, and then they were inundated with requests. Phillips also played lots of "white" music, having no qualms about playing top-40 hits if he liked the song. Thus on "Red, Hot and Blue" listeners heard the Delta blues of Howlin' Wolf, the crooning of Dean Martin, and the pop-country of Patti Page, without having to turn the dial. The format was best described as an "amalgamated hodge-podge,"[18] but Phillips kept it all together. It was a bouillabaisse of all of the elements that would become rock and roll.

Given that other on-air personalities of the time were defined by rigidity and stodginess, Phillips' unhinged style, loose grammar, slang and country twang, as well as the musical selections, made him all the more exciting. Phillips was so different from the usual white deejays that many early listeners wondered if he was black.[19]

Phillips threw out cornball non-sequiturs, intentionally botched pronunciations (e.g., the "mezzanine floor" in the Chisca Hotel, where he broadcast from, became the "magazine floor"[20]), and did impersonations and voices of different characters, sometimes speaking from different directions into the microphone. Listeners were not always sure who else was actually in the booth with him.[21] Phillips seamlessly integrated commercial pitches into his shows that were sometimes incoherent, yet funnier and more effective than anything Madison Avenue could ever dream up. In short, it is possible that no one better embodied the spirit of rock and roll than Dewey Phillips. A show excerpt is transcribed as follows:

> Whoa! Ya, that was "Dig That Boogie," Piano Red, kickin' it off Red, Hot and Blue, don't forget get P-B-K can't buy a better beer than good ol' P-B beer when you go to the baseball game you know it just ain't no baseball game unless you got a good ol' cold bottle of C-V in your hand or maybe a case on your left side now that cv beer is flat good I'm telling you when you go to your favorite tavern or just any ol' joint always order C-V, Champagne Velvet the beer with the million dollar flavor if you don't forget when ya' sittin' around home playin' canaska [*sic*] or I could say something else and your listening to the Red, Hot, and Blue always have cv just go back to the Frigidaire and if the ol' lady's got a crown full of ham eggs and all that just pull 'em out, lay 'em on the floor and put that CV in there and get it cold and al-ways serve your friends CV, CV the beer with that new 1952 taste, y'all taste that taste the beer that is lighter and buyin' it so don't forget to get CV al-ways say CV for me and CV for Phillips that's a good deal now wait a minute Phillips ya' got the wrongest request here ya' flat messin' up here.[22]

Phillips' show was an immediate hit.[23] *Memphis World* noted his "zestful expressions" and "punchy jives" in explaining his enormous success with black listeners.[24]

Phillips was every bit as popular with Memphis' young, white audience. While much of older, white Memphis may have hated the mixed-race format, Phillips' irrepressible humor and personality somehow made it tolerable for the white establishment. Phillips was apparently too funny, too likable, and too goofy to be seen as any real social threat. However, while never political,

Phillips crossed lines and opened eyes. He emceed some all-black shows on Beale Street and, amazingly enough, even openly entertained black folks in his home.[25] For younger Memphians, and similar to Charles Black's experience in Austin with Louis Armstrong, listening to black artists for the first time on WDIA and WHBQ was the first exposure to African Americans outside of the people mowing their lawns or cleaning their homes.[26]

Radio historian Rick Wright wrote that Memphians Phillips, Thomas, Williams, and other WDIA personalities, were the first to elevate deejaying to an art form.[27] Phillips became a phenomenon of sorts at precisely the time when deejays were wielding immense power, but before the payola scandal beginning in 1959 (which did not implicate Phillips). Phillips had a platform to reach virtually all of the youth of the mid–South, a special ear for hits, and a contagious enthusiasm for the evolving R&B/rock format. This meant that if Dewey Phillips liked a song, it would probably become a hit. Indeed, Phillips *made* hits. According to early Sun Records star Charlie Feathers, "If Dewey said the record had it, you could just go down and start

Dewey Phillips of WHQB, "Red, Hot and Blue" program, Hippodrome, Beale Street, Memphis (early 1950s) (Dr. Ernest C. Withers, Sr. Courtesy Withers Family Trust).

counting your money 'cause it had it. It meant he was gonna play it and that's all it needed."[28] Further, if there was a song Phillips was particularly passionate about, he would declare on air, "That is a hit," even if it wasn't actually selling yet, or had been released years before, just to generate excitement. With Phillips' blessing the cut invariably become a hit retroactively.[29] His only guiding principle, it seemed, was to play songs he was passionate about.

* * *

Across town, at 706 Union Avenue, was Dewey Phillips' best friend and soon-to-be Sun Studio founder, Sam Phillips. In 1949, Sam Phillips was twenty-seven years old and had already been listening to "Red, Hot and Blue" for a few months when he purchased a small auto body repair shop and turned it into a studio. Sam had been drawn to Memphis from rural Alabama for the same reason as Dewey: the music. As a teen, Sam, too, had visited Memphis, and when he and his friends drove down Beale Street late at night, he took in the sounds and the energy and was hooked. "I was 16 years old, and I went to Memphis with some friends in a big old Dodge. We drove down Beale Street in the middle of the night and it was *rockin'*! The street was *busy*. It was so active—musically, socially. God, I loved it!"[30]

Sam was educated as an electrical engineer and couldn't read music, but he had an intuitive feel for it. On Union Street, he converted his space into a 700-square-foot studio with a small, adjoining mixing booth. The narrow office area up front was scarcely big enough for his secretary and associate, Marion Keisker, and her desk. Business meetings had to be conducted at one of the tables at Taylor's Restaurant, the diner next door. With that, Sam opened the Memphis Recording Service in January 1950, Memphis' first successful studio. The slogan was "We Record Anything—Anywhere—Anytime." Weddings were Sam Phillips' bread and butter, but funerals paid, too.[31]

Sam worked at his studio during the day and then worked a late shift mixing big bands downtown at the Peabody Hotel for CBS affiliate WREC. Too much work and financial pressure led to a nervous breakdown in 1950. Phillips decided to forego the steady paycheck with WREC and, with his wife Becky's support, went all-in with the Memphis Recording Service.[32]

Like his buddy Dewey, Sam Phillips thought the black music of the Delta was as rich and compelling as anything he had ever heard—and certainly it was in a different league altogether from the popular music of the time. Sam also knew that these musicians had no other outlets or forums to be heard in beyond the local black juke joints and clubs in Memphis and the nearby Clarksdale, Mississippi, area. Thus, from the beginning, Sam's goal was to try to "develop new and different artists, and get some freedom in music, and tap some resources and people that weren't being tapped."[33]

Sam had plenty of reason to doubt that there would be a *mass* market for whites buying "race" music—it was unprecedented. Then again, Sam knew that he and Dewey were not the only ones to "get" what was going on; a great many whites had been listening to the blues "surreptitiously" for years.[34] Sam also realized that while white people were not likely to embrace or idolize a rural black man and his music as they would a white man, a crossover *could* happen. He famously stated, "If I could find a white man who had the Negro sound and the Negro feel, I could make a billion dollars."[35] It was a line that would linger and carry with it Phillips' sense of vision, but also questions of racial exploitation. Yet Sam Phillips knew it went beyond the simple dollars-and-cents equation—he was aware that most white artists were lacking something that black artists had. Phillips' comment reflected his vision of a revolutionary genre he knew was waiting to happen; he just did not yet know exactly what it would look or sound like.

In 1951, Phillips began recording a white hobo playing in the country blues tradition named Harmonica Frank. Frank came from a carnival and medicine show background, themselves early examples of white and black music melding together—except in the musical stylings of the 1920s. As Frank recalled, "Old Sam had one thing to tell me. Said it over and over. 'Gimme something different. Gimme something unique.'"[36] Early Sun rockabilly star Carl Perkins recalled Sam getting him to "try things I knew I couldn't do."[37] Phillips somehow, intuitively, knew something was just around the corner.

Once Sam had opened his doors, the talent from in and around Memphis poured in. The first slew of legends-to-be included B.B. King, Rufus Thomas, Howlin' Wolf, Junior Parker, Little Milton, Roscoe Gordon, Walter Horton, Ike Turner and others. Joe Hill Louis was a one-man band—with a harmonica in front of his face, drum pedals at his feet, and a guitar—playing his own unique, countrified blues; he even did some spoken-word, proto-rap over some proto-blues rock guitar on "Gotta Let You Go" (1950). The Prisonaires were a group of black inmates at the Tennessee State Penitentiary in Nashville. As a part of a prison rehabilitation program, inmates formed musical groups, and some, like the Prisonaires, even left the prison walls to perform and record. The Prisonaires' Sun recording, "Just Walkin' in the Rain" (1953), sold well.[38]

Sam and Dewey Phillips actually started their own record label ("Phillips") for a bit in 1950, although they quickly discovered they were in over their heads and the label folded within weeks. Nonetheless, Sam learned some lessons and, for the time being, fed his early recordings to the bigger

R&B labels of Chess in Chicago and Modern in Los Angeles, until eventually starting Sun Records in 1952.[39]

B.B. King first recorded with Sam and Sun quickly gained a reputation as a place where African American musicians were not only *allowed* to record but really embraced. It was so rare for a Memphis business or studio to open its doors to African Americans that many of the musicians at first assumed that they would have to pay Phillips for the privilege of recording.[40]

Black musicians were still conditioned to modify not only their social behavior, but also their music, depending on whether white people were present. Sun became known as a place where black musicians did not have to "whiten up" their sound, either consciously or subconsciously; Phillips actually wanted the raw, real sound of the Delta. He had an understanding that black artists, as he put it, "unfortunately did not *have* an ego," in that

Sun Records studio, Memphis, Tennessee (photograph by Carol M. Highsmith, 2008, Library of Congress).

"these were people that had dreamed, and dreamed, and dreamed ... and were afraid of being denied again."[41] Ike Turner reflected years later that the Sun studio was one place that he "never worried" about the color of his skin.[42]

Of course, Sam Phillips and Sun Records were a few years away from recording their real signature artists—the white rock and rollers. A complaint has been made, by Rufus Thomas in particular, that once Phillips' white artists started to hit it big, he abandoned recording black artists, including Thomas. Further, Phillips never had white and black artists collaborate together in the studio. Phillips himself admitted that it was "regrettable" that he did not continue recording black artists. He also, however, took great pride in crashing the color line the way Sun did. He stated that it was never about of a lack of respect for the black artists or a matter of his abandoning them, declaring, "[T]here was no way I could do that." Phillips pointed out that there were numerous labels recording black music at the time, but only Sun had the platform for whites to record this new sound.[43] Additionally, many of the first black artists at Sun (e.g., B.B. King, Ike Turner, and Howlin' Wolf) all left the South on their own for Chicago and elsewhere, presumably not because of anything Sam Phillips did or did not do but as business decisions—or simply because they were getting out of the South.

* * *

In 1951, Ike Turner was a talented, nineteen-year-old leader of his own R&B band, Ike Turner's Kings of Rhythm, playing the black music venues around Clarksdale. As Turner recalled, one day his friend B.B. King asked him, "'Man, why you not recording?' I said, 'I don't know how to record.' 'Well I know a man in Memphis named Sam Phillips.' He said, 'I am going to tell him to call you.'"[44] Sam called, and Turner and his band soon showed up at Sun Records with a rollicking new composition named after the fastest car on the road at the time: the "Rocket 88" Oldsmobile.

The precise authorship of "Rocket 88" is not clear. The finished product was partly derived from two previous R&B tunes—"Cadillac Boogie," by Jimmie Liggins, and an instrumental piece, "Rocket 88 Boogie," parts 1 and 2, by Pete Johnson. According to Turner, saxophonist and singer Jackie Brenston suggested the Rocket 88 as the topic; Turner then came up with the pounding boogie piano intro (later reworked as the intro for Little Richard's "Good Golly Miss Molly") and the first verse, and the band worked the rest out on the fly in the studio.[45]

"Rocket 88" sounds a little similar to other jump blues–inspired R&B songs of the era, but it is special. In fact, by most rock music historians' reckoning, it is *the* first rock and roll song. Some, however, argue that its shuffling drum rhythm prevents it from truly being First,[46] but more on that debate shortly. The basic rock template is certainly there. First, lyrically speaking, "Rocker 88" was one of the earliest songs to celebrate the American automobile and being young, with a hot rod synonymous with both youth and freedom, as well as being a metaphor for sexual prowess. That Southern black males were singing so confidently about a new, high-performance hot rod also says something about both radical racial and economic changes in America at the time, as well.

On "Rocket 88," Turner's band is raucous but in a groove. Turner provides the fast, boogie piano; Raymond Hill has two wailing tenor sax solos; Willie Sims' drums offer a shuffle and a strong back beat; and guitarist Willie Kizart plays the bass parts on the lower guitar strings and through a distorted amp, making the song extra heavy. On top of that, Brenston's vocals are raw, confident and loose.

All of the above made "Rocket 88" a true classic, and it hit number one on the 1951 R&B charts. One thing that makes "Rocket 88" *extra* special is its use of guitar distortion. Ironically, the distortion came about by accident. As the story goes, on the band's way to the Sun studio that day, either the amp fell off the roof of the car or it was damaged from sitting in the trunk. Kizart started to play only to discover that his amp was broken. Yet something about it sounded interesting. Phillips, always one to experiment, stuffed newspaper into the speaker cone. The result was better but still a heavily distorted sound. Instead of trying to bury the amp in the mix, Phillips brought the guitar to the forefront even more, giving the guitar a heavier and edgier sound, sounding like a guitar crossed with both a bass and a sax.[47] Still, as heavy as "Rocket 88" is, it still moves and swings: like a party on wheels. Thus "Rocket 88" certainly seems to both rock *and* roll.

After the recording of "Rocket 88" was sent to Chess for pressing, a decision was made that the record would be more marketable if the singer, Brenston, was given top billing.[48] Thus what was really Ike Turner's Rhythm Kings was credited as Jackie Brenston's Delta Cats. Today, Turner's contributions to the formation of rock and roll remain underappreciated.

Turner was a scout for Phillips for a while before moving on and marrying the future R&B/soul star Tina Turner of Nutbush, Tennessee. Ike was the bandleader and guitarist for the Ike & Tina Turner Revue, one of the biggest soul acts ever, with classics such as "River Deep—Mountain High" (1966) and "Proud Mary" (1971). However, the 1993 biopic loosely based on Tina's life, *What's Love Got to Do with It?*, highlighted Ike's spousal abuse, and his name became more synonymous with domestic violence than with the advent of rock and roll, at least until his later years.

Of all the performers who came through the studio at 708 Union, no one had more emotional or visceral impact than Howlin' Wolf (a.k.a. Chester Arthur). Sam Phillips later recorded Elvis Presley, of course, but to Phillips, Wolf was the greatest performer he had ever witnessed. In Phillips' words, Wolf sang from a place "where the soul of a man never dies."[49] Wolf set the standard for Sun.

Wolf was a presence, to say the least. At six-foot-three and weighing nearly three hundred pounds, Wolf walked into Phillips' studio seemingly right out of the Delta fields in worn overalls and shoes with holes cut out of them to accommodate his corns.[50] Along with a harmonica, Wolf incorporated his mentor Charley Patton's showmanship, as well as taking Patton's growling vocal style to new depths. Wolf was something beyond heartfelt or soulful, and more a force of nature.

After a stint in the army, Wolf had deejayed in West Memphis, where Phillips first heard him. With his impossibly deep and gravelly voice, and a world of emotion, Wolf perfectly conveyed life in the Delta: soulful, intense, sexual, and menacing. As music writer Cub Koda put it, "no one could match Howlin' Wolf for the singular ability to rock the house down to the foundation while simultaneously scaring its patrons out of their wits."[51] As for his signature song, "Smokestack Lightning," that it would be used in Viagra commercials in the 2010s says a lot.

Wolf started recording with Phillips, laying down singles such as "Moanin' at Midnight," "How Many More Years" and "Wolf Is at Your Door." Those singles were sold to Chess Records in Chicago, and Wolf himself left for Chess in 1953. Wolf recalled his exit from Memphis: "I had a 4,000 dollar car and 3,900 dollars in my pocket. I'm the onliest one drove out of the South like a gentleman."[52] With the electric blues of Chess and a back beat, Wolf later became well known for 1956 hits "Smokestack Lightning" and "Evil"; later he recorded "I Ain't Superstitious," "The Red Rooster," "Shake for Me," "Back Door Man," and "Spoonful," many of which were covered by later rock bands, from the Doors to Megadeth. Wolf's career waned in the late 1950s but saw a resurgence during the British Invasion. When the Rolling Stones played the TV show *Shindig!* in 1965, to honor Wolf's influence, they insisted that he appear with them. When Wolf performed, the Stones sat around the stage at his feet.

The First Rock Record

Pinpointing a specific point as the origin of rock and roll is probably impossible. One might hope to simply look for when the phrase "rock and roll" first showed up, see what song it was describing, and call it "The First." However, to paraphrase deejay Alan Freed, determining the precise start of rock is more like finding a river fed by many streams and then trying to determine which stream is responsible for the river.[53] At other times, identifying a first seems analogous to an automobile assembly line where someone sticks a proper windshield on an otherwise functioning car and is then named the inventor of the automobile.

First, what definition for rock and roll should one even use? Does it have to have a guitar? Does it have to have one particular type of rhythm? Is it when the blues and the big beat started to get loose and swing, which could be Ike Turner's band or someone even earlier? Or is it when R&B and western swing met up as the formal and literal meeting of "black" and "white" music, crossing the color line for good, either with Bill Haley and the Comets or with Elvis Presley? Further, the definition may shift over time. If you asked someone in the 1970s to define rock, for example, you might get one answer, but if you asked someone in the post-punk area, when the genre had vastly diversified, you might get a very different response. Each definition may lead to a different but legitimate candidate for the "First Rock Record."

In any event, *modern* rock, as most people think of it today, has generally been seen as based on an electric guitar with a 4/4 rhythm—virtually all of which can be traced directly back to Chuck Berry. Berry is a key architect of rock, though he was not the first, either. Before Berry, the blues, boogie, R&B, gospel, country and pop all gelled into what at several points could be identified as rock and roll. It is no wonder that blues and rock historian Robert Palmer decided that "one might as well call the first rock and roll record Trixie Smith's early blues record, 'My Man Rocks Me (With One Long Roll)' from 1922, citing its unmistakable lyric intent, and be done with the whole thing."[54] Even Ike Turner, the man apparently most responsible for what a consensus calls the first rock song, stated that he did not think "Rocket 88" was rock and roll; rather, it just made R&B more accessible to white kids.[55] Singer Ruth Brown may, too, have been squarely on point when she suggested that the morphing strain of R&B only became "rock and roll" once "the white kids danced to it."[56]

Of course, the very term "rock and roll" does not necessarily line up with the history of the music itself, with the terminology running on a separate but parallel track. That is, the term first came about sometime around the turn of the twentieth century, likely in the Delta, starting off as an African American slang term for sex long before the music emerged.[57] Yet the term does also in fact have *spiritual* roots, too, as a reference to spiritual rapture. In fact, the first known use of the phrase "rocking and rolling" on a record was in an obscure 1910 recording of an up-tempo spiritual called "The Camp Meeting Jubilee," credited to the Male Quartette. The quartet sings in the chorus, "rocking and a rolling in your arms/rocking and a rolling in your arms/in your arms of Moses." Again, the Holy Spirit/human spirit distinction remains hopelessly muddled. (For that matter, there are also nautical references with these words together, such as in Buddy Jones' "Rockin' Rollin' Mama," 1939.)

Two decades after Trixie Smith, any number of references to *rock* by itself followed, including a somewhat ambiguous use by Sister Rosetta Tharpe in "Rock Me" (1941), which may hint at both a secular and a sexual meaning. Roy Brown wrote and released the jump blues song "Good Rocking Tonight" in 1947, and Wynonie Harris made it a number one R&B hit the following year, as well as one of the most popular early references to "rock" as an obvious double entendre for dancing and sex. Harris' version is a strong early candidate for the title of "First." Later, in 1948, Wild Bill Moore's "We're Gonna Rock, We're Gonna Roll" was another call to cut loose, set to a boogie piano and employing a deep, honking sax. In 1949, Harris had the slower-tempo, shout blues hit, "All She Wants to Do Is Rock." In fact, the mid– to late 1940s could almost be called the first rock era, given that so many songs had a strong beat and plays on the word *rock* in their titles, *a la* Harris. At one point, *Billboard* even noted the "umpteenth" such variation.[58]

The man who has become most synonymous with the phrase "rock and roll" was another white deejay who played "black" music in the early 1950s: Alan Freed. Freed began as a jazz musician in Ohio until an ear infection ended his career. In 1945, he began working as a deejay at WAKR in Akron, with a pop and jazz format, before moving on to Cleveland's WXEL-TV in 1948. Freed had a feel for new and interesting music, and in 1950 the owner of a local R&B-only record store, Leo Mintz of Record Rendezvous, told Freed that R&B records were hot sellers with black teens and seemed to be drawing interest from white kids as well, even though they were taboo "race" records.[59] Freed subsequently started a new R&B show with WXEL-TV in July of 1951.[60]

Inspired by an odd instrumental piece by the street musician Moondog, called "Moondog Symphony," Freed adopted the name "The Moondog House" for his show and began calling himself "The King of the Moondoggers."[61] Freed first used the term "rock and roll" in 1951 to describe the music show itself, but he really used it to describe how the music made him and the fans *feel*. On air, Freed howled along to the music while sometimes yelling, "Rock and roll!," while he drank beer and knocked out a beat on a telephone book. Freed later renamed his show the "Moondog Rock and Roll Show," with the phrase "rock and roll" now a verb that reflected what the music inspired people to do: rock and roll and get crazy.[62]

It is reasonable to believe that Freed picked up the term from Billy Ward's use of it in his March of 1951 R&B hit, "Sixty Minute Man," a single that Freed had been playing.[63] Just as Dewey Phillips was experiencing with a similar format in Memphis, Freed's ratings took off. That success led to the first rock and roll–style concert on March 21, 1952: "The Moondog Coronation Ball" at Cleveland Arena. The lineup was mostly black but integrated, with headliners Paul "Huckabuck" Williams and the Dominoes, and an almost all-black crowd.[64]

According to Terry Stewart, president of the Rock and Roll Hall of Fame and Museum, the real problem was that tickets for a second show had been printed but the date had not been changed. Thus for March 21st there were tickets sold for more than twice what the 10,000-person venue could hold.[65] It was already a raucous, high-energy night, and when Freed took the stage, the crowd was shocked to see that this guy they had been listening to for nine months was white, and they went nuts. At the same time, a crowd was still trying to get in; those with tickets were understandably none too happy to be left outside, leading to a rowdy, overflow crowd as well. The arena doors were closed and people were still trying to get in, even breaking door windows, and the scene turned riotous. Fire hoses were used to disperse the crowd, and authorities almost shut the first rock show down before it started, but a couple of songs were played.[66]

The resulting uproar gave both Freed and the new musical style more notoriety, and Freed's ratings rose even higher. The music industry took note of Freed's success and in 1954 he landed a job in New York at WINS, which had taken on an exclusive "rock and roll-styled" format. At the time, *Billboard* magazine crowned Freed "the undisputed king of radio programming."[67] Freed was a true Pied Piper with an incredible knack for connecting with and unifying rock fans, white and black, and making people feel part of a hip community.

In New York, Moondog took legal action, and the Moondog Rock 'n' Roll Party became just the "The Rock 'n' Roll Party."[68] The term gradually gained acceptance, either as the grammatically challenged slang version to signify the genre's anti-establishment credentials, rock 'n' roll, or with the and spelled out. The Pull term "rock and roll" was in place by 1955. Today, it can be used to specifically refer to the first wave of rock music, anywhere from 1951 to 1960, or the genre in its entirety, with "rock" or "modern rock" sometimes used to distinguish the genre after that first wave.

Over the years, Freed became the deejay the public would most closely relate to rock's origins. Later on, the Rock and Roll Hall of Fame was founded in Cleveland in 1983, as opposed to Memphis, or possibly New Orleans or New York. This was in large part due to the city of Cleveland committing an enormous financial package to the Hall,[69] as well as a Cleveland radio station having heavily promoted an important *USA Today* newspaper poll to its listeners.[70]

Throughout the rest of the 1950s, Freed's popular shows featured Chuck Berry as a major headliner, along with Little Richard, Jackie Wilson, Buddy Holly, and others; Freed also played himself in a series of rock performance–related films. In 1958, at a Freed-produced show in Boston, he was cited for "igniting a riot." The police ordered the lights on to subdue the crowd when Freed purportedly told those gathered, "The police don't want you to have fun," agitating the teens even further.[71] This marked the beginning of the end of Freed's run, which would culminate with the "payola" scandal (more on that later) and alcoholism a few years later.[72] Freed was also in the habit of using his clout in promoting songs to leverage songwriting credits for himself (not uncommon in the business at the time) with both white and black artists. Thus, for example, Freed appears on the credits for Chuck Berry's "Maybellene" despite not having written any music.

Again, Freed's popularizing of the term "rock and roll" did not in and of itself mark any new musical sound—it described an exciting R&B genre that was already morphing into something different. Realistically, one could make a playlist of a dozen or more songs and make an argument for any one of them that could be considered the first of the new genre, from Wynonie Harris' "Good Rockin' Tonight" to Elvis Presley's "That's All Right Mama." Still, Freed's shows and his coining of the term helped legitimize, popularize, and solidify the movement. Further, doors were opened for black performers and black deejays across the country.

Making the music more accessible to whites also altered the very sound of rock and roll itself. Music historian Charlie Gillett wrote that "as the people producing the music became conscious of their new [white] audience, they changed the character of the music."[73] Thus, whatever R&B had been at the time, it began to pull in new influences and styles, conscious of the changing audience. Further, white artists were freed to embrace their own vision of the blues and R&B, and they ultimately created another, new strain of rock and roll, one with a strong country influence: rockabilly. Bill "Hoss" Allen, a white deejay from WLAC in Nashville (another mid–1950s R&B station that also played white country musicians drawing from "black music"), talked about the white take on the music: "They started trying to hold those guitar chords like the blues guys, play in minor keys and stuff, but it didn't come out like

Muddy Waters or Howling Wolf. It came out rockabilly, and from rockabilly came white rock and roll."[74] Thus at the very foundation of rock and roll in the 1950s were two primary strains: a more R&B-based strain and a rockabilly strain. There is loads of overlap, of course, and the distinction is somewhat irrelevant. Still having two strains can muddle the analysis and understanding each helps in clarifying how rock and roll first came about.

The R&B-based strain of rock started with "Rocket 88," along with the New Orleans artists Fats Domino, Lloyd Price and Little Richard, and it was shaped by Chess Records and the electric blues of Howlin' Wolf and Muddy Waters, and then Chuck Berry.

The crossover of these strains was such that in the mid–1960s, the Rolling Stones were referred to by the British press, and the Stones referred to themselves as a "rhythm and blues" group, even while their music obviously fell within the broader rock and roll genre.[75] This style is grittier, aggressive, and often more overtly sexual, while the rhythms are generally a low-swinging boogie. Examples include one of the Stones' most highly regarded albums, *Exile on Main Street*, with songs like "Rip This Joint" and "Hip Shake Thing." Later groups, such as Led Zeppelin, Aerosmith and Guns N' Roses, further exemplify this style.

The second thread of rock and roll has much the same Delta and R&B foundation, but it draws more from country, western swing, and pop: rockabilly. Rockabilly began with Bill Haley and Elvis Presley and the Sun rockabilly stars; Buddy Holly; and on to the early Beatles. Here the rhythm is, ultimately, more accommodating to pop harmonies and melody. This strain is embodied by everything from Johnny Cash, to the melodic folk rock of Simon and Garfunkel, to the power pop of Cheap Trick.

The distinctions between R&B and rock and roll were minimal to begin with. A key player in closing that gap was Fats Domino. Starting in 1949, Domino's "The Fat Man," a slow boogie piano piece with a strong back beat from drummer Earl Palmer, could really be classified as jump blues, R&B, or early rock and roll. From there, Domino's style shifted until 1955's "Ain't That a Shame," which featured dramatic stop time breaks, Domino opening up his vocals, a huge hook, strong tenor sax breaks, and a more pronounced beat. By that point, the major differences between the strains were gone.[76] Berry's sound coalesced when he took on some hillbilly sound (more on that shortly); Presley started with country and pop and then embraced the blues on "That's All Right Mama."

Getting back to determining rock's specific origins, certainly music became rock and roll when the above elements were present and, especially, then combined with raw emotion, something happens. To many rock performers and fans, at its core, the energy unleashed by rock music equates specifically to the physical act and the high of sex (e.g., Lewis' "Great Balls of Fire" and, later, AC/DC's "Let Me Put My Love in to You," and so on). Certainly rock is often about hedonism and self-indulgence. After all, the phrase "sex drugs and rock and roll," popularized in the 1960s, is meant to embody the rock and roll, and counter-cultural, ethos.

However, for others, the energy of rock can also represent the exhilaration of love in boy-girl relationships (or same-sex ones, though not openly early on, of course). Some rockers openly identify with organized religion (e.g., Little Richard, U2, Bob Dylan), have recorded straight gospel albums (Presley, Dylan, etc.), or have pursued spiritual paths outside of organized, Western religion (e.g., the Beatles' Hindu pursuits). Thus this kind of energy is more spiritual than the mere act of sex. It is fair to say that lust is not love, and love may transcend the purely physical act of intercourse and orgasms (e.g., the Beatles' "I Want to Hold Your Hand," "All You Need is Love," or even "Across the Universe"). According to soul legend and sex symbol-turned-Memphis Baptist minister, Al Green, "The physical drive of it, which we know is not the most important drive.... The physical drive is fine, but still, there's a greater drive than that. There's a more soulful, a more emotional inner drive that makes things possible."[77]

Of course, since love has physical and sexual components, it can all easily become confused, to say the least—and more so for hormone-addled teens. Thus the double entendres regarding dancing and sex in the jump blues were introduced to the (white) mainstream, and rock and roll continued to evolve from that. It is safe to say that rock and roll can definitely be sexual, but it may also transcend the physical act at the same time.

What *was* clear to the rock and rollers was that, in order to be freed from any stifling social codes, boundaries must be pushed, and thus risks taken. When the parental generation of the mid–1950s was, in many of their children's eyes, living dull, purposeless and robotic lives, often dictated by material or corporate interests or more invested in merely maintaining a façade of happiness, many quite logically asked: What exactly is there to lose?

In the rock and roll revolution, making mistakes was sometimes a small price to pay for some spontaneous, *real* expression. In this new culture, mistakes could even be seen as *positive*, as they were the result of having at least attempted to break out of the old and truly *live*. Future Sun star Carl Perkins, for example, related how he pushed himself in the studio at Sam Phillips' urging, inevitably making mistakes in the process. As Perkins himself described his and Phillips' conversations: "'Mr. Phillips, that's terrible.' He said, 'That's original.' I said, 'But it's just a big original mistake.' And he said, '*That's what Sun Records is.* That's what we are.'"[78]

To even better understand rock, it will help to jump ahead for a moment to the legendary 1963 cover of the garage-rock, party anthem, "Louie Louie," by the Kingsmen. This song offers a case study of the odd beauty of rock and roll. The lyrics of "Louie, Louie" are mostly indecipherable, which is okay because the song *feels* right, and you can sense what they are saying. "Louie Louie" sounds so raw, in fact, that many listeners assumed that it *had* to be obscene. The FBI even investigated the song for obscenity, only to determine that it could not be because the lyrics were "unintelligible."[79]

"Louie Louie" was written by Richard Berry in 1955, borrowing a rhythm from a 1950s Cuban song, "El Loco Cha Cha," by Ricky Rillera and the Rhythm Rockers.[80] The Kingsmen sound like they are playing in the late hours of a particularly good, if seedy, early 1960s frat party. Three basic chords. A Wurlitzer. An odd, syncopated bass line that provides a perfectly danceable beat. Impassioned but warbled vocals. At one point, singer Jack Ely screams to the band to give the crowd all it has, to really push it.

Before the final verse, the Kingsmen are repeating a riff as per another, earlier cover of the song by the Wailers. Ely jumps back in too soon, apparently per the Berry version, but then catches himself mid-line and has to stop singing and restart the verse. No matter. It was the only take and pressed because it captured the *feeling* just right, and that feeling otherwise eclipses one little mistake. In other words, "Lighten up. Have some fun."

The point, then, is that, along with instrumentation, lyrics, rhythm, and so on, the actual act of pushing things past boundaries is one, and maybe the most important, defining characteristic of rock. Thus it may be a defining characteristic of the first rock song as well, whichever song that may be.

* * *

The 1992 book *What Was the First Rock and Roll Record?* details fifty songs that have at various times been mentioned in this discussion.[81] Each song has interesting elements, though most fail an initial *I-know-it-when-I-hear-it* test. To give a few examples, in 1936, a Delta country blues group called the Graves Brothers recorded "Barbecue Bust," a number with some proto-rock guitar riffs and a loose, fun, slightly sloppy style. Yet the folk-country sound, the acoustic guitar, and (especially) the presence of a kazoo definitively mark "Barbecue Bust" as something pre-rock. Still, it does have that feel.

Sister Rosetta Tharpe's "Strange Things" (1944) is special, but it's still really gospel. Louis Jordan's 1945 hit "Caldonia" is nearly rock, but it also sounds more firmly entrenched in the jump and R&B genres it helps define. Also in 1947, Jack Guthrie and his hillbilly group, the Oklahomans, had a hit with the blues-influenced swing of "Oakie Boogie." Here the overall feel is country, the instrumentation is a pretty clear no (a fiddle serves as the main instrument), and Guthrie's vocals sound closer to a square dance call than a clarion call for the youth of the world.

Some would call Wynonie Harris the key figure here, pointing to his inspired cover of "Good Rockin' Tonight" (1948), with its strong back beat, boogie piano, brash vocals, and sexual references. It could well be rock and roll, and it certainly seems to mark a new era. Yet it, too, seems to lack the sound of something transforming into a brand new genre. It is certainly close, and it serves as a crucial building block.

Others of the era, such as two shout blues songs later popularized by Presley—Big Mama Thornton's version of "Hound Dog" and Arthur Crudup's "That's All Right"—have slower tempos and more loping rhythms than Presley's versions and, while great songs, are thus clearly in the shout blues genre.

In 1949, Fats Domino was discovered playing R&B on the piano in a dive bar in the 9th Ward in New Orleans. Domino went on to be a key architect of rock and roll and a giant throughout the 1950s and early 1960s. Domino's first hit, "Fat Man," co-written with Dave Bartholomew, had the required strong back beat, along with a rolling piano, subversive humor, and raw sexuality. Here Domino's combination of boogie and swing makes it the choice of some rock historians as First.[82] Still, the song has a slower beat, and although rock and roll does not necessarily have to be fast, it seems like a stronger sense of urgency or a bit of reckless abandon is needed to mark the beginning of a revolution.

For some boogie piano and very familiar-sounding, proto–Chuck Berry guitar riffs, Texan Goree Carter's "Rock Awhile" (1949) fits the bill and is certainly a top contender. Carter's song has *bursts* of rock guitar (and his guitar work probably owes a debt to "T-Bone" Walker), though the rest of the song feels more like R&B. Is that enough to be the first rock record?

If instead of a guitar, a squalling sax rocks enough for you, then Jimmy Preston's "Rock the Joint," also from 1949 and recorded in Philadelphia, could very well get the nod, with a boogie piano; a back beat; wild, loose vocals and screams; and scarcely veiled, pushing-the-social-norms sexual references.

Some believe that rock and roll did not really arrive until the true and literal crossing of the racial line. In discussing the explosive success of Elvis

Presley, Greil Marcus astutely noted that the white person who would really be original and have huge success, "had to be someone who toyed with race, the deepest source of limits in the South."[83] Marion Keisker of Sun Records said that Presley's music was like "the wedding of the Hatfields and the McCoys."[84] To play just black music was somewhat limiting, as was playing just white music. To open the sound up to embrace the best of both worlds was to broaden and elevate the scope and impact of the music. This adds weight to those songs that first explicitly crashed the racial boundaries and thus might favor Haley's 1952 cover of "Rock the Joint" or even Presley's "That's All Right" (1954), with the latter being the song that *Rolling Stone* said "started it all."[85]

* * *

Haley certainly warrants extra attention. In 1947, Haley was working as a musical director at a radio station in his hometown of Chester, Pennsylvania, and fronting the Four Aces of Western Swing. They put out some records, but when the group disbanded in the middle of 1949, Haley formed "Bill Haley and His Saddlemen." Haley was looking to branch out with the group's sound toward swing and the more hip, Hank Williams–type of hillbilly/country.[86]

In 1951, Hollywood Records owner David Miller talked the group into recording a cover version of Jackie Brenston and His Delta Cats' "Rocket 88." It is not an inspired version, and Haley had been opposed to recording it at all. Still, the recording was important for at least two reasons. First, it was the first white cover of a black R&B song. Second, it marked the beginning of a new phase in Haley's group's direction. Haley was already twenty-six years old (old to be a new pop star) and a little pudgy, with a moon-shaped face and an odd spit-curl of hair on his forehead—not what most would consider a proto-typical rock star.

Nonetheless, as the tides continued to shift in Memphis, Cleveland, New Orleans, and all across the country, Haley and company lost the cowboy hats, changed their name to Bill Haley and the Comets, and became an R&B act. They would soon be the first band to formally put themselves out as a rock and roll group.

Haley's 1952 version of Preston's "Rock the Joint" utilizes an early slap back bass, as the former swing band still had no drummer. There is a shuffling rhythm, and Comet guitarist Danny Cedrone pulls off some classic hillbilly/rockabilly riffs. The back-up vocals are right out of the shout blues of the time. In 1953, Haley had another major rock hit with "Crazy, Man, Crazy." All of this comes together so far as successfully marrying the blues and hillbilly sound, though the songs may lack some soulful energy and the transcendency of the music, as seen in many black R&B songs.

In 1954, Haley and the Comets released the swinging rockabilly song "Rock Around the Clock," at first a minor hit, and one of the great songs of the early rock and roll era. Next, Haley had a million-seller with a swinging and rocking cover of Big Joe Turner's classic jump blues/rock and roll song of the same year, "Shake, Rattle and Roll." From 1954 to 1956, Bill Haley and the Comets had nine songs crack the top twenty, and three made the top ten.

In 1955, "Rock Around the Clock" got a second life when it was used over the opening credits in the sensationalized juvenile delinquent film, *Blackboard Jungle*. The band was a hit, and its music defined the wild and reckless feel of rock and roll. When the film was first released in the U.K., teens were jumping out of their theater seats to dance to "Rock Around the Clock" (and in some cases tearing up the seats and damaging theaters). "Rock Around the Clock" was number one in the States for eight weeks, eventually selling 25 million copies worldwide, making it rock's first international hit and anthem.[87] The song helped connect rock's frenetic, *physical energy* with the white teen masses, unleashing the frustrations and libidos of a generation.

For a few different reasons, it is easy to overlook the edge and importance of Haley and the Comets, even though they were as relevant as anyone else at the time. Haley described his band's music as R&B being played with country and western instruments, with the result, in Haley's words, being "pop music."[88] Just a couple of years later, the group already seemed a bit out of touch, releasing, for example, an album called *Rockin' the Oldies*, in an effort to update pop standards like "The Dipsy Doodle" and "(I'll Be with You In) Apple Blossom Time."[89] Yet Haley and the Comets had indeed incited small riots.

* * *

So where does that leave the analysis of the effective and formal start of rock and roll? Who was first? Is there a first? In the late 1940s and early 1950s, rhythm and blues was getting energized and morphing into something different and more dynamic. The change was fueled by youthful rebellion, electric guitars and the big beat, and it was starting to crash both social and musical boundaries. The appropriation of the phrase "rock and roll" itself is not definitive in marking rock and roll's true birth, but it is helpful. Again, Freed's phrase and his wildly popular "rock and roll" shows certainly do suggest that, as a popular movement, it was already in gear by March of 1952.

Ultimately, then, the best definition may simply be when some down-and-dirty R&B got heavier, yet still swung loose, and clearly liberated fans at some new level. In Ike Turner's "Rocket 88," all of these elements are present. The sense of pushing into a brand new era is also there, but to keep the issue murky, at no point with the release of "Rocket 88," or any other song, did anyone explicitly recognize that an entirely new genre of music had just been born.

What even more clearly puts "Rocket 88" into rock and roll territory, though, is that not only did a broken piece of equipment not stop a recording session, but that the participants decided, Who cares?, and then went with it because it sounded and felt right—and it even made the resulting music *better.* That is as rock and roll as it gets. Rockabilly later opened up and broadened the palette of what rock and roll would be, and it popularized the music, for sure, but it was not the first. Still, to take rock to the next level, it would require a little more.

11

Mr. Presley

The Legacy

Elvis Presley left a vast and strange legacy. He arose dirt-poor from the Deep South to become the original and still biggest rock star ever. Presley's bold sexuality shocked America and the world in 1956 before he disappeared into the army, then faded into a disappointing eight years as a Hollywood B-movie star in the 1960s, followed by a comeback as a glitzy Las Vegas performer in the 1970s, before finally dying unexpectedly in 1977. Presley was the best-selling recording artist in history; only the Beatles and Michael Jackson are even remotely comparable in terms of both critical and commercial success, as well as their overall impact on popular culture. Taking rock and roll to worldwide prominence alone makes Presley arguably the most important performer of the twentieth century. That was the title bestowed upon Presley by composer and conductor Leonard Bernstein, who explained, "He introduced the beat to everything and he changed everything—music, language, clothes. It's a whole new social revolution—the sixties came from it."[1] From 1956 to 1958, with the ideal musical influences, talent, attitude, ambition, and voice to change music, not to mention the look, moves, and skin color to be effective in the new TV medium, Presley was perfectly positioned to bring rock and roll to the masses.

Still, despite Presley's accomplishments and his iconic status, his legacy is extremely convoluted. Presley biographer Peter Guralnick wrote that after Presley's death, the man himself was lost under "a cacophony of voices ... joined together to create a chorus of informed opinion, uninformed speculation, hagiography, symbolism, and blame."[2] With Presley's legacy and true story both obscured, rock's very origins, and a crucial piece of American history, remain obscured as well.

Presley's chapter requires a rather extended analysis. It will also help to again leap forward on the timeline for a moment to understand where and how this legacy got so twisted. Presley is such a central figure that this confusion clouds the entire history of rock and roll's origins. The "Elvis" legacy also serves as a Rorschach test for observers of American culture.

There are at least three factors that cloud the reality of Presley's life. First, his final years are defined by the tragic end to his unglamorous Vegas era: scarcely relevant musically; performing in unflattering, bejeweled jumpsuits; terribly overweight; and, as was widely reported, finally dying on the commode from what was understood to be a drug-induced heart failure. That image has persisted and overshadowed the rest of his story.

Second, Presley's legacy simply does not fit into any easy categories. He improbably found himself at the epicenter of some of the most volatile social issues in American history regarding shifts in culture, sexuality, and race, as well as in music. In part, Presley's talents made him a sensation, but his notoriety is also due to some amazing circumstances of geography and timing. The result has been that too often Presley has alternatively received either far too much or too little credit for his social impact. On the one hand, Presley is often dismissed out of hand and treated as a joke, but at other times he is deified and given attention to the point of eclipsing other important artists.

Third, and finally, Presley's Vegas years and ugly demise served to distance him from the rebellious cool of rock and roll, even though he had helped create it. Thus, throughout the 1960s and 1970s, Presley would scarcely even be linked with the ongoing rock and roll revolution that he had helped launch. Instead, he was often associated either with schmaltzy Las Vegas lounge lizards or with the original, but seemingly no longer relevant, "Golden Era" of rock and roll of sock hops and soda fountains.

Certain volatile issues were first raised in the 1950s and then crystallized in the 1960s, and many Westerners found themselves on one side or the other of a clear line of demarcation: the side of the establishment or on the side of the counter-cultural movement. But while the Beatles were facilitating the hippie/psychedelic movement and proclaiming that "All You Need Is Love," Mahalia Jackson was assuring civil rights marchers that "We Shall Overcome," Bob Dylan was informing politicians that "Times They Are a-Changin'," and Marvin Gaye asked everyone "What's Going On?," Presley was conspicuously absent, hanging out in Hollywood, presumably by the pool with a starlet and popping pills, while making a long string of forgettable movies.

Worse, in the late 1950s, the major labels turned away from the original African American–derived heart and excitement of rock and roll in favor of lesser, safer artists. Had not Presley himself ridden to success on some songs originally popularized by black artists—namely, "That's All Right" and "Hound Dog"—and in a style derived directly from African Americans?

In addition, even in death, timing and circumstances landed Presley squarely in the middle of another cultural epoch: a new era of celebrity and tabloid culture that would also alter his image forever. One of the odd, and perhaps sadder, ironies of modern pop culture is that even the most basic details and facts regarding the life of one of the most talked-about celebrities ever, have been obscured and eclipsed by so much hype and noise. The media, tabloids, and an often cultish fan base, created their own storylines in order to either preserve an image of Elvis, or create a new one. As a result, Elvis remained in people's faces prominently through the 1980s and 1990s, and he became an easy target for detractors.

Fairly portrayed or not, Elvis has come to symbolize not only the very best of America, but also the very worst, including greed, gluttony, insincerity and racial exploitation. The truth, of course, lay somewhere in the middle.

Presley's Early Life

Elvis Presley was born in 1935 to a poor family in the Mississippi Delta, in Tupelo, Mississippi. Presley and his parents, Vernon and Gladys, lived in a two-room "shotgun shack," a symbol of extreme poverty throughout the South. Presley's twin brother, Jesse Garon, was stillborn 35 minutes before Elvis. Presley went on to bear the hopes—and burdens—of two for the rest of this life. As Gladys always said, "when one twin dies, the one that lived got all the strength of both."[3]

The Presleys were described by those who knew them as somewhat unremarkable; church-going but insular.[4] Vernon Presley described the family as having friends and relatives, but the three "formed our own private world," with young Elvis in the center.[5] Gladys, four years older than Vernon, was the undisputed head of the family. Vernon was not particularly confident nor outgoing. He was known as someone who had trouble keeping jobs and, according to some friends, may have leaned too much on the bottle. One early girlfriend of Elvis described the family dynamics thus: "It was almost like Elvis was the father and his dad was just the little boy."[6] Elvis spoke of taking care of his parents one day, aspiring to lift them out of poverty. As an adult, he referred to his parents as "his babies."[7]

By all accounts, Gladys and Elvis had an overly close relationship. Even into Elvis' young adulthood, he and Gladys spoke to each other in "baby talk" (e.g., referring to ice cream as "iddytream" and milk as "butch").[8] One early acquaintance recalled a young Elvis as "quiet and he stuttered, and he was a mama's boy." In his youth, Elvis had few friends.[9]

In 1938, when Elvis was three, Vernon paid for a check-altering scam with an eight-month prison term. The crime was largely understood by friends and neighbors to be a one-time misstep by an otherwise decent but poor man enduring tough times. Nonetheless, the incident was shameful enough for the family to never discuss it, and it remained under wraps when Elvis first hit the limelight.[10]

Presley's first musical inspirations came at his Pentecostal church services at the Assembly of God in Tupelo. He later reflected on how the more reserved singers didn't seem to inspire much fervor, but others did: "They would be jumpin' on the piano, movin' every which way. The audience liked 'em. I guess I learned from them singers."[11] Presley also sang country ballads at school, often bringing his guitar with him. At eight years old, he calmly told classmates that one day he was going to play the Grand Ole Opry. As a ten-year-old, the shy Presley got up on stage to belt out a song in front of several hundred people at the Mississippi/Alabama Fair. At twelve, he found a mentor in Mississippi Slim, a brother of a classmate and a professional musician who played on East Tupelo's WELO radio station.[12]

In 1948, Vernon fell behind on the family's mortgage, and the Presleys had to move to a shack right next to the respectable but poor black section of Tupelo called Shake Rag. In the eyes of the rest of the town, the Presleys had formally become what today might be unfortunately referred to as *white trash*.[13]

On the weekends, the streets of Shake Rag came alive with the sounds from juke joint juke boxes, church sermons, and church choirs.[14] The Presleys' new home was just a few doors down from the black Sanctified Church, and here young Elvis was exposed to raw, unadulterated expressions of faith not entirely dissimilar to the outpouring of emotions and speaking in tongues of the Pentecostal church. Presley could not be a part of those services, of course, but the music both freed something inside him and emboldened him at the same time. When asked in 1957 about his rock and roll style, Presley explained:

> The colored folks been singing it and playing it just like I'm doin' now, man, for more years than I know. They played it like that in their shanties and in their juke joints and nobody paid no mind 'til I goosed it up. I got it from them. Down in Tupelo, Mississippi, I used to hear old Arthur Crudup [a Clarksdale, Mississippi, blues musician] bang his box the way I do now and I said if I ever got to the place I could feel all old Arthur felt, I'd be a music man like nobody ever saw.[15]

Presley's upbringing also forged a certain sincere humility (along with his class inferiority) within him, which he retained after becoming a superstar. It struck nearly everyone who met him. With Presley, everything was "yes, ma'm" and "no ma'm."[16] Father Vernon put it into perspective:

> There were times we had nothing to eat but corn bread and water but we always had compassion for people. Poor we were, I'll never deny that. But trash we weren't.... We never had any prejudice. We never put anybody down. Neither did Elvis.[17]

For Presley's freshman year in 1949, the family had to move again, this time to Memphis. As Presley later put it, "We was broke, man, broke"; his father "packed all our belongings in boxes and put them in the trunk and on top of a 1939 Plymouth. We just headed for Memphis. Things had to be better."[18]

Presley hailed from the direct social lineage of the hillbillies that the proper South was trying to ignore. Southern music writer Stanley Booth well captured Presley's element, to include his fellow and future white rockabilly superstars from the region:

> [L]ounging on the hot corners of a gas station on a Saturday afternoon, stopping for a second on the sidewalk as if they were looking for someone who was looking for a fight. You could see their sullen faces with a toughness lanky enough to just miss being delicate, looking back at you out of old photographs of the Confederate Army.... All outcasts with their contemporary costumes of duck-ass haircuts, greasy Levi's, motorcycle boots, T-shirts for the day and black leather jackets for evening wear. Even their unfashionably long sideburns (Elvis' were furry) expressed contempt for the American Dream they were too poor to be a part of.[19]

Those poor working-class whites of the South had long been seen, as Greil Marcus put it, as the South's "stepchild culture," and they were viewed by the rest of America as "a caricature of Bilbao [governor of Mississippi and Klan member in the 1930s] and moonshine."[20] Theirs was a demographic born into marginalization, and they knew it.

The Presleys moved into the Courts in Memphis, decent for public housing and actually a major step up for the family.[21] At Humes High School, Memphis' main white school, Presley was a bit of a misfit and loner, seen as an odd, poor kid from the wrong side of the tracks who sang hillbilly music.[22] Yet Presley was also gaining self-confidence and developing a vision for himself and a career in music with his own original and distinct style.

First, it was the slicked-up pompadour and long sideburns, which alone made him stand out anywhere he went. By his senior year, Presley had also taken to wearing the bold stylings of Lansky Brothers, purchased with money from his job at a furniture assembling plant, working from 3:00 p.m. to 11:30 p.m., and which also supplemented family bills. Presley sported black dress pants with a pink stripe down the side and a bolero jacket. In 1950s Memphis, when every other boy was wearing jeans, this was out there for a young, white male.[23] By the mid–1950s, Presley had additionally started wearing mascara, inspired by movie star Tony Curtis. After sharing a bill at Presley's only appearance at the Grand Old Opry in 1955, country singer Chet Atkins would comment, "I couldn't get over that eye shadow he was wearing. It was like seeing a couple of guys kissin' in Key West."[24] Presley told another story about his high school football team chasing him, trying to cut his hair for him so he would no longer look like a "squirrel."[25]

At that point, Presley was already a serious student of music and encyclopedic in his knowledge of the blues and religious music, including local Delta blues stars like B.B. King, Arthur Crudup, and Rufus Thomas. He was also well-versed in pop and country stars like Hank Snow, Bob Wills, and Roy Acuff. For a music fan in 1949, Memphis was about as good a place as one could hope for, especially if one wasn't worried about racial divides. A Memphian could enjoy musicians on the streets and in the parks, as well as on Beale Street, where whites attended special "Whites Only" nights. On the radio, one could tune into the legendary Grand Ole Opry from across the state in Nashville or KWEM from across the river in West Memphis, Arkansas, where blues legends-to-be Howlin' Wolf and Sonny Boy Williamson broadcasted. Among the Memphis stations, WHHM had Sleepy Eyed John's "Hillbilly Hit Parade"; WDIA, which had just switched to the "black" format the year before, had Nat D. Williams deejaying one show and B.B. King helming another; and WHBQ had Dewey Phillips' "Red, Hot and Blue."

On Sunday nights, WHBQ broadcast the famed Negro spiritual composer Reverend W. Herbert Brewster's sermons and music live, from East Trigg Baptist Church on South Bellevue Boulevard. In fact, during Presley's high school years, he and some friends would sneak out of their own church services at Memphis's First Assembly of God and head over to Reverend Brewster's and other black services. Brewster's sermons, and especially the choir and the music, were a far cry from the white church experience in Memphis. Presley and his friends were always welcome, and they respectfully sat in the back or in the balcony (as blacks would have to do at a white service) and soaked it in.[26]

Like so many other teens, Presley was also a huge Marlon Brando fan, especially after seeing the early biker gang film, *The Wild One* (1953), and he later became a fan of James Dean in *Rebel Without a Cause* (1955). From those characters, perhaps stronger and more dangerous versions of Salinger's alienated and angry Holden Caulfield, Presley learned what he understood as the new attitude of *cool*. Like Brando's gang leader character in *The Wild One*, who had famously responded to the question "What are you rebelling against?" with "What have you got?," Presley's persona was one of strong independence. He intentionally never smiled and instead developed a lip curl/sneer, which became a trademark of his live performances.

Becoming Elvis

After high school, Presley worked as a truck driver for Crown Electric in Memphis, something he expected to be his future. But then, in August 1953, the then eighteen-year-old Presley walked into Sun Records. He told Marion Keisker that he wanted to record something for his mother's birthday, though given that Gladys' birthday had passed in April, Presley was more likely just looking to be noticed. He recorded a pop music standard and a country song; he was unpolished and not overwhelming. Keisker, however, did sense something about Presley and his feel for music and made a note: "Good ballad singer. Hold." As incredibly shy as Presley was—Sam Phillips actually called him "the most introverted person that ever came into the studio"—he continued to stop by Sun to ask Keisker if Phillips had listened to his recording and if he wanted to hear more?[27]

Finally, in July of 1954, Phillips had a demo for a ballad, and Presley's name came up as a possible fit. Phillips paired Presley with two of his better house musicians: twenty-seven-year-old upright bass player, Bill Black, and twenty-two-year-old guitarist, Scottie Moore. Black was not a great musician, but he was loose and energetic, which Phillips loved, and Moore was an excellent guitarist who shared Phillips' desire to break into new sounds. Initially, neither Black nor Moore were overly impressed with Presley; he looked striking, but he had yet to find his own sound and was still too restrained. Moore noted that it was as if Presley could not find the words to say what he wanted, and the result was a lot of stammering and awkward pauses. Partly persuaded by Phillips' confidence in the singer, the pair agreed to record with Presley again the next night.[28]

Phillips' real genius lay in his ability to make musicians feel at home in his studio, giving them the time to relax and get comfortable. Since Phillips owned the place, he was in no rush to cram recording time in if he didn't feel like it. Time and again these relaxed sessions culminated in outstanding, more spontaneous expressions of feelings and of music. Black was the raw slap-bass player they would need; as for Moore, Phillips tried to keep him from veering off into displays of virtuosity, instead encouraging him to "simplify, simplify" his technique.[29]

Additionally, Phillips was an adept innovator in the recording booth. Despite not having the high-end equipment of some of his competitors, Phillips developed innovative microphone techniques, as well as the famous "Sun echo." This echo was created by "bouncing" the signal from one tape deck to the other, picking it up milliseconds later. The echo was almost imperceptible, but it gave the songs and the vocals, in particular, a dramatic resonance.[30]

In a now legendary story, the group started the session with a pop hit by Bing Crosby, then a country ballad, and Presley sounded okay, but there were no fireworks. The night started to drag on, and it looked like maybe Presley didn't have in him what Phillips had hoped for. Yet Phillips had seemingly endless patience. During a break late in the evening, Presley was filled with nervous energy and started messing around, accompanying himself on rhythm guitar and, as Moore would recall, "acting a fool." The song Presley started into was a frenetic take on the old blues song by Crudup, "That's All Right," something Presley might have heard on WDIA or WHBQ. As Moore would tell it, "We're just takin' a break deciding what to do.... Elvis just started with nervous energy started uh, absolutely just a-jumpin' around beatin' his guitar and singing, 'That's Alright Mama.' ... I had never heard the song, Billy had never heard it."[31] Black and Moore jumped in.

Phillips knew the song, but until then he had no idea that Presley had such a deep familiarity with the blues. Phillips popped his head out of the booth, asking, "What the hell are you doing?" None of the three musicians knew for sure, but they knew they had *something*. All were excited and a bit mystified by what had just occurred, and, according to Moore, "it really flipped Sam." Here is Phillips' version of what transpired:

> I heard this and I heard this rhythm just by himself and I said, "Jesus, Elvis! What have you been...." You know, just in jest. "You've been holding out on me all this time and have cost me this much time and look how grey my hair is getting," or some crazy something, you know. And he said, "You like that? You like that Mr. Phillips?" I said, "Man that thing is a hit," and you don't make statements like that. And even you don't know, "That thing is a hit."[32]

All four also seemed to instantly understand the barriers that had just been crashed, racial as well as standards of decency. Moore commented upon first hearing the recording, "Damn. Get that on the radio and they'll run us out of town!" Presley had started the session sounding unsure, mediocre and amateurish, but by the last take he sounded about as confident as a nineteen year old could ever possibly sound. The B-side was a stylistic mirror: Bill Monroe's bluegrass song, "Blue Moon of Kentucky," done with a faster beat and more R&B style. Everything had changed.

"That's All Right Mama" begins with Presley's ringing rhythm guitar line and Black slapping his bass and driving the beat. Moore virtually invents rockabilly guitar on the spot, with a perfect fusion of hillbilly and blues flourishes, but without detracting from Presley. Presley's voice instantly grabs attention, and the three throw themselves into the song. In his vocals, Presley leaves behind the tepid, lovelorn crooning of early 1950s pop. It is hillbilly, but, as Howlin' Wolf later said of Presley, he "made his pull from the blues."[33]

It is clearly a new sound and a landmark in the R&B/rock and roll continuum. It still sounds fresh sixty years later.

Crudup's original version of "That's All Right" (1946) was about a man wronged but moving on. His woman may have eaten his food and fooled around on him, but, hey, that's all right—Crudup is above it. His pride is still completely intact. This woman will not knock him off of his stride, and Crudup will move on down the road and keep doing his thing.

Presley's version (with slightly altered lyrics) laments that, yes, both his mother and his father had told him this girl was bad for him and he didn't listen, but "That's All Right," because, in the great American tradition, Presley is strong and independent with a detached cool. He is too cool to let some girl control his emotions; he's out of there anyway. Presley sneers his way through the lines and makes this kiss-off a little angry, but liberating and fun, as well.

Of course, while Crudup was free of his relationship, he was still black and in the Delta. Crudup's limited and intended audience was his fellow blacks in the Delta, the only people who really understood his experience. Black R&B and blues performers generally focused solely on their blues and R&B craft and had no real reason to be thinking about crossing over. Crossing over was out of black people's hands. African Americans were always dependent on white gatekeepers, be it Jon or Alan Lomax, Dewey Phillips, Sam Phillips, Alan Freed, or Dick Clark. Precisely when Presley was recording this cover song and launching his legend, Crudup had already returned to life as an itinerant farmer in Florida.[34]

Presley, however, is not just okay in his take on "That's All Right" ("That's All Right *Mama*"), but he is moving on anywhere he wants to go and the sky is the limit. And why not? As a white man, Presley could metaphorically and literally shout from the rooftops without being bothered or arrested, and the recording seems to reflect that. Presley was relatively free and did not know the same limits that Crudup did.

Presley had the vocal range, as well as the emotional depth, to combine both country and blues in the same song without losing his credibility in either genre. Plus, like any top gospel singer (which Presley was), he elevated the song as well. Last, for good measure, the song was such catchy pop that for the rest of the summer of 1954, Memphis teens greeted each other with Presley's catchy humming outro.[35] Although Presley did not *invent* rock and roll, he was the first to knock it out of the park.

Some early rock, like the original "Rocket 88," has the shuffle beat and maybe lacks a looser swing. Others, like Bill Haley's earliest R&B/rock recordings, lack something else. Haley is fun and can swing a blues song, but it lacks the visceral impact of the blues. As an example, in Haley's cover of Big Joe Turner's "Shake, Rattle and Roll," some of the lyrics were cleaned up, but even the raunchy double entendres that had snuck into the Haley version lost their meaning. Presley's "That's All Right Mama," however, solidified the sound.

Sam Phillips played the new cut for his friend Dewey Phillips that same day. Dewey was definitely interested but uncharacteristically quiet at first, not sure what to make of it.[36] That night, Dewey couldn't sleep; the next morning he called Sam and told him to press acetates to play on that night's show.[37] Dewey played the cut, and it caused an instant frenzy. The switchboard at WHBQ lit up, and Dewey went on to play the song some seven times in a row and more than a dozen times that night.[38] Sun Records had six thousand backorders before they had a single copy ready for sale.[39] All of this before anyone had even seen the stage show.

Presley was tracked down the next day to be interviewed on the air by Dewey. Listeners were not sure if Presley was white or black until Dewey asked him which Memphis high school he had gone to; Presley's response, "Humes," answered the unspoken question.[40]

Initially stations did not want any of Presley's songs, despite their being regional smashes. The country deejays thought he sounded too black for their white listeners, and the black deejays thought he sounded too hillbilly for their listeners. Presley was not even described as "rock and roll" at first, as the term was not in vogue yet, and no other category seemed to exist. Instead, he was variously billed as "The King of Western Bop," "The Hillbilly Cat" and "Bopping Hillbilly."[41]

Presley began to tour locally and around the South into 1955, including the Louisiana Hayride and the one time at the Grand Ole Opry. He was greeted with some confusion but also intense, screaming adulation of teenage girls, even exceeding the response to superstar crooner Frank Sinatra in the 1930s and 1940s, and he earned the respect and awe of teen boys. Presley's stage movements were influenced by any number of black, R&B artists whom he had seen since leaving Tupelo, in and around Memphis and on Beale Street, who were physically and sexually energized. Calvin Newborne, for example, used to perform the splits and other slick moves while playing his guitar. One noteworthy, non-black influence was James "Big Chief" Wetherington, a part–Caucasian, part–Native American gospel singer for the popular Memphis-based Statesmen Quartet. Wentworth mostly stood still when he sang, but he occasionally moved a leg around, which female fans loved.[42]

Presley had at first unconsciously moved his leg at an early show and was later told that the audience had responded strongly. Thus Presley began to let his moves come out naturally. The more Presley let loose, the wilder the audience response. Of course, he also happened to be devastatingly handsome, with sharp, dark features, and, obviously, he was white. To top it off, the trio soon added drummer D.J. Fontana, who complemented Presley's moves with beats mastered while playing in a strip club.[43] Presley and TV were a perfect storm waiting to happen.

* * *

As a small independent label, Sam Phillips and Sun actually had a bit of a problem with a success like Presley. At the time, the industry custom was for the label to pay for recording and manufacturing the records and then ship them to the retail record and department stores. The label only got its money once the retail outlets actually sold the records and paid up, often months afterward or otherwise at their leisure, while unsold records were returned for the label to eat. Thus a small label like Sun had to put up substantial cash outlays to get a huge number of records out to meet the demand for a big seller like Presley. Sam Phillips could not afford to be out that much cash and not have any money on hand to tend to the rest of his suddenly growing roster of Sun stars. Further, rock and roll, itself, as well as the unique-sounding and looking Presley, were still far from sure things outside of the mid-South region in the mid–1950s.

The big labels were more than intrigued, though, and approached Phillips about buying Presley's rights, first throwing out numbers in the $20,000 range, an astonishing figure at the time. RCA finally made an unprecedented offer to Phillips of $40,000 (including $5,000 for the rights to Presley's already released records), and Phillips took it. With that cash, he went on to perfect the "Sun Sound" with a stable of massive sellers and early rock icons—Jerry Lee Lewis actually rivaled Presley's sales for a while, and soon Johnny Cash, Carl Perkins, Billy Riley, Roy Orbison, and others all hit pay dirt as well. Phillips went on to make an even greater fortune in using that record money to become a ground-floor investor with his local friend's booming hotel chain, Holiday Inn.[44]

Through 1955, Presley was gaining popularity, but he was still a Southern act. In June 1956, a juiced-up song of blues fatalism, "Heartbreak Hotel," became Presley's first number one hit. It is a dramatic break-up song loaded with echo effects—a Sun technique that Presley took with him—and it had been inspired by lyricist Mae Boren Axton reading a newspaper story of a spurned lover's suicide jump from a hotel window.[45] It is dark but with a strong, swinging beat. Presley is singing deep blues, but he is an exciting rock and roller at the same time.

That same month, Presley had a second TV appearance on *The Milton*

Berle Show (1955–1956). The rest of the non–South U.S., and especially non-black U.S., had not seen anything like Presley and his Delta blues/R&B/hillbilly act. When Presley first performed on TV, popular singers had to that point stood motionless while singing. With no other point of reference at that time, it is not hard to understand why some early, dumbfounded critics at first wrote Presley's performances off as some sort of hillbilly freak show. The *New York Daily News* called Presley "vulgar" and declared that his performance was "tinged with the kind of animalism that should be confined to dives and bordellos."[46]

Not only was Presley's performance of "Hound Dog" on *Milton Berle* itself historic, but a couple of brief shots of the crowd from the TV footage illustrate precisely how Presley impacted the U.S. and the world.[47] The band is introduced by Berle, and they hit the ground running. Presley's whole body is rocking and swaying with the beat. One can hear audience noises of excitement and nervous laughter (and at least one person is laughing loudly). No one is quite sure how to react. Presley appears so nearly out of control that people seem to think that he *must* be clowning around. But he is not. Presley is totally confident and, as wild as he is getting, he has the presence of mind to coolly adjust and readjust his mic stand without missing a beat.

In the first TV camera cut to the crowd, five young women in their late teens or maybe early twenties are framed in the shot. The young woman on the bottom left is clearly a rock and roll convert already; she is thrilled, smiling, and bouncing up and down and clapping. Three of the other women are smiling and intrigued. But the young woman on the top left seems alarmed, confused, and unsure of how to respond. One can imagine her mulling over her options: "Leave the theater immediately—or rush the stage?" She is so ill-equipped to process the experience that she literally has to look to her friend on her left for some sort of cue. Once she sees that her friend is enjoying the show, she seems to decide that it is okay to experience what she is feeling after all.

During the instrumental break in the middle of the song, Presley cranks it up a few notches. He goes up on his toes and is, rather astonishingly, bumping and grinding to the slowed-down beat. In the next cut to the young women, the woman on the left is overwhelmed with emotion and actually covering her face out of embarrassment—yet laughing and thrilled at the same time. In two minutes and four seconds, Presley—and rock and roll—has practically liberated the young woman. Hopefully she exercised discretion in her love life in the days and years after she left the theater, but certainly she would have been less embarrassed, ashamed or even afraid of her own sexuality.

While abstinence was supposed to be the social norm in the 1950s, rock and roll turned things upside down as an "anti-inhibitor."[48] As one writer asked and answered, "What was it about rock and roll? In no small measure, it was the insistent beat, which relaxed and released the body, for dancing and, well, for sex."[49]

In another performance, a comic bit for comedian Steve Allen's TV show in June 1956, Presley allowed himself to be shown singing directly to an actual hound dog onstage (which Sam Phillips admonished him for afterward). The image may have resulted in a skewed image of the song "Hound Dog" for modern viewers. The meaning of "hound dog" at that time is probably best understood in today's vernacular as a non-profane version of m—f—.[50]

Presley's next performance was on the *Ed Sullivan Show* (1948–1971) in January 1957, with Sullivan's platform being *the* Sunday night event for families across America. Presley's appearance drew 60 million viewers and a record 82.6 percent of the U.S. television audience.[51] With that, the Elvis legend was cemented, and rock and roll was in virtually every living room in America.[52]

* * *

From the beginning, many African Americans questioned Presley's authenticity, originality, and true grasp of those black mediums—the blues, R&B and gospel. One African American columnist noted that Presley was "doing the things that such artists as T-Bone Walker, Lonnie Johnson, and others featured years before he was born." African American artists likewise voiced their frustration over Presley's success. Shirley Goodman of Shirley and Lee ("Let the Good Times Roll," 1956) stated, "It doesn't require much ability to steal a style, grab a guitar and get some shrewd managers who know how to sell you." And from Little Richard: "Elvis got paid $25,000 for doing three songs [in a movie] and I only got $5,000, and if it wasn't for me Elvis would starve." RCA reported that Presley at one point had fourteen consecutive million-selling singles.[53] Additionally, the *Wall Street Journal* reported that in the last few months of 1956 alone, just through merchandising, Presley earned $22 million ($182 million in 2011 dollars), dwarfing any other act.[54]

Still, the facts of Elvis Presley's life show him to have had a rather sterling record on race—despite the rest of white America. This is even true by almost any measure, and not just by an artificially low standard set for a white Southerner coming up in the 1950s. First, contrary to some assumptions, it is inconceivable that nineteen-year-old Presley, a shy, poor kid from Tupelo and the projects of Memphis, had calculated to embrace black style, when it was still taboo, so that he could single-handedly overturn the entire U.S. music industry for his own gain.

Second, Presley always clearly acknowledged his black inspirations and influences dating back to his first major interviews. A 1957 *Jet* magazine article quoted Presley as follows: "A lot of people seem to think I started this business, but rock and roll was here a long time before I came along. Nobody can sing that kind of music like colored people. Let's face it: I can't sing that kind of music like Fats Domino can. I know that. But I always liked that kind of music."[55] In another 1957 interview he explained, "I got my singing style listening to colored spiritual quartets down South."[56]

In 1959, Presley observed in another interview that rock and roll had already been around for many years before he started performing: "It used to be called rhythm and blues."[57] Further, he was always quick to correct anyone who suggested that he had invented rock music, and he never personally accepted the title of "The King of Rock and Roll."[58]

As to charges of being a cultural thief, again, a broad consensus and the word of credible peers clearly show that Presley was respected as an original performer and seen as true to, and respectful of, the spirit of his black influences. While Presley grew up dirt-poor, at or very near the bottom of an imposed class system, he never fully knew the "black experience." Yet, despite such significant differences in circumstances, Presley's feelings of alienation, emotional repression, and inequality, and the need to express himself and be heard, are universal to the human condition. Howlin' Wolf approvingly noted that Presley made his "pull from the blues." Per Nat Williams, "[Presley] had a way of singin' the blues that was distinctive. He could sing 'em, not necessarily like a negro, but he didn't sing 'em altogether like a typical white musician. He had somethin' in between and made the blues sort of different for Elvis Presley."[59] Finally, Reverend Brewster called Presley's version of Brewster's gospel composition, "Peace in the Valley," "one of the best gospel recordings I've ever heard."[60] As music writer Robert Hilburn put it, "Unlike many white artists ... who watered down the gritty edges of the original R&B versions of songs in the '50s, Presley reshaped them."[61]

Presley also enormously influenced black performers. Al Green declared that "Elvis had an influence on everybody with his musical approach." Even Presley's performing style, so obviously derived from black R&B performers, was still marked by originality and innovation. Jackie Wilson (a.k.a. "Mr. Excitement"), one of the all-time great stage performers in popular music, said of his friend Elvis Presley's style, "I took as much from Elvis as he took from me."[62]

On a *personal* level, the most respected African Americans of the Memphis music community at the time, and others, were unequivocal in their take on Presley. Sun Records alum and friend B.B. King wrote that at a time when white musicians, including some of the other rockabilly artists at Sun, could be "cool" to a black man, "Elvis was different"; he even addressed the older King as "sir," something King appreciated.[63] Giants James Brown and Muhammad Ali each talked about having deep, personal relationships with Presley; according to Brown, "I wasn't just a fan, I was his brother.... There'll never be another like that soul brother."[64]

A final story illustrates Presley's relationship with African Americans. Shortly after Presley's career had blown up, in December 1956, WDIA put on its annual Goodwill Revue to benefit needy black children at the Ellis Auditorium in Memphis. Presley showed up in support, the lone white figure in an all-black crowd of nine thousand and an all-black lineup, including B.B. King and Ray Charles, along with emcee Rufus Thomas. In Thomas's words, "for a young white boy to show up at an all-black function took guts."[65]

The result when Thomas introduced Presley was pandemonium. As Nat Williams reported, "A thousand black, brown, and beige girls in that audience blended in their alto and soprano voices in one wild crescendo of sound that rent the rafters and took like scalded cats in the direction of Elvis." Said Thomas, "The show was over. That was it. In a matter of moments all the aisles and the stage wings and exits were jammed with people trying to get to Elvis. They managed to get him out of there—somehow!"[66]

In a news article written the next day, Williams wondered whether at some level the response reflected a deeper societal conditioning toward acceptance of whiteness. In fact, like many other observers, Williams himself had written and spoken about the dilemma of black folks having been conditioned to hate their own race, thus making skin-lightening and hair-straightening products huge industries, for example. This was so deeply ingrained for many darker-skinned women, Williams wrote, that a woman had to consider the skin tone of a prospective husband because "she had to think in terms of how her children would look."[67] Still, Presley's gesture and his crossover impact were undeniable.

* * *

Before coming to any final understanding of the rock and roll phenomenon, Presley's personal story has to be put into focus. How did this legend fall so far, and so fast, both in life and in image? He first exploded on a global scale in 1956. In March of 1958, however, his career was sidetracked when he was drafted into the U.S. Army and then shipped overseas to Germany, and out of the American public's sight (though his manager continued to release already recorded material). The move to Germany was followed a few months later by the death of Presley's mother, Gladys. By most accounts, this was *the* defining moment of Presley's life, and he was never the same afterward.[68]

Presley had an exceedingly close relationship with Gladys, though she was also terribly overprotective; he was in fact a "mama's boy," and he remained so into his early adulthood. It is what psychologists today might call a severe form of *emotional enmeshment*.[69]

As Elvis was becoming a true superstar from 1956 to 1958, and the world began to take up more and more of her son's time, Gladys became nearly debilitated by anxiety and depression, as well as other health problems. She drank on the sly and quite heavily (and may have been for some time), and then she added "diet pills" (i.e., amphetamines) to the mix. Gladys' health deteriorated quickly, and, just a few months after her son had left for Germany, on August 14, 1958, she passed away at forty-six years of age. The cause of death was cirrhosis of the liver, though it was originally reported as a heart attack.[70]

As a public performer, Presley had already put himself way out there, truly into uncharted territory and beyond almost anyone's comfort zone. Now his overdependent relationship with his mother was gone. It seems that from this point on, Presley was adrift and at risk of becoming lost altogether.

Presley came back to Memphis on leave to the hospital, but his mother had already passed. He was hysterical and wailing loudly, as was his father. Presley kept hugging and touching Gladys' body until being asked to stop by hospital staff.[71]

Gladys Presley's funeral in Memphis was described by those in attendance as extraordinarily painful to watch. Elvis remained hysterical and inconsolable; it seemed he wouldn't make it through the ordeal. He flung himself at his mother's body, hugging and kissing her, pleading with her to come back and exclaiming, "Oh God, everything I have is gone."[72] Close friend Alan Fortas spoke of coming to the viewing and Presley greeting him: "When he got up to greet visitors, he just sat there with her, almost as if they were the host and hostess of their own little party. It was a pitiful thing to watch."[73] Even as the coffin was being lowered, Presley grabbed onto it, screaming, "Please don't take my baby away. She's not dead! She's just sleeping," before being pulled off. Presley did not leave the body for two days, even as friends and family tried to coax him away.[74]

Since 1955, Presley had already turned over all of his career decisions to the man who would manage him for the rest of his life: "Colonel" Tom Parker. Parker was a shrewd, cigar-chomping showman who first learned the entertainment business as a carnival barker. The "Colonel" title was honorary—a reward for work done on a Louisiana political campaign.[75]

Presley controlled every other relationship he was in, be it with his entourage or with the women he sometimes played like yo-yos, but Parker had a power over him described as near-hypnotic.[76] For example, Presley once related to a friend a recurring nightmare that the crowds were gone, Parker was gone, and he was left completely helpless and alone.[77] Presley's roots as so-called white trash left him with a certain inferiority complex and a tendency to be a bit in awe of men in power, which would become more evident in the years to come.

Jerry Leiber, of the legendary songwriting team Leiber and Stoller (writers of mega-hits "Hound Dog" and "Jailhouse Rock," among others), loved Presley as a person, but he also commented on Presley's underlying insecurity. Leiber recalled from the set of the film *Jailhouse Rock*:

> It happened when Elvis walked through an area where the extras and bit-part players were sitting around. As he passed by, someone told a joke and everyone began to laugh. Elvis wheeled around and angrily said, "I bet you think you're really hot." He had thought they were laughing at him. They weren't. I know; I was there. Elvis walked away, mumbling.[78]

As to Parker, Leiber recalled meeting the Colonel for the first time after Presley recorded "Hound Dog." Parker's control was so thorough that he would insist on "screening" people before they spoke to Presley, even people Presley was dying to meet, like Leiber and Stoller themselves. Leiber's take on the former carny was typical:

> He had a definite shtick ("Pick a number from one to ten"). He told dozens of canned jokes. I can't remember any of them except that they weren't funny. But it didn't matter that we didn't laugh, because the Colonel wasn't really conscious of us. Of course, he knew we were the songwriters of "Hound Dog" and the new songs for *Jailhouse Rock*. He knew more hit songs for Elvis meant more money for him. Beyond that, though, he was more interested in putting on his own show than getting to know us.[79]

Colonel Parker always truly believed in Presley as a talent and, career-wise, was unquestionably protective of his client's interests. However, Parker was also effectively tone-deaf when it came to interpersonal relations or Presley's personal well-being. Worse, while Presley relied on all of Parker's judgments, Parker was the one person he would not (or could not) confront. Parker regulated who came in and out of Presley's life, and, ultimately, it was showbiz itself that was everything. On the day of Presley's shocking death, Parker told colleagues shortly after hearing the news, "This changes nothing."[80] Immediately before the funeral, Parker cornered the distraught Vernon, explaining how crucial it was to immediately act to protect his son's image and marketing rights.[81]

In the 1960s, when not in Hollywood, Presley was holed up in Graceland, avoiding the crush of fans and media. His buffer from the world was the so-called Memphis Mafia—a group of male friends, hangers-on, and sycophants—along with an overabundance of speed (a habit picked up on guard duty in the army) and prescription drugs.[82]

Early on, Parker had anticipated the possible fading of Presley's career as an aging teen idol tied to rock and roll, which, as far as anyone knew in 1958, could have easily been a passing fad, like the hula hoop the same year. Instead of seeking special treatment for his army service, such as regularly performing at USO gigs, Presley followed Parker's direction and accepted a stint as a regular private. That humble act of patriotism set the stage for long-term, mainstream acceptance.[83] Presley's public persona, which had begun as an incredibly dangerous rock and roll rebel, shifted to a dutiful, all-American hero.

Presley carried on, but after that initial explosion from 1954 to 1958, he was largely contained and seemed trapped. He would describe feeling "imprisoned" in his film work, clearly losing the spontaneity and creativity that had made him a sensation to begin with.[84] Presley allowed Parker to co-opt that mercurial spirit and rebellious nature, turning him into a rather safe commodity in the world of pop culture. Presley helped knock down the first walls and got the ball rolling for those who would follow him, but he was no longer a true threat to anyone, certainly not to those institutions that still oppressed the spirit of American youth and African Americans, and he no longer challenged those living overly complacent lives in the mainstream.

Upon Presley's discharge from the army in 1960, he naturally moved to Hollywood. Despite what his many rock and roll fans might have wanted, Presley had always had big pop aspirations and stated that one of his biggest role models was pop crooner-turned-actor, Dean Martin. Presley wanted to follow Martin and other major stars who had successfully made the transition into film, including Bing Crosby and Frank Sinatra.

Presley showed some acting promise early on as a teen rebel in the tradition of James Dean and Marlon Brando; he had even memorized Dean's dialogue from his films. Yet, despite a stated desire to move into more serious roles, Presley's acting career never evolved. His earlier movies in particular were rather simple vehicles solely for him to sing a lot and to "get the girl," whether as an up-and-coming singer in New Orleans nightclubs, as a singing GI, or a singing boxer. On top of that, the songs in Presley's films were generally mediocre.

While artistically stagnant in Hollywood, Presley followed an incredibly profitable box office formula created by Parker. With a large, built-in fan base, these safe, lowest–common-denominator musicals meant sure-fire commercial success. In Presley's twenty-one films from 1960 to 1967, he was one of the most profitable box office stars in Hollywood. Parker also set up the publishing company Hill and Range, which further required songwriters to take a below-market cut if they wanted Presley to use their songs. It might have been a good deal in the short term for Presley, but it also dissuaded higher-quality songwriters from providing him with material.[85] Still, all of Presley's soundtracks were parallel chart smashes with the films, and Parker and Presley were a financial juggernaut. Parker upped his previous 25 percent take to 50 percent.[86]

Presley's personal life and legacy are in many ways embodied in Graceland, his famous estate in Memphis from 1957 until his death. Graceland is a white-columned, neo-antebellum Southern Colonial mansion. The home sits on fourteen acres, including a functioning horse stable, a racquetball court, and so on.

Graceland's famous, or infamous, interior design exemplified the flashy style that had first helped make Presley a sensation but later was associated with the gaudiness of the worst of Las Vegas. "Graceland is," as one writer put it, "how a poor boy lives rich."[87] Presley took ideas from the places he saw as a young star ("lavishly appointed theaters and auditoriums, luxury car and tour-bus interiors, Hollywood sets, and Las Vegas suites"), resulting in a home filled with "richly colored assemblages of thick carpet, costly fabrics, large-scale furniture, complicated lamps, and novelty accents."[88] Design critics and others have variously described Graceland as "[t]acky, garish, tasteless," "white trash"[89] and "particularly lurid kitsch."[90]

It has also been noted that the overwhelming feeling of Graceland, including wall-to-wall (even ceiling) carpet and heavy, perpetually drawn curtains, reflects an "intensifying need for enclosure and containment," as if Presley needed external forces to keep him from becoming unmoored.[91] Presley was not a practicing Christian in his adult life, though he did pursue various spiritual practices, including metaphysical literature and meditation, and he took his martial arts very seriously.[92]

* * *

By 1964, Presley's earning power could have enabled him to start taking artistic risks in his script selections. However, Parker decided, and Presley did not fight his choice, to turn the filmmaking over to producer Sam Katzman, who had the art of quick, no-frills filmmaking down to a science, earning him the nickname "King of the Quickies" and marking a further decline in Presley's film career.[93]

By comparison, after the release of *Kissin' Cousins*, the first wave of 1950s rock and rollers had already become dated and the British Invasion was in full swing. The Beatles teamed with director Richard Lester for a stylish, loosely autobiographical film, *A Hard Day's Night*. This movie captured the

Fab Four at their funniest and most charismatic, and it was a huge success, both commercially and critically.[94] Presley, the one-time world beater, was becoming irrelevant.

Presley's personal life also began to decline sharply at this time. He always had an innate ability to speak to someone and leave them feeling like they were the most important person in the world.[95] With the Memphis Mafia, however, Presley created an increasingly controlled and isolated, bubble-like existence. To become a part of his entourage and bask in his reflected fame and glory, one first had to get past Parker. Once inside the circle, one had to abide by Presley's rules to stay in.[96]

Presley was still an international sex symbol, though he especially liked the company of early-teen girls.[97] Oddly, he mainly enjoyed acting childish, even playing hide and seek, and having more compliant relationships than sexual relationships. In 1959, Presley, then twenty-five and in the army, met Priscilla Wagner, fourteen, a girl from a U.S. military family living in Germany; he secretly brought her to Graceland two years later, and they eventually married in 1967.[98]

Neither the Memphis Mafia nor Presley's girlfriends ever questioned his career moves or his drug abuse. If they did, any direct confrontation meant immediate expulsion from the inner circle. Thus Presley had no true confidants.[99] His crew jumped on board with whatever it was that Presley happened to be into at that time—be it a new book on self-discovery, martial arts, the NFL, whatever—and laughed at all of his jokes.[100]

Further, along with his speed habit, Presley learned the *Physician's Desk Reference* inside-out and befriended some questionable doctors. For years he prescribed himself and others loads of drugs.[101] He almost killed one friend, and once, after giving then-wife Priscilla a shot, she slept for two days while he refused to call a doctor.[102]

By 1968, as the British Invasion, Motown, folk and soul all dominated the music world, Presley had not performed live in seven years, and his Hollywood career was floundering. He had become largely lost to a younger generation and was a nostalgia act at thirty-three years of age.[103] It looked like he might be left behind for good when he agreed to do a 1968 Christmas television special with NBC. Director Steve Binder wanted to get Presley back to his raw, Memphis roots, and Presley agreed, while Parker was uncharacteristically less intrusive than usual.

Binder captured a swinging and electrifying Presley. Jerry Schilling, a friend of Presley, said that he was finally free to choose the people and songs: "He was out of prison, man."[104] Presley closed the show with a stunning rendition of "If I Can Dream," also notable for its quotations of Martin Luther

King, Jr., who had been assassinated just two months prior, putting Presley clearly on the side of the civil rights movement. The success of what became known as the Comeback Special led to a lucrative deal for Presley at the International Hotel in Las Vegas, the city he would perform in for much of the remainder of his career.

With his new momentum, Presley's first shows were major events once again, and he exceeded expectations. *Rolling Stone* called him "supernatural, his own resurrection."[105] Even his critics had to give him strong reviews.[106] In many ways Presley was perfectly suited for Las Vegas in that both were epic, even grandiose. Presley had a lot of flash, great emotional depth and range, a unique voice ("very nearly all at once a tenor, baritone and bass"), an ability to easily perform in multiple genres, and a genuine desire to reach *everyone*.[107] In Las Vegas, he was backed by a full rock band, a piano and two separate gospel vocal groups, the Imperials and Sweet Inspirations, meaning he could essentially cover the entire scope of American popular music.

Greil Marcus captured those Vegas years, writing that Presley embodied "the illusion that the American dream has fulfilled itself, that utopia is complete in an America that replaces emotion with sentiment and novelty with expectation ... the aesthetics of playing it safe.... Breaking loose and starting over cost more every time."[108] Biographer Peter Guralnick noted that Presley "continued to evolve," but he was "someone constantly reaching for something not quite within his grasp."[109]

An illustration of Presley's trajectory is found in his 1970 release, "Kentucky Rain," a song that reached number 16 on the pop charts.[110] It's a pop ballad with a full backing band and clearly dated as 1970s pop music, far removed from the cutting-edge and popular rock of the era, like the Doors and the Rolling Stones. Presley sings of an epic loss as he hopelessly seeks his lost love, searching in the cold "Kentucky Rain." He draws out the tension before belting out the climactic chorus to a blast of horns.

The song is moving and heartbreaking—for both intentional and unintentional reasons. Presley's earnest approach is to go bigger and bigger—seemingly to overwhelm the world, but perhaps also to overwhelm his own shortcomings. Like the song's protagonist, Presley is giving everything he has, but he also crosses into desperation, confusing schmaltz with real emotion. In the song and in real life, Presley was chasing something he apparently never found.

In 1973, Presley's drug abuse had become an open secret, and he was twice hospitalized for overdoses.[111] The Vegas shows became ever more grandiose. He opened them with Richard Strauss' *Also Sprach Zarathustra* (also known as the theme song from the film *2001: A Space Odyssey*) and readings from "How Great Thou Art," or lyrics from the Simon and Garfunkel hit "Bridge Over Troubled Water," all while wearing his outrageous jumpsuits laden with gaudy jewelry, capes, and diamond- and ruby-encrusted canes.[112] Elvis was becoming, to his fans, larger than life, but to his detractors he was a farce.[113] By 1977, the six-foot Presley's weight rose to over two hundred and fifty pounds, and he began to consistently bomb at his shows, sometimes rambling incoherently and sweating profusely. He was a very public mess.

At the same time, Colonel Parker was ill equipped to give Presley any help, as he himself was in the throes of a severe gambling addiction. One hotel president stated that Parker was losing one million dollars a year at the time.[114]

TV Guide referred to Presley's image in this era as not only a hick but also "a kind of poor ol' boys' Liberace," a performer who indeed influenced Presley's Vegas style. Liberace was a flamboyant, pop pianist and another Vegas star, biggest in the 1960s and 1970s. For those too young to remember, imagine Elton John, but far more flamboyant and, while highly talented, more camp. In other words, Presley had become a performer far removed from the rebel in a T-shirt, jeans, and leather jacket *a la* Brando and Dean, his roots in Tupelo, and the black experience of the Delta.

* * *

On August 16, 1977, forty-two-year-old Elvis Presley was found by then-fiancée Ginger Alden, face down, a few feet from the toilet in the upstairs bathroom of his home in Memphis. Presley had suffered heart failure while on the commode, crawled a short distance, thrown up, collapsed, and died shortly thereafter. Investigators found Graceland wiped out of any drugs, not even common over-the-counter ones found in medicine cabinets.[115] Presley was taken to the hospital, where administrators rushed to declare the cause of death as "cardiac arrhythmia due to undetermined heartbeat," even before the autopsy was finished, in an attempt to quell the coming media onslaught or any conspiracy theories.[116] That determination, however, was one that could never have medically been made without an autopsy, and the sloppy work fueled rumors of a cover-up for decades.[117]

Whether drugs *directly* caused Presley's death has been debated. What is not disputed is that fourteen drugs were found in his system, including toxic and near-toxic levels of codeine, Quaaludes, and other drugs.[118] Presley's main physician, Dr. George C. Nichopoulos, escaped criminal liability for his patient's death, but his license was temporarily suspended (and permanently revoked in 1991 for oversubscribing medications).[119] Presley's death was apparently an unsurprising result of years of intense prescription drug abuse, enabled by those close to him and numerous physicians.[120]

By 1977, Presley was already a staple of the *National Enquirer*, the supermarket checkout counter tabloid that regularly published flattering stories regarding Presley—the favorite son of its middle-class, white readership. Presley's death was a lead story worldwide and heralded a new era for the *Enquirer*, and tabloids in general, as well as a new *stalkerazzi* industry.

Upon Presley's death, the *Enquirer* flooded Memphis with reporters. After all, the very inspiration for the *Enquirer*'s approach to news had come when founder Generoso Pope, Jr., had driven by a car accident and noticed a long line of cars and rubbernecking drivers trying to glimpse the aftermath. At that moment, Pope saw a new industry.[121]

The *Enquirer* gave Presley's distant cousin Billy Mann a miniature "spy" camera and $18,000 to take a photo of his corpse in the coffin at the funeral, which Mann did.[122] Wire reports described near mass hysteria at Graceland. Fifty thousand fans descended on Presley's home for the funeral, and some eighty thousand lined the streets of Memphis as the body was delivered to Forrest Hill Cemetery.[123] A drunk driver plowed into the crowd outside Graceland, killing two and injuring one.[124]

Mann's coffin photo of Presley's body was the cover for that week's *Enquirer*, leading to sales of a staggering 6.5 million copies—more than the circulations of the *New York Times*, *Washington Post*, and *Wall Street Journal* combined.[125] Ginger Alden received $105,000 from the *Enquirer* for an exclusive interview, until she violated the exclusivity agreement and had to settle for a lesser amount.[126]

After the initial shock and grief stemming from a former hero's death, the ugliness of the later stages of Presley's life sank in with the public. Years later, even the RCA record executive in charge of selling Presley's back catalog had to acknowledge that "[t]he biggest challenge is to erase the memory of the caricature of Elvis, the one ingrained for so many years as a bloated icon."[127] For many, Presley's image was not one of a rebel with a cause, like John Lennon, or someone oozing sexuality like Mick Jagger, or even a tragic poet like Jim Morrison; instead, he had become synonymous with everything tacky, embarrassing, and overblown about the 1970s.

* * *

Graceland has long since become a multi-million-dollar tourist mecca, with loads of parking and additional museum wings. The estate is on Elvis Presley Boulevard, located smack in the middle of the economically depressed, mostly all-black neighborhood of Whitehaven in south Memphis. In 1957, Presley's obsessive fans had been swarming his home in town, making life miserable for him and his neighbors; thus Presley purchased Graceland before it was even Memphis proper yet and before there was any development around it.[128]

Despite being the site of Presley's untimely and ugly death (though the upstairs, where he died, remains off limits), thirty-eight years later, Graceland continues to see over six hundred thousand visitors a year, three times the number visiting the National Civil Rights Museum at the old Lorraine Motel across town (at less than half the admission price), and where Martin Luther King, Jr., was assassinated in 1968.[129]

The rest of the Graceland experience includes, among other things, the Graceland Wedding Chapel, the "Heartbreak Hotel and RV Park," and a tour through Presley's two airplanes. His gaudy Vegas-era jumpsuits (inspired by his martial arts uniforms) get an entire wing unto themselves. There is another, smaller building dedicated solely to Presley's two years of nondescript service in the army. Souvenirs run the gamut, including an "Exclusive Officially Authorized Elvis® Collectible Electric Train Collection Celebrates Elvis's® 75th Birthday!" (complete with a certified replica of Presley's birth certificate), an "Elvis Presley Signature Shot [glass] in Pink Classic Car Base," and so on.[130]

Elvis Presley Enterprises continues to consistently take in tens of millions of dollars every year.[131] It would seem that any one of the *sixteen* gift shops that cover Graceland take in more money than the combined sales of Charley Patton, Lonnie Johnson, Howlin' Wolf, and Muddy Waters, combined.

Into the twenty first century, as author Erica Lee Doss explained in her book, *Elvis Culture: Fans, Faith, & Image*, and through a "'transformative' ideology of consumerism," Elvis Presley Enterprises built Presley's image into what former BBC religion correspondent Ted Harrison referred to as no less than a "religion in embryo."[132] Country music legend Dolly Parton once said that where she is from in rural, eastern Tennessee, Presley is all but deified: "I don't think he will ever die down. He's considered by many to be like a religious figure, like Jesus.... I don't know how to explain it, but it's there, and it's real, and people love it."[133]

Through the remainder of the 1970s and through the 1980s and beyond, and partly stoked by the flawed autopsy, Presley conspiracy theories abounded among those who apparently could not accept life without the "King." As *Time* magazine put it, Presley is the "the only cultural icon to have inspired a passionate denial of the fact of extinction."[134] Tabloid newspapers and magazines sold millions of copies with headlines of reported "sightings" of Presley, whether in Canada, at a Burger King, or anywhere else. Books were published claiming that Presley's death was a hoax. His fame, in and of itself, was so huge that it literally took on a life of its own, complete with its own cadre of reporters.

Given such excessive attention, as Doss accurately summarized, a "cultural vilification" arose in the 1980s: "[s]niggering stereotypes about an obese pill-addicted Elvis and those that stigmatize his fans as delusional, middle-aged devotees, dominate public opinion and the popular press."[135]

The Presley phenomenon has had other implications. Even during his life he had been labeled by many fans as "The King of Rock and Roll," leading to the implication that Presley had transcended his roots; after all, a "King" could hardly *owe* anything to anyone. Given that the majority of fan club members and other Presley fanatics were white and concentrated in the Midwest and South, the implications of Presley's enduring fame had racial overtones. For many African Americans, the Presley phenomenon was a glaring and painful example of America's still-fractured race relations.

In 1990, the all–African American rock group Living Color delivered what was effectively a public service announcement in their song "Elvis Is Dead" (which was also in part a comment on Paul Simon's largely reverent "Graceland"). Aided by a guest rap from Presley contemporary Little Richard, the group pleaded for the cult-like following to stop obsessing over Presley: let the man rest already, and stop exploiting him in death. While the song is respectful of Presley personally, it also refers to a racial undercurrent of his deification. At the end of the song, singer Corey Glover questions whether people of a certain color would be accepted at Graceland.

Rapper Mos Def reasserted the black spirit at the heart of rock and roll with his 1999 rap polemic, "Rock and Roll." In the song, Def asserts that it is the black experience itself, and not Elvis or the Rolling Stones, that fuels rock music. That basic fact—an enormous chapter in American history—has in many ways been lost, and, again, Presley's *legacy* embodies that phenomenon.

That distrust and even resentment of Presley and his followers persists. In 2002, African American R&B star Mary J. Blige covered "Blue Suede Shoes" as part of a Presley medley on the VH1 cable television special *Divas Live*. Shortly afterward, Blige explained the song choice to the press:

> I prayed about it [performing the song] because I know Elvis was a racist. But that was just a song VH1 asked me to sing. It meant nothing to me. I didn't wear an Elvis flag. I didn't represent Elvis that day. I was just doing my job like everybody else.[136]

A review of a comment board on Blige's website a couple of years later, after her comments had been brought up again, is illustrative. Most commenters identified themselves as black, and their statements offered a snapshot of the feelings still evoked by Presley's name: "who cares about Elvis anyways. The man's been dead for decades"; "not only was he racist, he was a thief! ...

People worship this man like he was Jesus himself, and he died of a drug overdose!!"; "At the time when Elvis was alive many people where [*sic*] very racist"; "I'm not trying to just be rude to you ... but subjects like this touch a nerve for me."[137]

Finally, rap group Public Enemy produced perhaps the seminal rap song with their 1991 anthem "Fight the Power," and in it the group addressed the Presley legacy. The song had been commissioned as the centerpiece of Spike Lee's film *Do the Right Thing*, the acclaimed tome on the status of race relations in a post–civil rights America. "Fight the Power" had been the perfect merger of Public Enemy's heavy funk, dense music sampling, rapper Chuck D's social consciousness and outrage, and comic balance from a second rapper and "hype man," Flava Flav. Chuck D's lyrics are a rallying call to reexamine and challenge a society still dominated and defined by white power structures.

Chuck D's specific targets were what was seen as a sad complacency, as well as the images of two revered, white icons: Elvis Presley and movie cowboy John Wayne. While a hero to white America, Chuck called Presley racist, and Flava Flav punctuated this sentiment, profanely dismissing both Presley and Wayne.

In short, depending on whom you believe and how much, Presley might be a musical genius, an important civil rights figure, and possibly the Messiah—or he may instead be a no-talent, racist junkie and cultural thief. He may be a symbol of America's great promise, or he may be evidence of how very, very far it must still progress. Such is the Presley legacy.

Beyond the Noise

Clearly Presley could have been more vocal and more boldly aligned himself with the civil rights movement in the 1960s, and it may never be entirely clear why he did not. It could be that, on a personal level, Presley simply was not up to the challenge of what would have been an incredibly volatile position. One certainly has to keep in mind his personal limitations as a disenfranchised, lower-class, blue-collar man. Regarding that background, Presley himself once said, "You can't go beyond your limitations.... I stay with my own kind of people."[138] His makeup was such that he could never even stand up to Parker, whose only focus was the profitability of Elvis Presley Enterprises. Presley may simply have felt that, as a white man, it would have been presumptuous to assert himself into a high-profile role in that cause.

Further, in a time with clearly marked dividing lines, Presley really did not fit neatly into any class. He clearly aligned himself with the civil rights movement on social issues, although he was also drawn to powerful authority, law enforcement, and military figures, even in the middle of the Vietnam War. In the 1970s, Presley actually approached the FBI about obtaining an honorary federal agent badge, and he once called controversial FBI director J. Edgar Hoover "the greatest living American."[139] A visit with no less than the face of everything despised about the establishment, President Richard Nixon, led both to the badge and to one of the most infamous photo ops in American history—a picture of Presley and Nixon hanging out in the Oval Office. The photo undermined Presley's credibility even more.

Nonetheless, Presley did have strong personal relationships with African Americans. At the very least, Presley consistently acknowledged social justice in his performances throughout the 1960s and 1970s, regularly including the songs "In the Ghetto," "All My Trials," and Joe South's "Walk a Mile in My Shoes" in his set lists.[140]

Shortly after Presley's heyday, he was still seen in a largely positive light by most African Americans. The co-founder of the Black Panthers, Eldridge Cleaver, gave Presley credit in his influential 1968 book, *Soul on Ice*: "Presley dared to do in the light of day what American had been doing in the sneak thief anonymity of night—consorted on a human level with blacks." More recently, Chuck D has also acknowledged that while in his lyrics for "Fight the Power" he refers to Presley himself as racist, in truth, "there was always a great deal of respect for Elvis. As a black people, we all knew that." When Chuck D name-checked Presley, he was in fact referring to "the institution of Elvis," meaning the Presley presented by white people "as being the 'be-all' and 'end-all'" of this era of music.[141]

This appropriation and distortion of his image, though not Presley's fault, has helped make him, to some, the ultimate symbol of a gross neglect of African American perspectives and contributions. Thus, according to this viewpoint, Presley perhaps needed to be torn down completely for white America to even consider another perspective. Unfortunately, Presley would often be remembered with enormous skepticism or, worse, as a Southern white man who sold out to the glitz of Las Vegas, surrounding himself with an all-white, Southern male entourage, and posing with Nixon.

The main source of the long-running rumor of Presley being racist can be traced all the way back to the mid–1950s—and specifically to Presley's supposed statement, "The only thing a Negro can do for me is shine my shoes and buy my records." This rumor was first printed in April 1957 in *Sepia*, a white-owned magazine directed toward a black readership, in an article, entitled "How Negroes Feel About Elvis." *Sepia* attributed the quote to unnamed "people in the street." Another periodical geared toward a black readership, *Tan*, commented on the alleged statement, and in August 1957, *Jet*, a black-owned, black-read magazine, ran an article exploring the validity of the rumor: Had Presley made the "shoeshine" comment? The statement was reputed to have been made in Boston on the Edward R. Murrow TV show, *Person to Person*. Yet it was discovered that as of 1957 Presley had never even been to Boston, nor on Morrow's show. *Jet* concluded that the rumors had no basis in fact.[142]

In fact, *Jet* reported that Presley's personal record on race actually appeared to be quite good, citing black entertainers who knew him personally, including B.B. King, who vouched for Presley's character. But *Jet* also noted that the existence of the rumors did reflect racial resentments and frustrations of the black community.[143]

* * *

To really understand the Presley legacy, it has to be seen in a very specific context: that of a white man from Tupelo, Mississippi, right in the middle of one of the most racist regions in the world in the 1950s. At that time and place, Southern white men rarely had any use for black men or women unless they could exploit that relationship in some way. There was even the well-known Sam Phillips remark that *had* been made: "If I could find a white man who had the Negro sound and the Negro feel, I could make a billion dollars."[144]

In August of 1954 in Memphis, when Presley covered Arthur Crudup, it was mere weeks after the landmark school integration case, *Brown v. Board of Education*, which had first arisen with angry mobs just two hours west in Little Rock, Arkansas. And in September of 1955, while Presley's star was rapidly rising across the South, two white men were tried and acquitted by an all-white, all-male jury for the gruesome murder of fourteen-year-old African American, Emmett Till, two hours south of Memphis, in Webb, Mississippi.[145] At the same time, *Jet* magazine ran a photo of Till at the open-casket funeral a story worth revisiting.[146]

The Till photo finally gave the rest of the country and the world a haunting, unadulterated glimpse into the realities of the South and race, some ninety years after the end of slavery. Till's mother had wanted the photo to run in order to show the world what was happening. The resultant shock and uproar helped jumpstart the civil rights movement.[147]

Till, a lifetime Chicagoan, had been visiting family that summer in Webb. His Delta cousins couldn't believe that he freely talked to white girls in the North, and they dared him to speak to a young, white woman running a store in Webb. Till then allegedly told the woman, "See you, baby," as he left. The killers—the woman's husband, Roy Bryant, and his half-brother, J. W. Milam—went to Till's family's home, demanded Till from his great uncle, and took him away. By a river, they ordered Till to strip, brutally beat him, gouged out his eye, shot him in the head, and threw his dead body into the Tallahatchie River with a heavy fan wrapped to his head with barbed wire to sink his body. Bryant and Milam were not well liked by their peers before the killing, but they received strong support from the majority of the white community, resulting in their acquittal.[148]

Two months prior to Presley's big label debut and explosion, in January of 1956, an interview with Till's killers was published nationwide in *Look* magazine. Bryant and Milam were both safe from a second trial by constitutional protection against "double jeopardy" and spoke freely. They readily admitted to beating and murdering Till and were unapologetic. Milam stated that originally he and Bryant were only going to beat Till and scare him, but the problem, according to Milam, was that Till would not crack. Instead, Milam said that Till had told his tormenters, "You bastards, I'm not afraid of you. I'm as good as you are. I've 'had' white women. My grandmother was a white woman." To Milam, there was simply no choice in the matter:

> Well, what else could we do? He was hopeless. I'm no bully; I never hurt a nigger in my life. I like niggers—in their place—I know how to work 'em. But I just decided it was time a few people got put on notice. As long as I live and can do anything about it, niggers are gonna stay in their place.[149]

On December 1, 1955, Rosa Parks was arrested in Montgomery, Alabama, for refusing to leave her seat in the front, white section of a bus. Dr. Martin Luther King subsequently came to Montgomery and spoke to 15,000 black citizens at the Holy Street Baptist Church.[150]

The *Sepia* article on Presley came out in August of 1957, just a few weeks before Arkansas governor Orval Faubus' defiance of the U.S. Supreme Court's *Brown* decision and deployment of the state's National Guard troops to block the entry of nine black students into Little Rock High School through an angry mob. That incident only ended when President Eisenhower federalized National Guard troops and deployed the 101st Airborne Division to Little Rock to ensure the students' admission.[151] Also in August of 1957, popular African American singer Nat King Cole was attacked onstage at a concert in Birmingham, Alabama, by five members of the White Citizen's Council in protest of "bop and Negro music."[152] The same year in Birmingham, civil rights activist Reverend Fred Shuttlesworth and his wife Ruby attempted to enroll their children in an all-white school and were attacked in the street by the Klan, with police nowhere to be seen; Shuttlesworth was beaten with chains and brass knuckles, while Ruby was stabbed.[153]

Little Rock, Arkansas (1957). White youths throwing things across the street on the occasion of the Little Rock High School integration (photograph by Magnum Burt Glinn).

So why exactly is Presley's legacy so complicated? The blues, gospel, and R&B influences that made him so special and so exciting existed as a direct result of, and in direct response to, generations of harsh oppression. That music stood as testament to courage, perseverance, and the black experience itself. Yet, for decades, the black, Delta performers in particular had existed in obscurity, nearly invisible. Recall that even a talented entertainer like Ike Turner could not conceive of the idea that he would be *allowed* to record his music in the Delta, let alone be paid to do so.

Then, right out of the heart of the Delta, came a nineteen-year-old white kid adopting a largely black style and look, who achieved practically instantaneous worldwide success, fanatic adulation, and astronomical wealth. Not too surprisingly, Presley's success touched a painful place for a lot of African Americans, a place of distrust, and it still can.

* * *

As for Presley's inordinate popularity, in order for rock music to make inroads in America, it *had* to come from a white man to make it safe and as palatable as possible to obtain mainstream acceptance. As the studio owners, label heads, and TV hosts, whites were the gatekeepers. Only a white rock and roller could minimize the shock of rock and roll to the masses—and it was shocking. Going back to Presley on live TV, the notion of a black man performing the same bump-and-grind routine at the same time in U.S. history, with young women going nuts (let alone young *white* women), is not merely difficult to imagine—it is truly unimaginable.

Only after Presley brought black music into America's living rooms would white America allow the door to stay open for black artists like Big Joe Turner, Ray Charles, Chuck Berry and Little Richard, so that they could finally be accepted into the mainstream. This fact does not make Presley a hero, but it is a reality reflecting a society often overtly racist and carrying enormous racial baggage, both consciously and subconsciously. Presley was just doing his thing.

12

Mr. Berry and the First Wave of Rock

Where Elvis Presley was the "spark" for rock music, Chuck Berry was rock's first great composer and, for many, rock and roll's most crucial figure. Berry's songs transcended early R&B and early rockabilly to establish the template for the guitar-centric sound of rock and roll for decades to come. Lyrically, he gave rock and roll its original voice and attitude, capturing the spirit of American youth in the 1950s, both black and white. As a black, electric blues performer incorporating white hillbilly music influences, Berry further completed the circle racially, mirroring the career trajectories of Presley and Bill Haley.

Chuck Berry was born in 1926 in St. Louis, the fourth of six children, to a strict, church deacon father and a high school principal mother. His family was middle class in a virulently racist and segregated time and place. Later in life, Berry offered insight into how powerful an effect Jim Crow had on him: "I feel safe in saying that NO white person can conceive the feeling of obtaining Caucasian respect in the wake of a world of dark denial, simply because it is impossible to view the dark side when faced with brilliance."[1]

As a sophomore in high school, Berry sang a blues song called "Confessin' the Blues" at a school function and received a huge response. Soon after, he picked up and mastered the guitar, and his musical destiny was set. Before reaching fame, however, he ran into trouble. A weekend road trip with two high school buddies ended with their car breaking down; the three then stole a car at gunpoint, landing Berry in a juvenile detention center for three years.[2]

Upon Berry's release in 1947, he began playing clubs in East St. Louis, quickly gaining notoriety as a top musician and showman. He covered a lot of Nat King Cole numbers, as well as drawing from the Delta and electric blues, and even white country stars like Red Foley, Bill Monroe and Bob Wills. Initially, Berry was playing to all-black crowds, and on occasion he would throw in some hillbilly music, almost as a lark, as it was such a novelty for a black man to be playing in that style. To his surprise, the black crowds loved it. Berry integrated the sound into his regular sets, and soon he was drawing white fans, too.[3] By 1954, he was a regional star and headed for Chicago, home of the electric blues and Chess Records.[4]

Berry had a brief meeting in Chicago with his idol, Muddy Waters, who pointed him to Leonard Chess, president of Chess Records. Berry made a crude demo for Chess and was amazed to discover that Chess was particularly interested in his revamped version of "Ida Red," an old country fiddle song. Berry had reworked it and given it a stomping blues beat.[5] Where rockabilly had a clippety-clop rhythm, Berry set it in his R&B style and smoothed it out. He established the trademark 4/4 rhythm that would become the rock and roll standard, and then he added a blistering but fluid guitar solo. As *Rolling Stone* later declared: "Rock & roll guitar starts here."[6]

Berry added original lyrics to the song as well, using the car/sex metaphor and changing the name to the less hillbilly-sounding, "Maybellene." Once again, the symbolic freedom and excitement of the open roads of America, the opposite sex, and a great car all spoke to the freedoms that 1950s teens were seeking and finding in rock and roll.

When Alan Freed brought Berry to his mixed-race rock and roll shows in New York, the hits started to flow. From 1955 to 1959, Berry released "Roll Over Beethoven," "Thirty Days," "Too Much Monkey Business," "Brown Eyed Handsome Man," "You Can't Catch Me," "School Day," "Carol," "Back in the U.S.A.," "Little Queenie," "Memphis, Tennessee," "Johnny B. Goode," and "Rock and Roll Music."

Virtually every rock and roller who has followed Berry is indebted to him, and none more so than the Beatles and the Rolling Stones. Both bands covered Berry songs, with the Stones including a Berry cover on each of their first four studio albums. As John Lennon would say, "If you tried to give Rock and Roll another name, you might call it Chuck Berry."[7] One of rock's greatest composers, Brian Wilson of Beach Boys fame, stated that Berry wrote "all of the great songs and came up with all the rock & roll beats." Probably nothing better embodies the spirit and feel of rock music than the opening guitar riffs of Berry's classics, like "Johnny B. Goode": hard rocking and explosive. These songs would be the clarion call for a generation to let loose.

"Goode" is a classic American rags-to-riches story, wherein a poor country boy rides his guitar to stardom. It was essentially autobiographical, as a reference to Louisiana refers to Berry's grandfather from Louisiana; Berry specifically cited New Orleans due to its role as a primary port in the slave trade, as well as its musical importance. He also changed the original lyric

Chuck Berry (1957) (New York World-Telegram & Sun Collection, Library of Congress).

about a colored boy to reference a country boy in order to ensure radio play.[8] The message of "Goode" is that, even given humble beginnings, if you are original, and if you can rock hard, you can succeed in America—even if you are black, rural and poor.

In Berry's 1957 hit "School Day," he describes the miserably mundane life of a 1950s teen stuck in school; yet he delivers it with an underlying joy. The tedious school hours are made tolerable because Berry knows he just has to hang in there until the three o'clock bell. From there, the books are exchanged for the juke box and bliss.

Berry captures the angst but also the fun that America's teens were experiencing through rock music and everything that went with it, including cars, the big beat to dance to, and the opposite sex. Through rock and roll, Berry finds a new lifestyle not beholden to the staid rules and institutions that were seen as stifling or simply false.

Rock and roll had arrived, and Berry, a "colored" country boy from St.

Louis, planted its flag right in the middle of America. He sang in the confidence that no one could stop him, not even old Jim Crow and the rest of the nightmares from days gone past. Berry wasn't so naïve as to imagine that he had life beat—and later he would suffer in his dealings with the establishment—but he knew that nothing would ever be the same, either. In his music, Berry was almost giddy, and he relished every word he sang. Jim Crow was on life support, and rock and roll was kicking the cord out of the wall.

Berry did not carry an overt civil rights message; simply being a black man with confidence, swagger, and loads of white admirers was his statement. His 1955 hit, "Brown-Eyed Handsome Man," amounted to what was then a statement of black pride, or "Brown Is Beautiful," if you will. The song was surprisingly uncontroversial, partly because the lyrical message falls short of any specific call for revolution, and partly because it was so bold for its time that it may not have even registered to white listeners that a black man would make such a brash statement. Most listeners interpreted the song as being about males who happen to have brown eyes, not even thinking of the color of the man's skin. In each verse Berry recounts women in history falling for brown-eyed men, concluding with the triumphant last verse, in which a brown-eyed man hits a home run to win the game.

* * *

There is plenty of evidence to suggest that integration was the real, often glacially slow, but possibly inevitable "Manifest Destiny" of America. Jackie Robinson integrated "America's Pastime," baseball, in 1947; the U.S. military was integrated under President Truman's executive order of 1948; by 1957 popular Beat writer Jack Kerouac had written in *On the Road* that he "wished he was negro" because the white world was "not enough"[9]; and Norman Mailer was writing of white hipsters adopting black culture in his 1957 essay, "The White Negro."

Still, someone had to actually knock the door down all the way. It had been over fifty years since a fictional Huck Finn rejected the deeply rooted and religiously justified racism of his Southern culture ("All right then, I'll go to hell!"). By the 1950s, Southerners were replacing often overt hatred of blacks with, if not *pure* hearts, certainly an open love and appreciation of black culture and black music. Blacks and whites were even standing side-by-side with one another on stage and in the music venues. This was change coming from the heart, an often deeper and sometimes more significant form of change than that which comes from the highest court.

Indeed, to Southern segregationists, the surge of rock and roll's popularity could hardly have been more threatening. Rock was literally crashing lines, such as velvet-rope-divided dance floors, but it was also an obvious metaphor for integration on the broader scale. In the early 1950s, touring black artists were still wary of the South or avoided it altogether due to the threat of arrest or violence, or simply horrible treatment.[10]

Yet three hundred years of core Southern cultural beliefs were being washed away, and there was scarcely anything to be done about it. Many Southern white preachers saw this movement as the result of a lack of proper religious indoctrination and appreciation of segregation.[11] The Citizens' Council distributed flyers charging that rock and roll was an NAACP conspiracy in its attempt to "mongrelize" the country.[12] In Birmingham, Alabama, the KKK wrecked a broadcast tower belonging to a radio station that played "mixed" music, vandalizing the building with KKK and "Nigger" graffiti.[13] Southern affiliates of ABC TV got Alan Freed's 1957 rock and roll dance show, *The Big Beat*, cancelled after just two episodes when singer Frankie Lymon was shown dancing with a white girl. Dick Clark's *American Bandstand* was mostly segregated as well, though Clark later played up the presence of the occasional black kids on the set.[14]

But Freed and others continued to stage wildly popular rock and roll tours through the mid– and late 1950s, with mixed-race lineups and white and black kids showing up to see the same artists. Southern cities often prepared for the shows by deploying a dozen or so police officers to ensure that one race occupied the balcony of the venue while the other occupied the floor, or else there would be a roped-off "race line" in the middle of the dance floor. Despite these dividers, white teens still clamored to get into forbidden areas, in clear violation of the segregation laws,[15] and it became harder and harder to prevent co-mingling on the dance floor.

A 1956 concert in Houston featured Frankie Lymon and the Teenagers, who performed first, followed by Carl Perkins, before a mixed-race crowd. Black teens were already occupying the dance floor when Lymon finished his set and Perkins came on. Perkins exhorted the crowd, "Let's everybody in here rock and roll," and the white kids burst onto the floor, with the police helpless to stop them. The concert continued without incident and was one of the first shows in which black and white couples were allowed to dance on the same dance floor.[16] Nearly as telling was the government effort to suppress any public mention of the event.[17]

Little Richard reflected on those early tours as follows: "I've always thought that rock and roll brought the races together. Although I was black, the fans didn't care. I used to feel good about that. Especially being from the South, where you see the barriers, having all these people who we thought hated us, showing us all this love."[18] White kids idolized many of the black performers and wanted to interact with them. Berry recalled white fans hanging around after shows to meet him and his band while security looked on, dumbfounded.[19]

Not that America's racial issues disappeared once rock and roll came onto the scene. A few hundred years of cultural and social devastation would not go away with a few killer tracks. Little Richard was once arrested after a multi-racial show in Armadillo for "improper posturing,"[20] and white rockabilly artists like Carl Perkins and Elvis Presley endured taunts accusing them of being "white niggers" and "nigger-trash."[21]

While these rock and roll tours created indelible bonds, there were also frictions. For example, Chuck Berry and Jerry Lee Lewis feuded a bit.[22] There was also tension (and, on occasion, some fighting) between white and black fans, but most often the conflict was between the teens and the police trying to enforce segregation.[23]

On the other side of the coin, black performer Billy Eckstein recalled one show in the South at which two white girls expressed interest in meeting up with him after the show. Eckstein had to hide in the men's bathroom for forty-five minutes after the show not only because he was happily married but also out of fear for his life.[24] Chuck Berry had a similar, rather chilling incident at a frat-house show in 1957.[25]

In the 1960s, and reflecting longstanding social and cultural factors, rock and roll and popular music began to splinter into new sub-genres, often falling along racially distinct lines (though still with enormous crossover sales, like Motown, and some integrated bands, like Stax records legendary soul house band, Booker T and the MG's). Soul, R&B, funk and Motown were essentially "black" genres, whereas the British Invasion, folk-rock and psychedelic rock were largely "white" genres. Still, rock and roll was an unquestionable victory for race relations. When Little Rock was enduring a stand-off between state and federal troops, and blacks were being denied seats in restaurants even in the nation's capital, rock and roll had already integrated a significant part of society.

Somewhere Between Heaven and Hell

> "If I do not return to the pulpit this weekend, millions of people will go to hell."[26]
>
> —televangelist and cousin of Jerry Lee Lewis, Jimmy Swaggart

> "If I must set it down—my career and the money and the popularity and the ladies—then I will."[27]
>
> —soul legend-turned-minister, Al Green

"How can the *Devil* save souls?"[28]
—Jerry Lee Lewis

"It's all God's music—the Devil ain't got any music."[29]
—gospel/soul legend, Mavis Staples

Little Richard

Little Richard was born Richard Penniman in Macon, Georgia, in 1932, the third of twelve children. The Pennimans were poor blacks living deep in the stifling world of the Jim Crow South, and it was the Depression. Richard also happened to have some effeminate characteristics and showed homosexual leanings as a young teen, while his family had strong ties to the Pentecostal church. To top it off, Richard was also born with a gimpy leg. His father, Bud, was a moonshiner and disciplinarian who was shot and killed outside a bar when Richard was nineteen. When Richard's sexuality had first become known at age thirteen, Bud had kicked him out of the house. In short, Richard Penniman's life did not look like it was going to be particularly easy, nor was he going to fit into any traditional societal track.

From the beginning, Richard responded to his circumstances by becoming a clown and an entertainer, and especially by embracing the music in the church and singing and learning the piano. As he put it later, "See, there was so much poverty, so much prejudice in those days, people had to sing to feel their connection to God. To sing their trials away, sing their problems away, to make their burdens easier and the load lighter. That's the beginning. That's where it started."[30] The young Penniman sang to Louis Jordan's "Caldonia," shrieking out the name of a woman, as he would do later in "Good Golly Miss Molly" and "Long Tall Sally."[31] The previously mentioned meeting and opportunity to play with Sister Rosetta Tharpe was, in Richard's words, "the best thing that ever happened to me."[32]

Richard jumped around from group to group, surviving and singing across the local circuit of black clubs, theaters and juke joints, performing in latter-day minstrel shows, carnivals, and even the King Brothers' Circus.[33] With King Brothers, Richard teamed up with the flamboyant and wildly dressed showman known as Dr. Mobilio. Richard sang to attract a crowd, while the doctor captivated the crowd with prophesies and produced a "Devil's Child," described as a "dried-up body of a baby with claw feet like a bird and horns on its head."[34] With Mobilio's encouragement, Richard learned to combine the best of both worlds.

By 1952, the twenty-year-old Richard was performing at the Tick-Tock

Club in Macon, a wide-open club, and a racially integrated one at that, as it catered to the already-integrated military bases nearby. There was even cross-dressing, and Richard's wild, gender-bending style, including eyeliner and a slicked-up pompadour, was accepted without question.[35]

Richard did not break out creatively or commercially until 1955, when the rock movement began in earnest. That year, at a recording session at the Dew Drop Inn in Macon, Richard finally unleashed a lewd raver that, up to that point, he had only played on the club circuit and at underground gay clubs in the area. A local lyricist was called in to clean the song up so as to remove references to "good booty," and the like.[36] Richard famously kicked the song off at top gear with the vocal explosion (possibly a vocal approximation of a drum riff): "Womp-bomp-a-loom-op-a-womp-bam-boom!" Presumably there was some glossolalia in there, as well. That was followed by Richard himself pounding out the rhythm on the piano, and from there rock and roll got really wild. "Tutti Frutti" is so exhilarating, sexually charged, and out of control that some have called it the *real* defining moment for rock and roll. It is arguably the sound of the music becoming fully unhinged and free.

Richard produced other seminal songs, including "Lucille," "Long Tall Sally," and "The Girl Can't Help It." He also performed a live, raucous version of "Long Tall Sally" in the 1955 film *Can't Stop the Rock*, where he was shown blowing the minds of the white teen fans in the audience.

It is impossible to capture the full influence of any of these seminal rock performers because they are the very foundation for everything that followed. For Richard, his direct influence, both musically and spiritually, but also as an explosive genre- (and gender-) challenging performer, can be plainly seen in superstars Michael Jackson and Prince; yet you are just as likely to hear Richard's praises sung by a proto-punk legend like Lou Reed or a proto-thrash metal icon like Lemmie Kilmeister of Motorhead.[37]

Richard has acknowledged that during those early days in Macon, he engaged in lots of cocaine and a promiscuous sex life (with both men and women) after shows. During an outdoor show in January 1958, he saw a flash of light across the sky (it turned out to be Russia's *Sputnik* satellite reentering the atmosphere). Richard was spooked by the sight and had a revelation that led him back to gospel music; he even became a preacher. It would be an ongoing back-and-forth struggle between the sacred and the secular for Richard, who at various times identified himself as straight, gay and bisexual in the decades to come. At one point he was married to a woman for a while so that he wouldn't "go to hell."[38]

Jerry Lee Lewis

Jerry Lee Lewis was born to Elmo and Mamie Lewis in 1935, on the Louisiana side of the Delta, in Ferriday. The parallels between Lewis and Elvis Presley's upbringings, in particular, are striking. Both were poor white guys from the Delta, and both lost brothers young, putting even greater pressure on them to achieve something with their lives. At the age of three, Jerry Lee Lewis witnessed his seven-year-old brother get hit by a truck. Both Lewis and Presley also had parents who worshipped them, and both had overly-dependent mothers.[39] As Lewis' sister noted, "With all that attention, all that treatment, Mama and Daddy put something inside of Jerry. In a way—in a nice way—they put a hell in him."[40]

Elmo Lewis was a hard drinker. Lewis' sister, Frankie Jean, described Elmo as angry with a sometimes "uncontrollable temper."[41] Elmo was a cotton farmer until times got hard and he began moonshining, for which he did some prison time. For that matter, not only did Lewis and Presley—and Little Richard—share Pentecostal roots, but Lewis' and Richard's fathers were also in the moonshine business, and both Lewis' and Presley's dads did stints in jail.

Like Presley, Lewis believed that big things were in store for him and that his voice was going to be heard. And, of course, the Lewis' were devout churchgoers who belonged to the local Pentecostal church; Jerry Lee was also heavily influenced by local sanctified, black church music, along with the blues.

Jerry Lee's parents were musically inclined, and Elmo sang and played the guitar, in addition to listening to Jimmie Rodgers, one of Jerry Lee's major influences. When Jerry Lee was eight, his parents mortgaged their home to buy him a third-hand upright piano.[42] He shared piano lessons with his two cousins: the future country star Mickey Gilley and future hugely successful (and controversial) televangelist Jimmy Lee Swaggart. A ten-year-old Jerry Lee Lewis showed remarkable aptitude, and the family already believed stardom was in his future.[43]

That hellion Jerry Lee Lewis, who as an adult would be known as "The Killer," and TV preacher Jimmy Lee Swaggart were raised virtually as brothers is another one of the great factoids of American music history. Growing up, Swaggart's father was domineering and controlling, to the point that, as Lewis' sister put it, "Jimmy was not allowed to think, act, or breathe like a normal human being." Yet Swaggart also loved to hear his grandmother's story of her first experience with the Holy Ghost, again and again; thus he found his calling.[44] Swaggart and Lewis would always remain close, though Swaggart would later reference Lewis on his TV show specifically as a bad example for his audience not to follow.[45] After all, both men, and even Lewis in his rock and roll heyday, had a profound fear of the potential eternity of "blood, and fire, and vapour of smoke."[46]

By the end of the 1980s, however, the entire televangelism industry had become a national joke, with many leading figures more associated with greed, glitz, and sex scandals than the word of Christ. In 1988, after publicly lambasting fellow televangelist (and competitor) Jim Bakker for his adulterous affairs, Swaggart himself admitted to encounters with a prostitute. He was arrested for solicitation again in 1991.[47]

The young Jerry Lee, not too surprisingly, was impulsive, a troublemaker, and a bad student.[48] In their teens, he and Swaggart burglarized local businesses.[49] On the radio, Lewis listened to the Grand Ole Opry and Roy Acuff, as well as bluegrass stars like the Louvin Brothers. In 1948, the Louisiana Hayride radio show brought Hank Williams and the R&B of Fats Domino into Lewis' world. A local black pianist known as Old Sam showed Lewis the boogie technique that became his signature. Due to poverty and an overwhelming yearning for excitement, at fourteen Lewis worked at a local honky tonk, the Hilltop Club, in nearby Natchez, Mississippi, and he played there and at some other places. Also in Natchez, Haney's Big House was an all-black club owned by Lewis' uncle, although when bigger acts came through, including B.B. King, an area was roped off for white folks.[50] The owner allowed the young Lewis to watch the black acts through a window, as famously depicted in the 1989 bio-pic, *Great Balls of Fire.*

Lewis embraced the wild energy of the music of the Pentecostal services and its ecstatic impact. Stylistically, he played a rock-solid boogie pattern with his left hand while his right hand played the high keys with gospel fervor and flash.

Lewis' mother had believed that her son was on an unholy path, so she enrolled him in a Bible college in Waxahatchie, Texas. Shortly after arriving, Lewis launched into a wild boogie-woogie rendition of "My God Is Real" at a church assembly; he was gone by the next morning. Still, that Pentecostal fear of damnation would always remain with him.[51]

In 1955, Lewis and a friend saw Elvis Presley perform in a concert in Presley's hometown of Tupelo, and Lewis was blown away. At twenty years of age, Lewis had been thrown out of college; had failed both as a farmer and as a sewing-machine salesman; had been turned down by most Nashville-based record companies, as well as the Louisiana Hayride; and had already been married *twice* before he was eighteen (and he'd been a bigamist to boot). He was also a high school dropout who'd been in jail once for stealing a gun, and about all he was left with was an unwavering belief that he was the next Big Thing.[52]

In 1956, Lewis showed up at the then-red-hot Sun Records in Memphis. His first single was a hopped-up rendition of Ralph Mooney's "Crazy Arms," and it sold respectably. In 1957, Lewis broke out with "Whole Lotta Shakin' Goin' On," which went to number two on the pop charts, and followed it up with "Great Balls of Fire," "High School Confidential," "Breathless," and on. Lewis took boogie piano to new levels of both insanity and artistry. Lewis' sales rivaled Presley's. By the end of 1957, with Presley soon to ship out, Jerry Lee Lewis, the wild man with the flailing blond hair, was being sized for the crown of rock and roll.

In the Deep South in the 1940s and 1950s, marrying young was legal and not uncommon, both to avoid "living in sin" and because living in poverty often meant kids needed to get out on their own quickly to work. In fact, Lewis' sisters had married at eleven and fourteen years old, respectively.[53] Swaggart was seventeen when he married a not-even-pregnant fifteen year old. Lewis met his younger cousin, Myra Gale Brown, in December 1957, when she was twelve, and the two married when Jerry Lee was twenty-two and Myra was thirteen, which she looked every bit of.

Prior to embarking on a tour of England in 1958, Sam Phillips begged Lewis not to let anyone know of the marriage, but he refused to hide his wife.[54] Once the British press figured out who the young girl with Lewis was, the story blew up. Lewis was heckled badly at his next show as a "cradle robber," and the U.S. press had a field day. Sam Phillips and Lewis ran an apology in *Billboard*, and Phillips tried to make a joke out of it all with a misguided novelty hit, "The Return of Jerry Lee." But sex scandals did not go away in those days—and certainly not ones involving thirteen-year-old cousin/wives. *American Bandstand* stopped booking Lewis, and overnight he went from arenas to small clubs. The man who was to fill Elvis' void was done on the big stage. Lewis was out of the spotlight for years, though he would eventually occupy his spot as a rock and roll legend.

More Icons

By the mid–1950s, rock and roll was the place where the boldest, brashest, most high-energy young musicians all came together. In *The Sound of the City: The Rise of Rock and Roll*, Charlie Gillett identified five distinct styles of rock and roll that developed from 1954 to 1956: (1) northern band rock and roll (e.g., Bill Haley); (2) New Orleans dance blues (Lloyd Price,

Fats Domino, Little Richard); (3) Memphis country rock—that is, rockabilly (Sun); (4) Chicago R&B (Chess); and (5) vocal group rock and roll, including doo wop and various crooners. These five styles came about largely independent of one another, but all shared common blues roots and got their dance beats from the black music of the time.[55]

Fats Domino

Antoine Domino was born in New Orleans in 1928. The name "Fats" came in 1947, as a tribute to either of the legendary pianists, Fats Waller or Fats Pichon, and for the fact that Domino was a fireplug at 5 feet 5 inches tall and 220 pounds.[56]

Domino was raised in a musical family, and at fourteen he was playing for small change at juke joints in the Big Easy. He developed a unique, lolling boogie style on the piano, which worked perfectly with his smooth, mellow baritone and down-to-earth attitude. Domino was not the wildest or most electrifying performer, but, with his Dixieland-born rhythm and outstanding songwriting, and collaborating with partner Dave Bartholomew, he was both a pillar and an original architect of rock and roll.[57] He and Bartholomew also played on and elevated the early music of classic New Orleans rock and roll artists, such as Lloyd Price ("Lawdy Miss Clawdy," who later added hits "Staggerlee" and "Personality"), Shirley & Lee ("Let the Good Times Roll"), and Little Richard.

Domino became a dominant force in rock, beginning his career in the late 1940s with his proto-rock, New Orleans boogie. In the mid–1950s, Domino was playing essentially the same music that he had always played. The new rock era dovetailed perfectly with Domino's style, and in 1955 he had a huge hit with "Ain't That a Shame," hitting the pop top ten.[58] Pat Boone covered the song the same year, and it went to number one.

That success was followed by Domino's cover of an old jazz number, "Blueberry Hill" (1956), which became his biggest single, as well as "Walking to New Orleans," "Whole Lotta Loving," "I'm Walking," "Blue Monday," and many others.[59] Domino hit the pop chart 63 times and sold more rock records in the 1950s than anyone but Elvis Presley.[60]

Bo Diddley

Right there with fellow early guitar heroes Muddy Waters, Chuck Berry and B.B. King was Bo Diddley. According to *Rolling Stone*, Diddley developed "a new kind of guitar-based rock & roll, soaked in the blues and R&B, but owing allegiance to neither."[61]

Diddley was born Elias McDaniel in 1928 in McComb, Mississippi, adopted by a sharecropping family that moved to Chicago in 1934. Diddley began studying classical violin, but after hearing bluesman John Lee Hooker, he shifted gears for good.[62] He was signed by Chess subsidiary Checkers in 1955. Diddley added a West African drum rhythm that formed his distinctive hambone rhythm; some tremolo and distortion; and a lot of swagger that reverberated through not only R&B and rock, but also funk and even rap.

Diddley's syncopated groove was all about rhythm and his chugging freight train sound. In the late 1950s, he scored hits with "Who Do You Love?" "Roadrunner," and "Mona." Diddley left behind for good the monikers that Southern white men used for black men—"boy" and "Uncle"—with his emphatic "I'm a Man" and his biggest hit, the exultant "Bo Diddley," both released in 1955.

Many subsequent rock hits have been constructed using Diddley's simple, off-beat, five-accent rhythm (bomp, ba-bomp-bomp, bomp-bomp), including Buddy Holly's "Not Fade Away," the Who's "Magic Bus," Bruce Springsteen's "She's the One," and George Michael's "Faith."[63] The Rolling Stones covered at least seven Diddley songs. In Diddley's own words, he used his Delta roots "mixed up with spiritual, sanctified rhythms"[64] Another song, "Say Man," was a joking verbal sparring between Diddley and his maraca player engaged in "signifying" or "doing the dozens" (black folk traditions dating back to the time of slavery), which sounds something like an early rap battle.[65] Diddley did not have quite the commercial success of some of his peers—or even many of those who adopted his style—but he was a living rock legend until he passed in 2006.

Carl Perkins

Carl Perkins was another crucial Sun artist, writing and performing one of the key songs in the Sun canon with "Blue Suede Shoes" (1956) and otherwise producing a series of rockabilly classics such as, "Matchbox" (1957) and "Boppin' the Blues" (1956). The Beatles, in fact, recorded five Perkins songs, the most they covered from any songwriter.

Perkins grew up in a poor sharecropping family near Tiptonville, Tennessee, in 1932.[66] He worked side-by-side with African American laborers, laboring from sunup to sundown in the summers.[67] When he finally purchased a guitar, a black sharecropper named John Westbrook taught him the blues and black gospel.[68]

As young men, Carl Perkins and his brother Jay formed a band around the rough-and-tumble Jackson, Tennessee, honky tonk circuit, with Carl working during the day at factory jobs and as a pan greaser at a baking company at night. In 1953, Perkins already had his own juiced-up version of Bill Monroe's "Blue Moon of Kentucky." When he heard Elvis Presley's version over the radio the next year, Perkins heard his calling and made a beeline for Sun Records.[69]

"Blue Suede Shoes" captured the electricity of the blues-country fusion and was one of the most important songs of the era. The song has the swagger of the poor Southern male who may not have a lot, but he damn well is not going to let you scuff up his slick shoes on a Saturday night. Perkins' own recording of "Blue Suede Shoes" (1956) put him near the top of the pop, country and R&B charts simultaneously. Soon after, however, a car crash on the way to his big TV debut in New York took him out of the spotlight, and Presley's version of "Blue Suede Shoes" would be the better remembered of the two. The song endowed the image of the hillbilly with style and an indelible, new, rock-inspired swagger and cool.

Perkins, too, has been slightly overlooked, partly due to bad luck, and partly because his authentic, "Dixie Fried"–style became lost when rock moved past the Sun sound to a more homogenized, mainstream path. Thanks to a drinking problem and the shift away from rockabilly, Perkins career was derailed until a revival in the 1960s. He eventually beat the booze, toured with Johnny Cash's entourage in the 1960s and 1970s, and performed off-and-on until his death in 1998.

Eddie Cochran

Eddie Cochran's career was tragically short, though he produced enough great music by his death at just twenty-one years of age to be inducted posthumously into the Rock and Roll Hall of Fame. Cochran was born in Minnesota in 1938; his family relocated to California when he was in his teens.[70] Cochran was a gifted country guitar player, but, like Lewis, Buddy Holly, and others, once he heard Elvis Presley he went straight to rockabilly. Cochran and his partner, Hank Cochran (no relation), even auditioned at Sun, though unsuccessfully.[71]

Despite not being a Southerner, Cochran instantly grasped the rebellious and liberating nature of the new sound. Along with excellent guitar skills, Cochran brought some abandon, as well as humor, to his music. In 1956, his star took off when he performed "Twenty Flight Rock" in the Jayne Mansfield film *The Girl Can't Help It*, a song about a teen climbing twenty flights of stairs to see his girl, only to discover by the time he gets to the last flight that he is too tired to finish his quest.[72] The next year, Cochran released his ode to bored teens, "Summertime Blues," cracking the top ten, followed on the charts by "C'mon Everybody" (1958) and "Somethin' Else" (1959).[73]

Cochran died when the London taxi he and fellow rock and roll star Gene Vincent ("Be-bop-a-Lula") were riding in crashed on April 17, 1960. Vincent survived, though with a bad limp; after early success, his career slowly faded out as the first rock era ended.[74]

An additional note on rockabilly should be made here: Cochran, along with Presley, Lewis, and Richard, in particular, produced the foundation of rock and roll, but also the seeds for the punk rock movement of the mid–1970s, as well. Cochran's "C'mon Everybody" is a prime example.

In "C'mon Everybody," Cochran captures so many teens' dream come true: Mom and Dad are out of town. The song is an open invitation to stop caring, have friends over, dance, and get crazy. The wild rockabilly music abruptly stops, giving way to the chorus of four yelled/sung words, in which Cochran effectively captures the essence of the rock and roll movement: "Who cares? *C'mon everybody!*"[75] And the anarchic fun kicks in again.

A little over twenty years later, Sid Vicious, the admittedly talentless bass player of the seminal British punks known as the Sex Pistols, produced a fairly faithful but transformative version of Cochran's song. The Pistols had made Vicious their second bass player, and while he could barely *play* the bass (his playing only made it onto one recorded song[76]), he embodied the punk rock aesthetic (or, more specifically, that most nihilistic aspect of punk) as much as any other person.

Vicious sang just three songs with the Sex Pistols on their post-breakup, 1979 release. His vocals on "C'mon Everybody" elevate the original to an entirely new level of, if not artistry, at least abandon. It is a funny and exuberant take, but Vicious also sends it off the rails, recklessly flirting with oblivion. In other words, it is a nearly perfect punk rock song. Who cares, indeed?

Sadly, Vicious himself went far off the rails shortly thereafter. After being charged in the stabbing death of his fellow heroin addict girlfriend, Nancy Spungeon, he died of a heroin overdose before he went to trial. To underscore the insanity that was Vicious' life, the heroin was scored by his mother.[77]

Everly Brothers

The Everly Brothers, with hits like "Wake Up Little Suzie" (1957), have also been somewhat underrated, being perceived as more light pop. Yet Phil and Don Everly were in fact a crucial early rock act, representing the other side of rock's gritty Delta blues guitar influence. Along with a country flavor and the two-part harmonies that helped define the Beatles and Simon and Garfunkel, among many others,[78] somewhat surprisingly, they were a major influence on the Rolling Stones as well.[79] From 1957 to 1960, more hits followed, including "Bye Bye Love" and "All I Have to Do Is Dream," and the duo helped bring some pop sensibility to rock and roll without it losing its soul.

Link Wray

A final guitarist of note is Link Wray, inventor of the so-called power chord. Ray's ominous and jagged chords sounded so threatening that his most famous song, "Rumble" (1958), was banned from several cities despite being an instrumental, perhaps a pinnacle achievement in rock guitar history.

Wray captured the menace of the Delta bluesmen like Wolf and Waters in particular, and made it his own. He thus helped provide major tools for hard rock acts like the Who, and effectively every punk, hard rock and heavy metal act that followed.[80]

Screamin' Jay Hawkins

Jay Hawkins was a talented R&B and rock performer but who would come to embody rock's vulgarity. Hawkins, a Cleveland native, began singing opera and was a boxer before transitioning to R&B and rock in the mid–1950s. Mostly by accident, he was the first to illustrate the genre's capacity for over-the-top theatricality. Hawkins created a funny/morbid stage show, right on the edge of pure gimmick, and about as vulgar and shocking to parents as anything at the time.

Hawkins set out to record a serious ballad called "I Put a Spell on You" in 1955, but not before he and the entire band became extremely inebriated. The final version caught on record surprised Hawkins as much as anyone else when he heard it.[81] His drunkenness comes out more as oddly sexual, with the feel of a voodoo witch doctor.

With the surprising success of "I Put a Spell on You," Alan Freed encouraged Hawkins to embrace a new persona for his live show, including emerging from a rented coffin.[82] Hawkins added his own touches, with gold and leopard-skin costumes and voodoo stage props, including a smoking skull on a stick and rubber snakes.[83] His show harkened back to the early American circus and carnival acts, and, further, were much like the comic books of the time that already horrified many parents. In the mid–1950s, comic book titles like *Tales from the Crypt* and *Crime SuspenStories* appealed to the cruder interests of adolescent males. Those comics were finally subdued under the comic industry's self-censoring Comics Code Authority in 1954.[84]

Hawkins' new image detracted from his legitimate musicianship, but he had a successful career and continued to tour successfully, including stints with Fats Domino and the Rolling Stones. Hawkins influenced and otherwise paved the way for the more theatrical and outrageous rock performers who followed, such as Alice Cooper, Kiss, the Cramps, and Marilyn Manson, in particular.[85]

Buddy Holly

Buddy Holly's recording career lasted just eighteen months, from the spring of 1957 until the winter of 1958–1959, but he left an outsized impact on rock and roll and popular music. Holly was born in Lubbock, Texas, in 1936, the youngest of four children. He took up the guitar, banjo, and mandolin early and was publicly performing in a duet at age fifteen. Holly listened to a lot of blues and R&B on the radio and local juke boxes; by the mid–1950s he was into what was considered "western and bop." Fellow Southern white musician Elvis Presley was, of course, then helping carve out the rock and roll sound, and Holly was blown away; he even opened for Presley, and the pair met in Lubbock in early 1955.[86]

In 1956, Holly formed Buddy Holly and the Crickets, with himself as the primary songwriter, singer, and lead guitarist. The group ended up a trio in late 1957, and by 1958 Holly went solo to fully realize his quickly evolving vision for the future of rock music.

Buddy Holly (1958) (photograph by James J. Kriegsmann, Library of Congress).

At first, the group was more country than rockabilly and a bit tame, but they switched it over for good with the release of the single "That'll Be the Day," which went to number one in the summer of 1957. Holly and the Crickets developed into a full-on rock band and began to show a somewhat harder edge, as evidenced on a song like "Rave On" (1958). They had enough blues credibility to win over a skeptical all-black crowd at the Apollo Theater in Harlem.[87]

Holly has gone down in history as a legendary songwriter, having written or co-written about half of the band's forty-nine recorded songs, and reaching the top ten with originals "Oh, Boy" (1957) and "Peggy Sue" (1958). This was another breakthrough for rock, as the norm in popular music had long been to leave songwriting to professionals. Yet here was twenty-one-year-old Holly not only writing songs but also elevating the sophistication of the genre. Holly and the Crickets both inspired the Beatles' name and provided them with a blueprint of sorts for their first 36 original songs, each a boy-girl love song much indebted to Holly's style.

In the studio, Holly had a huge impact with innovations such as double tracking vocals, and he was already embarking on a grander, more complex vision for rock, particularly on "Well … All Right" (1958). As music writer Bruce Eder wrote, "Holly advanced rock & roll's range and sophistication without abandoning its fundamental joy and excitement."[88]

It has been surmised that Holly's manager, Norman Petty, did not handle the books well, possibly ripping Holly off, so that Holly was surprisingly low on cash by 1958. At the same time, Holly had a new, and soon pregnant, wife, Maria. Holly decided to earn some cash by signing on to play a low-budget Winter Dance Party package tour in the Midwest.[89] On February 3, 1959, while flying to Moorhead, Minnesota, in a snowstorm, Holly, Ritchie Valens, and deejay J.P. "Big Bopper" Richardson were all killed in a plane crash, effectively ending the first wave of rock and roll.

Doo Wop and Pop

African American vocal groups of the 1930s and 1940s, such as the Mills Brothers and the Ink Spots, often combined pop, jazz and barbershop quartet influences. Those influences were then absorbed into the jump blues, creating a new vocal style of R&B, eventually labeled "doo wop" in the early 1960s. Doo wop first charted with Billy Ward and the Dominoes' "Sixty Minute Man," in 1951.

Doo wop usually featured three- to six-part *a capella* harmonies, often with backup vocalists providing a harmonic background and wordless onomatopeia (mimicking instruments). Young males in eastern urban centers like Chicago, New York, and Baltimore took to the sound and could practice anywhere with decent acoustics—in school bathrooms, under bridges, and on stoops and street corners. When done in swing time, early doo wop became a popular form of rock and roll, and it was often slowed down to provide dance hits throughout the 1950s, and the genre was personified by successful groups like The Coasters and The Drifters.

The Penguins had the first big vocal group, rock and roll breakout with "Earth Angel" (1954), followed by The Orioles ("Crying in the Chapel") and The Platters ("Only You" and "The Great Pretender"). In 1956, Frankie Lymon and The Teenagers performed live on national TV, playing their number one hit, "Why Do Fools Fall in Love?," which sat on the charts alongside Presley and Carl Perkins. Because doo wop/vocal group songs were relatively simple to perform, it was was one of the first sub-genres to be extensively covered and re-created for white artists at a much greater profit, including the Chords' "Sh-Boom," covered by the Crew-Cuts in 1954, and the Moonglows' "Sincerely," covered by the McGuire Sisters in 1955. Italian American vocal groups followed, including Dion and the Belmonts ("I Wonder Why," 1958) and, into the 1960s, the Four Seasons ("Sherry," 1962).

Rock and Soul

Ray Charles and Early Soul

Ray Charles was born in Albany, Georgia, in 1930, and he grew up in Greenville, Florida. Charles was introduced to music as a small child through a local boogie woogie pianist and through regular attendance at Baptist church services. Music helped Charles in dealing with serious childhood traumas. First, he developed glaucoma at four or five. And when he was five years old, his brother George (age four) drowned in a laundry tub. Finally, at seven, Ray Charles went completely blind.[90]

Charles was enrolled at the Florida School for the Deaf and Blind, where he learned classical piano and excelled. His mother kept him doing the same chores as any other kid, telling concerned neighbors, "He's blind, but he ain't stupid."[91]

While still in his teens, Charles began touring the chitlin' circuit throughout the South.[92] Early on, he modeled himself on pop-jazz vocalist Nat King Cole, finding success between 1949 and 1952, when he landed on the R&B charts with "Confession Blues" (1949) and "Kissa Me Baby" (1952). Charles signed with Atlantic in 1952, while developing a jump blues and boogie style, and by 1954 he had found his own voice and style.[93]

Church-inspired, secular R&B stars Sam Cooke and Jackie Wilson laid the foundation for soul, and Charles built on that. His new version of R&B

was part church and part rock and roll, complete with soulful moans and propelled by a bouncing horn section. Charles put it all together with "I Got a Woman" (1955) and hit number two on the R&B charts.[94] As Charles remarked, the shift between sacred and secular was not all that hard: "You just change Jesus to baby, and you got the blues."[95] Along with the feeling of the church, Charles created soul music.

Among Charles' other hits of the era, "What'd I Say" hit number six on the R&B chart in 1959.[96] "What'd I Say" further broke down the sacred-secular line and gave another jolt to the rock era. This song, too, was soulful, wildly energetic, almost proto-garage rock, but expertly written and arranged, as well.

John Lennon noted that guitarists trying to re-create Charles' electric piano on "What'd I Say" changed the future of rock guitar. Further worth noting is that the very early Beatles used to hone their chops and build band chemistry with extended workouts of "What'd I Say," sometimes for an hour and a half, as part of their six-hour marathon sets in clubs in Hamburg's red-light district.[97]

Charles became known as Brother Ray, or sometimes just "The Genius."[98] He later exhibited his strong jazz influences and country roots as well, on the way to becoming one of pop music's most renowned performers.[99]

Another soul pioneer of note, Jackie Wilson, assumed the position of lead vocalist when Billy Ward left the Dominoes in 1953, although the band was not experiencing major commercial success. In 1956, Wilson struck out for a successful solo career and found minor success with "Reet Petite," co-written by a young Detroit songwriter, Barry Gordy. Gordy went on to start his own black-owned, black-run label, of course, the powerhouse Motown, and teamed with another Detroit singer-songwriter, Smokey Robinson, for the label's first nationwide hit, "Shop Around" (1960).

James Brown

James Brown also arose from incredibly humble origins. Brown was born on May 3, 1933, in Barnwell, South Carolina—right into Jim Crow, the Great Depression, abject poverty, and a broken home. From the age of four onward, Brown lived in Augusta, Georgia, raised by his Aunt Honey, the madam of an Augusta brothel. As a young child, Brown scrapped for money, including dancing for soldiers at nearby Fort Gordon, picking cotton, and shining shoes. At twelve years old, he was dismissed from school for "insufficient clothing."[100]

Brown's sacred/secular conflict caused him to throw himself into the church (especially church music and the choir), as well as crime. At the age of sixteen, he was sent to prison for three years for car theft. While in prison, Brown met future longtime partner Bobby Byrd and formed the first incarnation of the Famous Flames.[101] Coming as he did on the heels of the first wave of rock and rollers, Brown would soon pick up the R&B/soul torch from Ray Charles.

The Famous Flames moved to Macon, Georgia, in 1955, and Brown, who idolized Little Richard, reached out to his hero. As a result, Richard set Brown up with his own management team. Richard also wrote a "song" on a napkin that consisted of a mere three words or really, one word repeated three times: "please, please, please," and gave it to Brown.[102] Brown hung on to it and eventually worked out his breakthrough hit, "Please, Please, Please," recorded at King Records Studios in Cincinnati in 1956.

Brown went on to place 114 total entries on *Billboard*'s R&B singles charts.[103] He accurately wrote in his memoir, "Others may have followed in my wake, but I was the one who turned racist minstrelsy into black soul—and by doing so, became a cultural force."[104] Brown himself would become the "Godfather of Soul," define the Black Pride movement of the 1960s and 1970s, and take live performances to a level of excitement that few have matched.[105] Brown and his group's records gained new life with an enormous influence on hip hop and heavy sampling of his songs by hip hop acts in the 1980s and beyond.[106]

In the 1980s and 1990s, Brown faced problems with spousal abuse, drug possession, and the IRS.[107] Still, he became one of music's most important and most explosive performers in pop history.

13

A Changed World

For all of the United States' wealth, powerful institutions, and worldwide influence, the unbridled popularity of rock and roll suggested that American youth could not be controlled. The American establishment saw rock music as, at best, a serious threat to society; at worst, it was quite literally the Devil's music. As Robert Pattison wrote, rock and roll "knocks the props out from under religion, first by shifting the focus of faith from God to self, and secondly, by depriving sects and churches of their claim to exclusive revelation."[1] Funnily enough, while the U.S. establishment saw rock as possibly a communist threat, the communists saw rock as a depraved Western plot to undermine the East, and American racists saw it as an NAACP plot.[2] In truth, rock was simply a revolution of the spirit.

In the mid–1950s, the world was still sifting through the aftermath of World War II. One explanation for fascism and the Holocaust was that a charismatic orator like Hitler, with powerful and emotional rhetoric, could create some sort of mass-mind control that somehow led millions in even the most destructive of directions. What else could explain an entire nation allowing and even collectively committing such atrocities against an entire class of people? For many, only a similar kind of voodoo could explain the younger generation's unrest and the popularity of rock and roll. A 1956 *Time* article explicitly noted that rock music bore "a passing resemblance to Hitler's mass meetings."[3] The *New York Times* quoted a psychiatrist who referred to rock as "cannibalistic and tribalistic."[4] In 1957, respected novelist Gay Talese declared rock fans to be "addicts."[5]

The mini-riots resulting from the use of "Rock Around the Clock" in *The Blackboard Jungle* had helped put rock and roll in the crosshairs of parents, the government, and church officials, as the song topped the charts.[6] An editorial at the time, which appeared in the influential *Music Journal*, concluded that teenagers were "definitely influenced in their lawlessness by this throwback to jungle rhythms. Either it actually stirs them to orgies of sex and violence (as it did for the savages themselves), or they use it as an excuse for the removal of all inhibitions and complete disregard of the conventions of decency."[7] By the end of 1957, rock and rollers virtually owned *Billboard*'s top ten.[8]

America's juvenile delinquency fears had actually begun prior to rock and roll's commercial breakout, beginning with Brando and Dean. Statistically, there was a rise in juvenile crime, though overstated, that really began in the middle of World War II, when the country's fathers had gone off to fight in Europe and the Pacific.[9] In the mid–1940s, comic books were blamed for this development and became the scourge of decent society, leading to bans, comic burnings, and ultimately the comic industry's self-censorship.[10] In February 1954 (still before rock and roll's breakout), R&B "rock" records were the subject of legislation introduced in Congress "to ban the mailing of certain records through the U.S. mail" and to have "certain rock records … added to the list of 'pornographic' materials that are illegal to send through the postal service."[11] In 1954 and 1955, the raunchiest of these records, or "smutty songs," were targeted for letter-writing campaigns and congressional discussions of possible censorship.[12]

Elvis Presley's look and sound represented the culmination of every establishment fear, brought front-and-center. Rock and roll was the epitome of "freedom without responsibility," or worse.[13] New York's *Daily News* described rock and roll music as "a barrage of primitive jungle-beat rhythm set to lyrics which few adults would care to hear."[14] Monsignor John B. Carroll, the head of the Catholic Youth Organization, concluded, "There is no doubt but that the byproduct of rock and roll has left its scar on youth."[15] Another *New York Times* columnist commented, unknowingly ironically, "What is it that makes teenagers throw [away] their inhibitions as though at a revival meeting? Is this generation going to hell?" From the conservative *National Review*: "May the Lord have mercy on us."[16]

The establishment was so caught off guard that in 1956, a Columbia Records A&R executive confidently assured listeners that rock was a fad and "quality show tunes" were already pushing rock out of the picture.[17] Pop superstar Frank Sinatra initially called Presley's music a "rancid smelling aphrodisiac."[18] Even key liberals of the time embraced consensus and conformity as the prime societal ideals of the time. The Reverend Dr. Martin Luther King, for example, saw the rock music revolution as having more morally destructive force than benefits as a racially integrating force, writing that playing the new music "often plunges men's minds into degrading and immoral depths."[19]

Opponents of rock and roll cited it as the worst and lowest form of human expression, a place where impressionable youth rejected the sound moral authority of their elders. Cultural critic Dwight Macdonald wrote in 1953 that where the youth were lacking direction, "morality sinks to that of the most brutal and primitive members, it's taste to that of the least sensitive and most ignorant."[20] As Tocqueville had warned of a loss of a central moral, authority pantheism: "It naturally attracts their imagination and holds it fixed. It fosters their pride and soothes the laziness of their minds."[21] Who could say where it was all leading? Cities such as New Haven, Jersey City and Santa Cruz all had bans on rock and roll shows for a time.[22]

The *New York Times* columnist Jack Gould wasn't a fan of rock and roll or of Elvis Presley, but he had a different analysis. Gould expressed dismay that younger children were being exposed to Presley's sexualized behavior during primetime TV, but he also suggested the following: "In the long run, perhaps Presley will do everyone a favor by pointing up the need for early sex education so that neither his successors nor TV can capitalize on the idea that this type of routine is somehow highly tempting yet forbidden fruit."[23]

According to Alfred Kinsey's reports of the late 1940s and early 1950s, 50 percent of men wanted to marry virgins, and 80 percent of American women saw premarital sex as unethical; yet 50 percent of women had engaged in it. Kinsey concluded that this all reflected a lot of confusion and guilt surrounding the subject of sex.[24]

By the mid–1950s, middle-class teens had access to the family car and thus freedom to roam about with the opposite sex—with rock and roll on the car radio. Further, the widespread availability of condoms and penicillin—the birth control pill would not come until 1960[25]—rendered the old, standby parental scare tactics obsolete. Parents were going to have to find a new way to steer kids in the desired direction.[26] Thus, they looked to expert psychologists, books and magazines, like *Parenting Magazine*, for help, as well as encouraging their children to read teen-targeted magazines like *Seventeen*, which offered moral advice, often from the perspective of other teens.[27]

* * *

The corporate response to the overwhelming commercial and cultural success of rock was to cash in big. Along with the music of the initial wave of rock giants, white cover songs, in the "vocal group" style of the more visceral, and sometimes raunchy, black R&B and rock and roll records that sanitized the lyrics and softened the sound.[28] Lighter music, with less emotional commitment, and more focus on light melodies, minimized the threat, perceived or otherwise. The listeners' physical connection with the music was minimized, and the music itself was conducive to slow and more restrained dancing—not the gyrations or the thrill of a Presley or a Little Richard. It was a poppy and popular strain of rock that could be consumed by the white masses with far less parental outrage.

This "whitewashing" of rock had gone as follows: black performers recorded exciting and groundbreaking rock and roll, and those records got crucial radio play, which drove sales. However, when white artists released covers of those songs, deejays stopped playing the black versions and switched to the white versions, so that sales completely shifted. This was fine for songwriters' royalties, but not for the original performers. Also, if black artists wanted to compete in the pop realm, they, too, had to soften and smooth over their own style to compete with those covers, focusing more on melodies and orchestrations that would be acceptable to white audiences. Black political messages in early rock were nearly nonexistent.

While Little Richard acknowledged Pat Boone's success in opening up the bigger markets, he was also quoted as saying that Boone "took [his] music."[29] In Richard's view, "They needed a rock star to block me out of white homes because I was a hero to white kids. The white kids would have Pat Boone upon the dresser and me in the drawer 'cause they liked my version better, but the families didn't want me because of the image that I was projecting."[30]

Some of this more pop-oriented strain was very good rock and roll, including the rise of doo wop. Much, however, was simply a watered-down commodity, often from teen heartthrobs, readied for mass distribution, and labeled by some as "schlock rock."[31] Topics of top hits shifted to love and immortality: "Earth Angel," "Teen Angel," "Book of Love," "The Chapel of Love," "Teenage Crush," and "Sixteen Candles," which assuaged many parental concerns.[32] With rock records as the growth engine, the record industry saw sales nearly triple from $213 million in 1954 to $613 million in 1959.[33]

The corporate story of early rock is epitomized by TV personality Dick Clark and singer/actor Pat Boone. Both Clark and Boone were white, had matinee-star good looks, oozed decency, and were entirely uninterested in threatening the status quo—in fact, both were proud conformists. Each helped bring rock and roll into mainstream America, for better and for worse, and each made a fortune in the process.

Clark had moved from New York State to Philadelphia to be a radio host in 1952, and in 1956 the twenty-six-year-old had a chance to take over as the host of a local, teen-oriented music and dance television show called *Bandstand*. The show broadcast every weekday afternoon at 46th and Market Street with the most popular acts performing, while local kids danced the latest dances, like the pony and the Watusi, and rated the new records. Clark hosted and conducted brief interviews. In 1957, ABC picked up the show nationwide, and Clark changed the name to *American Bandstand*. He found out what the kids wanted to hear, and, in turn, the artists increased their audiences to the tune of twenty million (mostly school-age) viewers every day.[34] The record ratings segment spawned the famous catchphrase: "It's got a good beat, and you can dance to it."[35]

The cordial and polished Clark was accepted by teens; yet he was as clean-cut and nonthreatening as any parent could wish. As the sheer shock of Elvis on Ed Sullivan wore off, Clark helped rock and roll stay in the mainstream. By and large, Clark was, as he himself later jokingly put it, a "fluffmeister."[36] Still, along with giving breaks to local Italian American crooners from South Philadelphia High School (i.e., Frankie Avalon and Fabian), Clark presented early rock luminaries such as Johnny Cash, Eddie Cochran, and Buddy Holly, and he also provided important screen time for black artists such as Jackie Wilson, Sam Cooke, and the Drifters.[37]

Clark later broke another South Philly alum, Chubby Checker, and helped launch "The Twist" dance craze in 1960. He moved the show from Philadelphia to Los Angeles in 1964 and went on to become an American pop culture icon and entertainment business mogul.[38] Before all of that, however, Clark had to survive the payola scandal in 1959.

When the mind-control theory of rock's popularity did not pan out, and mainstream America did not otherwise run away from the rock and roll revolution, the establishment got very nervous. Congress thus next began to blame the music and music publishing industries. The "payola" practice involved deejays accepting cash from record labels and song publishers to play their songs on the nation's airwaves and drive sales. Thus, it was assumed, rock music was being force-fed to America's youth—not because the kids actually wanted to hear it.[39] One music professor testified to Congress that "the growth of a healthy music culture in the United States had been retarded."[40]

Also by the late 1950s, the power of television and mass media had reached new heights. The payola scandal happened to come right after notorious quiz show scandals in 1958, when several national game shows were exposed for fixing the outcomes of their supposedly honest competitions and hoodwinking the entire nation, and garnering congressional attention.[41] Along with having the power to put Elvis Presley in every living room in America, the mass media industry, in general, was suspect.

Further, powerful interests from Tin Pan Alley and Hollywood were seeing rock and roll completely take over the music business they had long dominated.[42] According to *Billboard* at the time, "frustrated music men—out of step with current song and recording trends" started to "blame their plight on rock and roll and construe that rock and roll is an outgrowth of payola," and thus pushed Congress to put an end to it.[43]

In 1959, the U.S. Senate launched its payola investigation. The practice had rarely been talked about much in public, but it predated rock and roll, going back to early radio in the 1920s.[44] The immense power of congressional prosecutors was then seen as a means of stopping the rock rebellion.

At the time, Dick Clark had significant investments in music publishing and recording interests, thus he could use immense leverage to negotiate a financial stake in the songs and acts that he would champion on *American Bandstand*. It was a clear conflict of interest, and really just one step removed from being payola. Clark, however, was already a popular and hugely profitable entity, and ABC gave him a heads-up prior to the start of congressional investigations. Clark then divested himself of those holdings and formally swore off any further associations. That was enough for Congress to ignore him.[45] *American Bandstand* became a Saturday afternoon staple into the 1990s, and Clark was one of the most prominent faces on network television, heading his own hugely successful production company and hosting TV game shows and a New Year's Eve special into the 2010s.

Conversely, Alan Freed was the most visible, and was perceived as the most dangerous leader of the dark side of rock music. Freed thus became Congress' primary target. Freed was eventually convicted of commercial bribery, which was only a misdemeanor, but it was enough to tarnish his reputation, effectively blackballing him and ending his career in the mainstream. His personal life went downhill fast, and his drinking problem worsened. Freed ultimately died from cirrhosis of the liver in 1965, at forty-three years of age.[46]

* * *

Pat Boone was one of the top-selling artists of the late 1950s, regularly covering black artists' rock and roll originals. Boone had 38 top forty hits, including covers of "Tutti Frutti" and "Ain't That a Shame," and he also hosted his own TV show from 1957 to 1960.[47] Boone was straight-laced, to say the least, and he had a straightforward, Christian take on the issues facing teens of the day. Boone became a *de facto* spokesperson for an idealized and conformist teen lifestyle and even wrote a best-selling lifestyle guide for teens.[48]

While Boone's Christian values were clear and sincere enough, what was not clear was how he felt about the deeper and more complex questions that American youth were really grappling with at the time: questions regarding religion and spirituality, emotional/psychological problems, the difference between "good" (legal) drugs and "bad" (illegal) drugs, family dysfunction, racism, moral issues of materialism and personal integrity, the military-industrial complex, fighting far-flung wars for murky reasons, the nuclear build-up and potential Armageddon, or repressed sexual feelings. One of Boone's overriding principles that was clear: do what your parents say. As he put it in one interview, "For the record, your parents had to be teenagers [themselves] at some time." Besides, resisting authority was, said Boone, like a "large dog" pulling on a choke chain: "the more he struggles and pulls, the tighter the collar gets."[49]

Boone also adopted a corporate philosophy throughout his life. In one of his books, Boone refers to himself (the father) as the "CEO," and his wife as a "VP." Boone's 1957 film *Bernadine* included gratuitous product placement for Coca Cola, and even specific references to the drink in the dialogue.

Along with *Bernadine*, Boone starred in another illustrative 1957 film, *April Love*, which extolled clean and obedient lifestyles for teens, as opposed to a life of rock and roll degeneracy and juvenile delinquency. His character, Nick, is a city boy obsessed with hot rods and driving too fast. After being caught "joyriding," part of Nick's probation is to stay with some of his family out in the country for a while, in hopes that this will settle him down. In one scene, strict but wise old Uncle Jed callously and mindlessly rides Nick for not being more responsible. Nick *almost* speaks out, but he quickly falls back in line. Later, Nick seeks to apologize to Uncle Jed for having *almost* rebelled.

Whatever might have been troubling young Nick before he committed his joyriding crime is never addressed. Nick's lesson is that if you follow your elders' directions, you will be successful. In this case, Nick wins the big harness race at the fair and falls in love. Any other problems or questions a teen in the late 1950s might have are ignored.

As for morality or confusing feelings regarding relationships and sexuality, Boone's religious beliefs and married status made him uncomfortable kissing a woman on screen.[50] In *Bernadine*, Boone sang his hit "Love Letters in the Sand" by himself in the boys' clubhouse, and in *April Love* Boone and love interest Shirley Jones never actually kiss, although Jones' character sneaks a kiss onto his cheek and they *almost* kiss on a Ferris wheel.

There was a bright side of sorts to the corporatization of rock. Once again, it was undoubtedly going to take white artists to be recognized by white gatekeepers before the mass white audience would ever embrace black rock and rollers. To his credit, Boone showed more socially conservative, white audiences that rock and roll really was not so alien, nor always so immoral, thus paving the way for broader acceptance. In fact, Little Richard and Fats Domino themselves have acknowledged the positive impact of Boone. In the late 1960s, at a show in New Orleans, Domino brought Pat

Boone onstage with him, pointing to a diamond ring on his own finger and joking that Boone had bought the ring for him.[51]

Despite Clark and Boone's successes, white consumers soon realized that they were being sold weak imitations of what really spoke to them. In 1955, Little Richard put out his raucous "Long Tall Sally," a song so beyond what his imitators could even attempt to re-create that the original outsold Boone's version, marking the beginning of the end of that phase of rock. Still, by the conclusion of the 1950s corporate interests had created a rock and roll market that was becoming, overall, tame and rather bland.[52]

Eventually, attempts to depict rock music as dangerous and rock musicians as villains largely backfired. Whatever one thought of the music, attempts to demonize individuals like Elvis Presley fell flat. In interviews, Presley could hardly come across as anything less than sincere, respectful, or polite. Not only were these "crazed hillbillies" and "wild Negroes" maybe not such bad influences on America's youth, but it also became impossible to avoid one obvious conclusion: they *were* America's youth.

Presley's third performance on Ed Sullivan's show in 1957 was restricted in that the camera only showed his upper body (to spare America the sight of his swiveling hips). By the end of that show, however, Sullivan addressed the audience as follows: "This is a real decent, fine boy. We've never had a pleasanter experience on our show with a big name than we've had with you.... You're thoroughly all right."[53] Frank Sinatra, too, would quickly change his mind, becoming a fan of rock music and performing with Presley on TV after Presley's return from the army, and later covering songs by the Beatles and other rock musicians.

Rock and roll encountered other roadblocks in the late 1950s, seriously calling into question whether it would be anything more than a passing (albeit highly successful) fad. By 1960, the biggest of the pioneering rock stars were already out of the limelight for various reasons: Presley, of course, was in the army, and Chuck Berry was convicted under the (selectively prosecuted) Mann Act after a young woman who had come with him across state lines to work in his nightclub turned out to be sixteen and a prostitute. Jerry Lee Lewis was mired in scandal for marrying his thirteen-year-old first cousin. Little Richard was doing gospel. Carl Perkins was injured in a car crash on the way to a crucial TV performance, effectively sidelining him (later he was further sidetracked by alcoholism). Buddy Holly, Ritchie Valens, and the Big Bopper all died in 1959. And, finally, in 1960, Gene Vincent and Eddie Cochran were in a car accident in London, badly injuring Vincent and taking the life of Cochran.[54]

It is an alarming sequence of events. Yet the impact of the first wave of rock and rollers had only just begun to reverberate. In many ways rock and roll's critics were on point: the music was sometimes thoughtless, unrefined, overindulgent, and, of course, *primitive*. But the whole point of rock was to be primitive—that was precisely what so many were longing for. Despite all of the genre's substantial faults, the music provided an enormous public service. Rock spoke to that dark, empty place of alienation and anxiety that was only becoming more pronounced, just as Louis B. Seltzer noted in his op-ed in the *Cleveland Press* and as President Truman had noted in his State of the Union. The great rock and rollers were able to experience that anxiety, and, instead of suppressing or ignoring it, they gave it a voice. Otherwise, what good were institutions and popular music that could not adequately accommodate self-expression or allow for challenging a failing status quo? In 1956 *Cash Box* was so stunned by rock and roll's meteoric ascent that it declared that rock could be a "great unifying force" in society.[55] Rock and roll certainly had incredible numbers of followers, and it would solidify much of America's youth culture into the 1960s and beyond. Yet the genre also ended up on one side of a dividing line in the nation's most divisive era since the Civil War.

Rock music and its attendant attitude and culture provided direction and language for youth looking for alternatives to the norms and institutions of their parents. Sexual feelings would no longer be ignored; moral hypocrisies would be challenged and illegal drugs used; institutionalized segregation was out; military service and the military-industrial complex would no longer be blindly served; and alternatives to both corporate ideals and traditional religions were to be explored. Those new directions saw varying levels of success—and failure—over the decades that followed. Rock did not necessarily have all of the answers, but it was absolutely necessary.

The thriving leftist folk scene of the 1950s (exemplified by Lead Belly, Woody Guthrie, Pete Seeger, and Lonnie Donagan and skiffle music in England) would likewise be transformed in the rock era, becoming another direct influence on 1960s rock. By the early 1960s, the new folk scene provided another deeply rooted American art form and helped create a political soundtrack for a youth movement.

Philadelphian Chubby Checker was featured on Dick Clark's *Bandstand*, launching a national dance craze and loosening up young and old white America's hips with "The Twist."[56] Hard-rocking garage bands, epitomized by "Louie, Louie" and the Troggs' "Wild Thing," found their footing as well. Across the Atlantic, a generation of young Brits couldn't get enough of American blues, R&B and rock and roll records. Those influences were absorbed and brought back to the U.S. in the form of the British Invasion, marked by the arrival of Beatlemania in 1964 on *The Ed Sullivan Show*.

The Beatles' connection to those early years can be encapsulated in their 1964 hit, "Can't Buy Me Love." The song is indebted to the blues and Chuck Berry, but it is also written in the more traditional Buddy Holly style. Additionally, George Harrison's guitar riffs and solo are pulled directly from idol Carl Perkins' rockabilly songbook, and, vocally, Paul McCartney channels some of the spiritual energy and sexuality of Little Richard. In fact, if you want to know where the Beatles got their overwhelming joy and energy from every time they shrieked and shook their mop tops, look no further than an early (1964) cover of "Long Tall Sally." Little Richard taught the Beatles how to blow it out, much like people did back in the Southern, black churches. Combining all of the above, the Beatles practically took over the world. Fellow Brits, such as the Rolling Stones, the Who, Pink Floyd, David Bowie, Eric Clapton, the Kinks, the Yardbirds, the Animals, the Dave Clark Five, and more, were all right behind them.

Conclusion

Rock and roll has, of course, evolved and changed in myriad ways since 1960, dominating the pop music charts and pop culture for decades. Although the rebellious music was not immune to corporatization, the movement continued to be an enormous force, and it has been deeply intertwined with many of the social, political and cultural issues of the times. Rock would continue to reinvent and reinvigorate itself, regularly and organically, through various major movements, including soul, glam, funk, reggae, punk, rap, indie rock, grunge and so on, and spawning hundreds of sub-genres, from ambient rock, to Brit pop, to symphonic black metal. But *that* story is a whole other book.

The impact of this *initial* explosion of rock and roll reverberated across the world, and it is still being felt, for both good and ill—but mostly good. The new rock and roll ethos facilitated a fresh approach to life, with little regard for the establishment's existing mores and institutions—a new era of individual expression, self-actualization and personal freedom, along with some recklessness, overindulgence, and, at times, devastating self-destruction. Rock and roll has significant shortcomings, namely, a lack of structure, limits, and, quite possibly, moral direction, but, beyond being fantastic entertainment, rock has allowed its fans both to feel and to connect with one another, despite times of severely repressed emotions and rampant alienation. Four more short vignettes will hopefully capture some of that impact.

Mystery Train

In his 1989 film *Mystery Train*, director Jim Jarmusch explored themes of dislocation, the allure of Elvis Presley, and Memphis, through three separate stories. Each story takes place in one evening in and around a tired, rundown hotel on a forgotten Memphis block. The film is named for Presley's 1955 cover of the 1953 song written and performed by Junior Parker. Both versions were recorded at Sun studio. Many consider this song one of Presley's finest moments: haunting (and enhanced by the Sun echo), thrilling, distinctly bluesy but with a rockabilly beat, and Presley putting everything on the line and whooping it up at the end like the hillbilly that he was.

The song title itself is a bit of a mystery, as the phrase "mystery train" never appears in the song itself. The first verse references the singer riding the train that is also taking his girl away. The second verse mentions the girl being taken away (possibly referring to death?). In the final verse, the train is bringing his girl home. The song seems to collectively capture the not-sure-if-one-is-coming-or-leaving dislocation of the rails, loss, Memphis, and the Delta. It can all be sad and confusing, especially if one is not feeling grounded and with direction in life. But the song can also be about a fresh start—something exciting, freeing, and full of promise. "Mystery Train" is thus a sort of mini-parable for a fast-changing and strange twentieth century.

One of Jarmusch's three stories features two Japanese tourists, both rockabilly fanatics. The late-teen girl, Mitsuko, is as perky as her eighteen-year-old boyfriend, Jun, is depressed. Mitsuko constantly tries to brighten Jun's mood, but to no avail. She is a die-hard Presley fan, whereas he cannot stand Presley (apparently one can become oversaturated with Presley in Japan as well). Jun wants to go to Graceland first but only to get it out of the way. He is a fan of Carl Perkins and all of the early rock stars *except* Presley.

Jun does not feel any better after visiting any of Memphis' tourist destinations or buying a souvenir to show his friends back home. Jun doesn't even take pictures of the places they visit; he explains that he will remember those places without photos. Instead, Jun takes pictures of the inside of the hotel room: the bed, the alarm clock. The real world.

As the pair walk around downtown Memphis, the lethargic Jun tells his girlfriend that the relatively spread-out Memphis is exactly like their unexciting hometown of Yokohama, except "minus sixty percent of the buildings." That night, Jun stares out the window at empty streets while a train rolls by. Now, he decides, Memphis is not Yokohama, because, unlike Yokohama, "It feels cool to be eighteen and in Memphis."

What finally clicks for Jun is the realization that he is feeling precisely the same sense of malaise and alienation in Memphis that he did in Yokohama—and that is precisely what those rock and rollers had felt when they walked the same Memphis streets. They were not superhuman; they were just like him. Jun knows this to be true because he felt it through the music that spoke deeply and directly to him. His deep feelings are finally validated; he is not alone. In that shared alienation and angst, the music can transcend it all. That is part of the magic of rock and roll. So long as people are feeling marginalized, disconnected and anxious, rock can provide a kind of cure.

"Jenny"

The designations used in the title of this book—"Devil's music," "holy rollers" and "hillbillies"—are all pejoratives, or at least each was originally intended as such. Each term was used to mock those on the fringes of respectable American society. These were the outcasts that would bring rock and roll to the forefront and beautifully expressed some long-repressed aspects of the American psyche.

More classic testimony to the special qualities of rock comes in the 1970 Velvet Underground song "Rock & Roll," written by group singer Lou Reed. Reed has said that the song is essentially his own story, though here it is told through the eyes of a girl named Jenny.[1] It is a fairly simple, gritty, and swinging homage to early rock. Reed sings that already by the age of five, Jenny was stuck in a malaise that she assumes will be her life story. But eventually rock music comes to her through a New York radio station, and, just like that, Jenny goes from a bleak worldview to dancing to a brand new sound.

The simplicity of the story (Reed repeats the same verses twice) only enhances the power of both the message and a relatively simple but emotionally resonant music. Jenny's new reality is that through this music she can get past her old barriers, be more spontaneous, and know that her life may actually be okay. Whatever is in store for Jenny in her life, it is certainly better than not feeling alive.

Roots

Rock music permanently altered popular music with regard to race, and the integration and cross-pollination of music between white and black artists continued long past the initial surge. Yet major divisions remained. This was also reflected in the rest of society, of course, such as with a continued "white flight" from the cities to the suburbs and both *de facto* and illegal segregation and "redlining" in the cities.[2] While popular music was transformed across the board by the rock revolution, new genres, such as Motown, funk, and soul music, would be seen as "black" genres, while country, folk, garage and psychedelic were seen as "white" genres. The term *rock* itself has become largely associated with white folks, and specifically long-haired white guys with guitars, and less with the interracial amalgamation it began as.

The word "rock" thus developed two distinct definitions. The first definition is simply an abbreviation of "rock and roll," which can refer to everything that has occurred between the original commercial breakout from the mid–1950s to the present. This initial timeframe began with previously mentioned recordings such as "Hound Dog," "Tutti Frutti," "Johnny B. Goode," "Blue Suede Shoes," and "Great Balls of Fire." So much of popular music since that time can be seen as lying at least partly under this enormous umbrella, whether called pop, soul, or whatever. Rock music allowed for the melding of genres, a new beat, and a new swaggering attitude. Thus, although James Brown is regularly referred to as the Godfather of Soul, he is still rock and roll and was a no-brainer inductee into the Rock and Roll Hall of Fame. "The King of Pop" (Michael Jackson), "The King of Country" (Johnny Cash), and arguably country superstar Garth Brooks all fall under the *rock* heading. Even many of the pure pop stars from the hit TV show *American Idol* (2002–2016), including Carrie Underwood and Kelly Clarkson, fall under it.

A second, newer definition of the term "rock" characterizes what is effectively a sub-genre of the original rock and roll movement. This second use emerged in the aftermath of the British Invasion and 1960s guitar-based rock, often played by white men with long hair, and all heavily indebted to Chuck Berry. This alternative definition speaks of a genre that still clearly falls under the original classification but runs parallel to other sub-genres. (The term can be broken down even further, including "modern rock," meaning post–Beatles [or at least post–*Sgt. Pepper's Lonely Hearts Club Band*], "album-oriented rock," and so on but that is not necessary for the purposes of this book.)

In the mid–1980s, the re-segregation of popular music had in many ways hit bottom. MTV sprang up in 1981 and, for various reasons, excluded black performers for its first few years. Since the 1970s, hard, traditional "rock" had less to do with dancing, while dance music (like disco, funk, and soul) was more synonymous with black artists. There were so few African Americans engaged in this version of rock that a group led by guitarist Vernon Reid of Living Color formed specifically to provide support for black "rock" artists.[3]

Still, the roots of all of the above genres can be traced back to the initial breakthrough. That first era was a musical crucible through which the previous, often disparate genres of popular music all passed. They came out the other side transformed, and from there a multitude of sub-genres were created anew.

Consider a short-lived rock band from Toronto in 1964 named the Mynah Birds. The group began by covering songs from early rock and R&B masters. The young band's recordings especially reflect the influence of the early work of the Rolling Stones, whose style was directly derived from some jazz rhythms, the Delta blues, Sun Records, and Chess Records. The Mynahs' singer, Ricky James, who happened to be African American where the rest of the band was white, came from across the border in Buffalo. James was strongly influenced by the Stones' Mick Jagger; Jagger, in turn, had been, ironically (or not), considered by many to "sound black."[4]

The young Mynahs had serious talent, and even more so after bringing in a new lead guitarist in early 1966: Neil Young. That same year the Mynahs signed a deal with Motown in Detroit, and an album was cut. Unfortunately, when James had left Buffalo, he had also left the U.S. Navy. The FBI came and picked him up in Toronto later that year and took him back to the U.S. James and Young had a strong personal and professional bond, and they had even lived together for a time. The Mynahs lasted a little longer after James' departure, but their recordings were eventually shelved by Motown.[5]

Nonetheless, the individual members of the Mynah Birds did, in fact, go on to great things. Drummer Nick Nicholas went on to play in the hugely successful classic rock band, Steppenwolf, best known for the proto-metal, rock anthem, "Born to Be Wild." Bassist Bruce Palmer and Neil Young went to California and formed the folk-rock supergroup Buffalo Springfield. Young, who became one of rock's iconic figures and one of its greatest songwriters, later played with folk-rock giants Crosby, Stills, Nash, and Young before embarking on a hugely successful solo career. Young's future, heavier musical output (particularly when backed by the heavy roots rock band Crazy Horse) also led to him becoming known as the "Godfather of Grunge." The grunge genre, which took off in Seattle in the early 1990s (e.g., Pearl Jam, Nirvana, and Soundgarden), comprised aspects of punk, hard rock, and heavy metal.

Ricky James dropped the "y" and became superstar Rick James, one of funk's biggest figures. James was best known for the monster hit, genre-defining and Grammy-winning "Super Freak" (1981). James was also a successful songwriter and producer for notable soul/pop Motown acts, including the Temptations and Teena Marie.[6] Of course, funk is one of the "blackest" genres of all; James called his style "punk-funk."[7] Yet all of the former Mynahs indeed had much the same roots in that initial wave of integrated rock.

Bringing Noise in the Free World

The advent of the black-defined genre of rap in the mid–1970s, and its ascension to mass popularity in the 1980s, raised more racial classification questions. In the mid–1980s, rappers Public Enemy expanded on the style and music of the first wave of rap. The group's ground-breaking production crew, the Bomb Squad, took production and song sampling to new levels of artistry and sophistication. The group also hardened the sound of rap, politicized their lyrics, and visually presented a menacing, Black Panther–influenced stage show. The wall of noise, the infusion of politics and anger, and the menacing tone marked a whole new era of protest music.

Public Enemy's sound was made up of a collage of agitating noise, as well as samples of funk guitar riffs and drum beats (often taken from James Brown and his band). The result is intensely rapped vocals and often unsettling, effects-heavy music, with a deep funk undertone. It is a stark, in-your-face challenge to the American status quo.

In their 1987 song, "Bring the Noise," Chuck D delivers his rapid-fire baritone, offset by the wild humor of Flava Flav. The song is intense and noisy enough to be punk, but with a complex layering of sounds. It also feels like heavy metal (they later built a song around a riff borrowed from thrash metal band Slayer), with its frenzied intensity.

Rap and rock had already crossed streams, most notably when the rap stars Run DMC, who regularly sampled rock guitar riffs, had a hit cover and collaboration with Aerosmith on the latter's "Walk This Way," in 1986. Yet "Walk This Way" felt more like a fun, one-off experiment than a new genre. "Bring the Noise" was different.

Heavy metal and the black, urbanized experience of rap, in particular, at that time had relatively few fans in common. The former worshipped the electric guitar; the latter did not even play guitars, relying instead on a deejay spinning and cutting records on two turntables, and an emcee not even singing but rapping.

A few years after the initial release of "Bring the Noise," Chuck D happened to notice another successful thrash metal band, Anthrax, who were known to be fans of Public Enemy. Anthrax had already done one collaboration with rappers U.T.F.O., and even recorded their own jokey but reverential rap song, "I'm the Man" (1987). In 1991, Chuck D reached out to Anthrax, and the two groups got together to record a new version of "Bring the Noise." The wall of heavy funk combined with the contagious intensity of Anthrax was a perfect fit. The groups made a popular live-performance music video of the song for MTV, as well, and followed that up with a successful co-headlining world tour.

In "Bring the Noise," Public Enemy's message is as "rock and roll" as anything else. In essence, the title is a call to speak truth to power, even if you have been politically marginalized, even if your culture's icons are ignored, and even if the music you love is dismissed as a novelty. What is important is to find your voice, speak out, and keep bringing the noise. Thus the rock ethos can inspire or simply agitate in the face of power. It can be a cure for lethargy and passivity.

Neil Young's anthem, "Keep on Rockin' in the Free World" (1989), is in the same vein. Young wrote the song long before 9/11, but here Young comments on U.S. indifference to a hatred being engendered toward it in foreign nations, as well as gross inequalities existing within the U.S. itself.

On the one hand, the song is overtly political and particularly draws attention to the plight of the poor and the oppressed. Young is highly critical of then-president, George H.W. Bush, mocking his well-known "thousand points of light" speech, the state of American social justice, the lack of effectiveness in dealing with the crack cocaine epidemic of the 1980s, and a persistent overreliance on the military-industrial complex to solve problems. Yet Young also explicitly calls out the Democratic Party, specifically referencing and mocking the Reverend Jesse Jackson's "Keep Hope Alive" motto.

Even if Young does not necessarily lay out a detailed political plan of action, he has a political message. His intensity, wild guitar solo, and relentless title-chorus are an all-out assault on complacency and a demand for action—not just the mouthing of otherwise empty rhetoric about "points of light" and "hope." The music gets listeners' attention, for sure, and it certainly did wake some people up, and that is a lot. Also of note, in Young's acclaimed and incendiary live performance of this song on the TV show *Saturday Night Live* (1975–present) in 1989, he sported an Elvis Presley T-shirt.

* * *

In sum, rock and roll music helps fans get in touch with that place deep within themselves that no one else can touch, repress or manipulate—thus allowing them to feel more alive. I would even be so bold as to suggest that rock and roll fits into a long arc of Western history in which so-called rebels carve out a place for themselves despite establishment pressures and artificial societal divisions: from Protestantism, to the American republic, to Romanticism, to Pentecostalism, to jazz, to the civil rights movement, to rock and roll. This is a process meant to better afford each individual an autonomous existence and unrestrained voice at the deepest and most personal of levels. It is a narrative that is still playing out today.

Rock and roll is, at its best, an inclusive, mostly pure expression of an irrepressible spirit set to music. Few things can be more relevant than that. The Great American Experiment, with all of its imperfections, has facilitated and allowed this movement to happen, transcending numerous boundaries along the way.

Chapter Notes

Introduction

1. Mark Haefeli, dir. *Paul McCartney in Red Square*. A&E Home Video, 2003. DVD.
2. Alexis de Tocqueville and Harvey Claflin Mansfield. *Democracy in America*. Chicago: University of Chicago Press, 2000. 184.
3. David Willey. "Vatican 'Forgives' John Lennon." *BBC News*. November 22, 2008. Accessed July 28, 2015.
4. Robert E. Voorst. "Ritual." In *Anthology of World Scriptures*. 6th ed. Australia: Thomson Wadsworth, 2008. 158.
5. "You Can't Kill Rock and Roll." Official Ozzy Osbourne Site. Accessed October 5, 2015. http://www.ozzy.com/us/music/diary-madman/you-cant-kill-rock-and-roll.
6. Harvey Cox. *Fire from Heaven: The Rise of Pentecostal Spirituality and the Reshaping of Religion in the 21st Century*. Cambridge, Mass.: Da Capo Press, 2009. 59.
7. "Sister Rosetta Tharpe—Up Above My Head." YouTube. Accessed October 5, 2015. https://www.youtube.com/watch?v=JeaBNAXfHfQ.
8. Gayle Wald. *Shout, Sister, Shout! The Untold Story of Rock-and-Roll Trailblazer Sister Rosetta Tharpe*. Boston: Beacon Press, 2007. 86.
9. "Pennsylvania Governor Rendell Proclaims Sister Rosetta Tharpe Day on January 11, 2008 to Honor the Gospel Music Legend." *WebWire*. January 2, 2008. Accessed October 5, 2015. http://www.webwire.com/ViewPressRel.asp?aId=56002.
10. Charles White. *The Life and Times of Little Richard: The Authorised Biography*. 3rd ed. London: Omnibus Press, 2003. 17; "CNN Larry King Live Family Members and Country Stars Remember Johnny Cash." CNN. November 11, 2003. Accessed October 5, 2015. http://www.cnn.com/TRANSCRIPTS/0311/11/lkl.00.html; and "Johnny Cash Accepts Induction." Rock and Roll Hall of Fame. Accessed October 5, 2015. https://rockhall.com/inductees/johnny-cash/transcript/johnny-cash-accepts-induction/?flavour=full.
11. Wald, 88.
12. Ibid., 82.
13. Ibid., 82 and 143.
14. Ibid., 70.
15. Ibid., 69, fn38.
16. Ibid., 70, fn36.
17. "Sleepy Labeef Rocks and Rumbles with Honky-tonk Authenticity." *Chicago Tribune*. October 31, 1985. Accessed October 12, 2015.
18. Cox, 58, 68–71.
19. Bobbie Gillespie. "Chuck Berry: Hail. Hail, Rock'n'roll." *The Guardian*. January 23, 2010. Accessed July 28, 2015. http://www.theguardian.com/music/2010/jan/24/chuck-berry-bobby-gillespie.
20. Henry Ford Sr. *The International Jew: Being an Abridged Version of a Series of Articles*. Johannesburg: Global Publishers, 1997. 163; and Michael T. Bertrand. *Race, Rock, and Elvis*. Urbana: University of Illinois Press, 2000. 51.
21. "Primitive." *Merriam-Webster*. Accessed July 29, 2015. http://www.merriam-webster.com/dictionary/primitive.
22. Dwight D. Eisenhower. "Radio and Television Address to the American People on the State of the Nation." April 5, 1954. Online by Gerhard Peters and John T.

Woolley, American Presidency Project. Accessed July 28, 2015. http://www.presidency.ucsb.edu/ws/?pid=10201.

Chapter 1

1. Robert Palmer. *Rock & Roll: An Unruly History*. New York: Harmony Books, 1995. 16.
2. Glenn C. Altschuler. *All Shook Up: How Rock 'n' Roll Changed America*. Oxford: Oxford University Press, 2003. 9.
3. W.H. Auden. *The Age of Anxiety: A Baroque Eclogue*. New York: Random House, 1947.
4. Quoted in Eric Frederick Goldman. *The Crucial Decade: America, 1945–1955*. New York: Knopf, 1956. 218.
5. Ibid.
6. Ibid.
7. "People: The Younger Generation." *Time*. November 5, 1951. Accessed November 15, 2015. http://content.time.com/time/subscriber/article/0,33009,856950,00.html.
8. Ibid.
9. Ibid.
10. Ibid.
11. Ibid.
12. Ibid.
13. "The 'War to End All Wars,' 100 Years Later." *CBS News*. Accessed August 4, 2015. http://www.cbsnews.com/news/the-war-to-end-all-wars-100-years-later/.
14. Paul Battersby and Joseph M. Siracusa. *Globalization and Human Security*. Lanham, Md.: Rowman & Littlefield, 2009. 10–11.
15. Battersby and Siracusa, 150; Lawrence Sondhaus. *World War I: The Global Revolution*. Cambridge: Cambridge University Press, 2011. 31.
16. Battersby and Siracusa, 11.
17. "Destruction at Hiroshima—Japanese Reports." *The Guardian*. August 9, 1945. Accessed November 15, 2015. http://www.theguardian.com/century/1940-1949/Story/0,,127720,00.
18. U.S. Department of Energy. Office of History & Heritage Resources. *The Manhattan Project: An Interactive History*. "The Atomic Bombing of Hiroshima." Accessed May 15, 2010. https://www.osti.gov/opennet/manhattan-project-history/Events/1945/hiroshima.htm.
19. ACHRE Report. "The Aftermath of Hiroshima and Nagasaki: The Emergence of the Cold War Radiation Research Bureaucracy." Accessed August 3, 2015. https://ehss.energy.gov/ohre/roadmap/achre/intro_6.html.
20. David Halberstam. *The Fifties*. Reprint ed. New York: Ballantine Books, 1994.
21. Ibid., 26.
22. Center for Defense Information. "U.S. Military Spending, 1945–1996." Accessed November 27, 2010. http://academic.brooklyn.cuny.edu/history/johnson/milspend.htm.
23. Halberstam, 98.
24. Einstein interview with Alfred Werner, published in *Liberal Judaism* 16 (April–May 1949), as cited in Ralph Keyes. *The Quote Verifier: Who Said What, Where, and When*. New York: St. Martin's Press, 2006. 284.
25. Robert Pattison. *The Triumph of Vulgarity: Rock Music in the Mirror of Romanticism*. New York: Oxford University Press, 1987. 19. Quoting William Barrett. *Irrational Man: A Study in Existential Philosophy*. New York: Doubleday, 1958. 145.
26. Daniel Smith. "It's Still the 'Age of Anxiety.' Or Is It?" *New York Times*. January 14, 2012. Accessed August 3, 2015. http://opinionator.blogs.nytimes.com/2012/01/14/its-still-the-age-of-anxiety-or-is-it/?_r=0.
27. Leo Tolstoy. *The Kingdom of God Is Within You. What Is Art? What Is Religion?* New York: T.Y. Crowell, 1899.
28. "Sermon on the Mount." In *A Dictionary of the Bible*. Edited by W. R. F. Browning. Oxford Biblical Studies Online. Accessed August 6, 2015. http://www.oxfordbiblicalstudies.com/article/opr/t94/e1725.
29. Pub.L. 83-396, Chap. 297, 68 Stat. 249, H.J.Res. 243, enacted June 14, 1954.
30. U.S. Department of the Treasury. "History of 'In God We Trust.'" Accessed November 6, 2011. https://www.treasury.gov/about/education/Pages/in-god-we-trust.aspx.
31. Terry Whalin. *Billy Graham: A Biography of America's Greatest Evangelist*. New York: Morgan James, 2015. xv.

32. Angela M. Lahr. *Millennial Dreams and Apocalyptic Nightmares: The Cold War Origins of Political Evangelicalism*. New York: Oxford University Press, 2007. 33–36.

33. Kevin Rafferty, dir. *The Atomic Cafe*. Docurama, 2003. DVD.

34. Ibid.

35. Ibid.

36. Ibid.

37. Doug Gilford's Mad Cover Site, http://www.madcoversite.com/mad030.html.

38. "When Debates First Flowered." *Washington Times*. August 6, 2015. Accessed August 9, 2015. http://www.washingtontimes.com/news/2015/aug/6/editorial-harold-stassen-was-a-true-debater/.

39. Halberstam, 617.

40. PBS, Nova Online, http://www.pbs.org/wgbh/nova/venona/dece_hiss.html.

41. John Philip Jenkins. "Julius Rosenberg and Ethel Rosenberg | Biography—American Spies." *Encyclopedia Britannica Online*. Accessed August 9, 2015.

42. Arthur Herman. *Joseph McCarthy: Reexamining the Life and Legacy of America's Most Hated Senator*. New York: Free Press, 2000. 51.

43. Ibid., 220.

44. "Congress Passes Communist Control Act." History.com. Accessed August 9, 2015. http://www.history.com/this-day-in-history/congress-passes-communist-control-act.

45. Wiener, Time, "U.S. Tells How It Cracked Code of A-Bomb Spy Ring" Published: July 12, 1995 http://www.nytimes.com/1995/07/12/us/us-tells-how-it-cracked-code-of-a-bomb-spy-ring.htm; Andrew, Christopher M., and Vasili Mitrokhin. *The Sword and the Shield: The Mitrokhin Archive and the Secret History of the KGB*, 591. New York: Basic Books, 1999 .

46. Herman, 189–90.

47. Michael McKenna. *Real People and the Rise of Reality Television*. Lanham, Md.: Rowman & Littlefield, 2015. xxv.

48. "Joseph McCarthy Dies." History.com. Accessed August 9, 2015. http://www.history.com/this-day-in-history/joseph-mccarthy-dies.

49. "The History of the Office of the Secretary of the Defense, Vol. III: Strategy, Money, and the New Look, 1953–1956." 2001. Accessed August 9, 2015. http://history.defense.gov/Portals/70/Documents/secretaryofdefense/OSDSeries_Vol3.pdf.

50. "Korean War." History.com. Accessed August 9, 2015. http://www.history.com/topics/korean-war.

Chapter 2

1. Christopher Conte and Albert R. Karr. "Outline of the U.S. Economy." Accessed August 9, 2015. http://usa.usembassy.de/etexts/oecon/chap3.htm.

2. Halberstam, 117.

3. Ibid., 135.

4. Ibid., 132.

5. Ibid., 136.

6. John Keats. *The Crack in the Picture Window*. Boston: Houghton Mifflin, 1957. 7.

7. Halberstam, 141.

8. Ibid., 127.

9. Ibid., 123.

10. Ibid.

11. James T. Patterson. *Grand Expectations: The United States, 1945–1974*. New York: Oxford University Press, 1996. 316.

12. U.S. Department of Transportation, Federal Highway Administration, Highway Statistics 2003.

13. Kenneth T. Jackson. *Crabgrass Frontier: The Suburbanization of the United States*. New York: Oxford University Press, 1985. 4.

14. Daniel Gross. "Ray Kroc, McDonald's, and the Fast-food Industry." *Forbes Greatest Business Stories of All Time*. Accessed August 9, 2015. http://www.wiley.com/legacy/products/subject/business/forbes/kroc.pdf.

15. Halberstam, 171.

16. John C. Stauber. "Smoke and Mirrors: How Tobacco and PR Grew Up Together." PRWatch.org. 2004. Accessed August 9, 2015. http://www.prwatch.org/files/pdfs/prwatch/PRWatchQtrlyVol1No4.pdf.

17. Ibid.

18. Ibid.

19. Ibid.

20. Gene Borio. "Tobacco Timeline: The Twentieth Century 1950–1999." Tobacco BBS. Accessed October 17, 2015. http://

archive.tobacco.org/resources/history/Tobacco_History20-2.html.

21. "Stanford Research into the Impact of Tobacco Advertising." Stanford Research into the Impact of Tobacco Advertising. Accessed October 17, 2015. http://tobacco.stanford.edu/tobacco_main/images.php?token2=fm_st042.php&token1=fm_img1055.php&theme_file=fm_mt013.php&theme_name=Women's Cigarettes&subtheme_name=Marlboro.

22. Ibid.

23. Ibid.

24. Adrian Shirk. "The Real Marlboro Man." *The Atlantic*. February 17, 2015. Accessed August 9, 2015. http://www.theatlantic.com/business/archive/2015/02/the-real-marlboro-man/385447/.

25. "Meet the Real 'Mad Men': Leo Burnett." *Fortune*. Accessed August 9, 2015. http://archive.fortune.com/galleries/2009/fortune/0908/gallery.real_mad_men.fortune/4.html.

26. Marie Brenner. "Jeffrey Wigand: The Man Who Knew Too Much." *Vanity Fair*. May 1, 1996. Accessed November 16, 2015. http://www.vanityfair.com/magazine/1996/05/wigand199605.

27. Borio, "Tobacco Timeline: The Twentieth Century 1950–1999."

28. David Riesman and Nathan Glazer. *The Lonely Crowd: A Study of the Changing American Character*. Abridged and rev. ed. New Haven, Conn.: Yale University Press, 2001. 8.

29. Sloan Wilson. *The Man in the Grey Flannel Suit*. New York: Simon & Schuster, 1955.

30. William Hollingsworth Whyte. *The Organization Man*. New York: Simon and Schuster, 1956.

31. "Number of TV Households in America." Last visited May 23, 2010. http://www.tvhistory.tv/Annual_TV_Households_50-78.JPG.

32. Stephanie Greco Larson. *Media & Minorities: The Politics of Race in News and Entertainment*. Lanham, Md.: Rowman & Littlefield, 2006. 22.

33. Steven D. Stark. *Glued to the Set: The 60 Television Shows and Events That Made Us Who We Are Today*. New York: Free Press, 1997. 110.

34. Gregory Curtis. "Leave Ozzie and Harriet Alone." *New York Times Magazine*. January 19, 1997. Last viewed June 14, 2010. http://www.nytimes.com/1997/01/19/magazine/leave-ozzie-and-harriet-alone.html.

35. Norman Vincent Peale. *The Power of Positive Thinking*. New York: Prentice-Hall, 1952.

36. George Vecsey. "Norman Vincent Peale, Preacher of Gospel Optimism, Dies at 95." *New York Times*. December 25, 1993. Accessed October 17, 2015.

37. Kirk Bjornsgaard. *The Encyclopedia of Christian Literature*. Edited by George Thomas Kurian and James D. Smith III. Lanham, Md.: Scarecrow Press, 2010. 515.

38. Gerhard Peters and John T. Woolley. "Ronald Reagan: Announcement of the Recipients of the Presidential Medal of Freedom." American Presidency Project. Accessed November 15, 2015. http://www.presidency.ucsb.edu/ws/?pid=39548.

39. Weekly Compilation of Presidential Documents (Date: January 3, 1994).

40. "The Religious Issue: Hot and Getting Hotter." *Newsweek*. September 19, 1960.

41. Eric Pace. "Benjamin Spock, World's Pediatrician, Dies at 94." *New York Times*. March 17, 1998. Accessed November 16, 2015. http://www.nytimes.com/learning/general/onthisday/bday/0502.html.

42. Michael S. Green and Scott L. Stabler. *Ideas and Movements That Shaped America: From the Bill of Rights to "Occupy Wall Street."* 3 vols. Santa Barbara, Calif.: ABC-CLIO, 2015.

43. Vecsey.

44. Daniel Murphy. "*The Power of Positive Thinking*—A Book for Today." January 31, 2011. Accessed August 15, 2015. DANIELRMURPHYCOM; see also Tim Challies. "The False Teachers: Norman Vincent Peale." Challies.com. April 2, 2014. Quoting John Krumm. Accessed October 17, 2015. http://www.challies.com/articles/the-false-teachers-norman-vincent-peale.

45. Peale, 113.

46. Ibid., 13.

47. Ibid.

48. Vecsey.

49. Ibid.

50. Green and Stabler.

51. Peale, 131–32.
52. Ibid., 50.
53. Ibid., 13.
54. Ibid., 110.
55. Murphy; see also Challies.
56. Peale, 212.
57. Kyle Eustice. "The Death of the Rock Star—Everyone's Sober Now." *Vice*. December 6, 2012. Accessed November 16, 2015. http://www.vice.com/read/the-death-of-the-rock-star.
58. *Alcoholics Anonymous: The Story of How Many Thousands of Men and Women Have Recovered from Alcoholism*. 3rd ed. New York: Alcoholics Anonymous World Services, 1976.
59. Halberstam, 272–75.
60. Ibid., 278.
61. R. Scott Appleby. *Catholics in the American Century: Recasting Narratives of U.S. History*. Ithaca, N.Y.: Cornell University Press, 2012. 92.
62. Michael S. Kimmel. *Manhood in America: A Cultural History*. New York: Free Press, 1996. 183.
63. Ibid., 252–55.
64. Steven Watts. *Mr. Playboy: Hugh Hefner and the American Dream*. Hoboken, N.J.: Wiley, 2008. 210.
65. Peter Conrad and Joseph W. Schneider. *Deviance and Medicalization: From Badness to Sickness*. St. Louis: Mosby, 1980. 61.
66. William E. Leuchtenburg. *A Troubled Feast: American Society since 1945*. Boston: Little, Brown, 1973. 778.
67. Molly Wellmann. *Handcrafted Cocktails: The Mixologist's Guide to Classic Drinks for Morning, Noon & Night*. Cincinnati: F+W Media, 2013. 59; and E. Freye. *Pharmacology and Abuse of Cocaine, Amphetamines, Ecstasy and Related Designer Drugs: A Comprehensive Review on Their Mode of Action, Treatment of Abuse and Intoxication*. Dordrecht: Springer, 2009. 112.
68. Paul McFedries. *Word Spy: The Word Lover's Guide to Modern Culture*. New York: Broadway Books, 2004. 169.
69. J.D. Salinger. *The Catcher in the Rye*. New York: Little, Brown, 2001. 19.
70. Todd Gitlin. *The Sixties: Years of Hope, Days of Rage*. Toronto: Bantam Books, 1987. 37–41.
71. Ibid.

Chapter 3

1. "Delta Blues." Allmusic.com. Accessed September 4, 2015. http://www.allmusic.com/style/delta-blues-ma0000002549.
2. James C. Cobb. *The Most Southern Place on Earth: The Mississippi Delta and the Roots of Regional Identity*. New York: Oxford University Press, 1992. 319
3. Ibid., 325.
4. http://www.britannica.com/place/Mississippi-state#ref1018485.
5. Cobb, 47.
6. Neil R. McMillen. *Dark Journey: Black Mississippians in the Age of Jim Crow*. Urbana: University of Illinois Press, 1989. xv.
7. Ibid., 5.
8. Ibid., 37.
9. Ibid., 37, fn7.
10. David M. Oshinsky. *Worse than Slavery: Parchman Farm and the Ordeal of Jim Crow Justice*. New York: Free Press, 1997. 52.
11. Cobb, inside cover.
12. Ibid., 155.
13. Ibid. (title of book)
14. Alan Lomax. *The Land Where the Blues Began*. New York: Pantheon Books, 1993. xv.
15. Ibid., 20.
16. Ibid.
17. Ibid., xv.
18. Ibid., 1.
19. William Ruhlman. "Lead Belly." Allmusic.com. Accessed November 15, 2015. http://allmusic.com/cg/amg.dll?p=amg&sql=11:jifqxq95ld0e~T1.
20. Lomax, 18–19 and 405.
21. Ibid., 17.
22. "Robert Johnson Biography." Rock and Roll Hall of Fame. Accessed October 6, 2015. http://rockhall.com/inductees/robert-johnson/bio/.
23. Lomax, 17.
24. Ibid., 16.
25. Ibid.
26. Barry Lee Pearson and Bill McCulloch. *Robert Johnson: Lost and Found*. Urbana: University of Illinois Press, 2003. 54.
27. Ibid., 14–15.
28. Ibid., 14.
29. Ibid., 49.
30. Ibid., 47.

31. Ibid., 48.

32. John Nova Lomax. "49 Experts Agree: That Third Photo of Robert Johnson Is Not Authentic." *Texas Monthly*. May 29, 2015. Accessed November 10, 2015. http://www.texasmonthly.com/the-daily-post/49-experts-agree-that-third-photo-of-robert-johnson-is-not-authentic/.

33. Steve Cheseborough. *Blues Traveling: The Holy Sites of Delta Blues*. 3rd ed. Jackson: University Press of Mississippi, 2009. 145–46.

34. Pearson and McCulloch, 54.

35. Ibid., 89.

36. Ibid., 92–93.

37. Ibid., 7. See also Elijah Wald. *Escaping the Delta: Robert Johnson and the Invention of the Blues*. New York: Amistad, 2004. 110.

38. Ibid., 9–10, 14, 16, and 59.

39. Greil Marcus. *Mystery Train: Images of America in Rock 'n' Roll Music*. New York: E.P. Dutton, 1975.

40. Pearson and McCulloch, 6–7; Elijah Wald, 110.

41. Pearson and McCulloch, 14.

42. "The 50 Albums That Changed Music." *The Guardian*. Accessed October 6, 2015.

43. Cobb, 284.

44. Pearson and McCulloch, 76–77.

45. Ibid.

46. Ibid., 84–85.

47. Elijah Wald, 176–79.

48. Ibid., 163 and 267.

49. Cobb, 289.

50. Ted Gioia. *Delta Blues: The Life and Times of the Mississippi Masters Who Revolutionized American Music*. New York: W.W. Norton, 2008. 164.

51. Pearson and McCulloch, 72.

52. Lomax, 139.

53. Trudier Harris. "The Trickster in African American Literature." TeacherServe®, National Humanities Center. Accessed November 8, 2015. http://nationalhumanitiescenter.org/tserve/freedom/1865-1917/essays/trickster.htm.

54. Lomax, 139.

55. Ibid.

56. Ibid., 58.

57. Ibid.

58. Ibid., xv.

Chapter 4

1. Adam Bernstein. "Historian Altered Understanding of Slavery." *Washington Post*. July 14, 2009. Accessed August 16, 2015. http://www.washingtonpost.com/wp-dyn/content/article/2009/07/13/AR2009071303130.html.

2. Ulrich Bonnell Phillips. *Life and Labor in the Old South*. Boston: Little, Brown, 1929.

3. "Ulrich Bonnell Phillips." World Heritage Encyclopedia. Accessed October 18, 2015. http://www.worldheritage.org/article/WHEBN0002718588/Ulrich%20Bonnell%20Phillips.

4. Ulrich Bonnell Phillips. *American Negro Slavery: A Survey of the Supply, Employment and Control of Negro Labor as Determined by the Plantation Regime*. Baton Rouge: Louisiana State University Press, 1966.

5. William L. Deburg. *Slavery & Race in American Popular Culture*. Madison: University of Wisconsin Press, 1984. 82.

6. Phillips, *American Negro Slavery*, 341–42.

7. George M. Fredrickson and Christopher Lasch. "Resistance to Slavery." *Civil War History* 13, no. 4 (1967). 315–29.

8. "Ulrich Bonnell Phillips," World Heritage Encyclopedia.

9. Phillips, *American Negro Slavery*, 287.

10. Ibid., viii.

11. "The Capture and Sale of Slaves." International Slavery Museum, Liverpool Museums. Accessed November 15, 2015. http://www.liverpoolmuseums.org.uk/ism/slavery/africa/capture_sale.aspx.

12. "Quick Guide: The Slave Trade." *BBC News*. March 15, 2007. Accessed November 15, 2015. http://news.bbc.co.uk/2/hi/africa/6445941.stm.

13. Amiri Baraka. *Blues People: Negro Music in White America*. New York: W. Morrow, 1963. 4.

14. Ibid., 2–3.

15. Ibid.

16. Ibid., 31.

17. Ibid., 25.

18. Ibid., 26.

19. Kenneth M. Stampp. *The Peculiar Institution: Slavery in the Ante-bellum South*. New York: Knopf, 1956. 361.

20. Ibid., 57–58.

21. James H. Cone. *The Spirituals and the Blues: An Interpretation.* New York: Seabury Press, 1972. 30.

22. Stampp, 187.

23. Ibid., 174 and 178.

24. Ibid., 144–45.

25. Ibid., 261.

26. Ibid., 146.

27. Ibid., 147.

28. Ibid., 198.

29. Ibid., 344.

30. Ibid., 343.

31. Ibid., 351.

32. Werner Sollors. *Interracialism: Black-White Intermarriage in American History, Literature, and Law.* Oxford: Oxford University Press, 2000. 128.

33. Cone, 27.

34. Ibid., 26.

35. Stampp, 109.

36. Samuel A. Cartwright. "Diseases and Peculiarities of the Negro Race." In *The Cause of the South: Selections from De Bow's Review, 1846–1867*, edited by Paul F. Paskoff, 26–43. Baton Rouge: Louisiana State University Press, 1982.

37. Howard Thurman. *Deep River and the Negro Spiritual Speaks of Life and Death.* Richmond, Ind.: Friends United Press, 1975. 16.

38. Stampp, 162.

39. Ibid., 158.

40. Ibid., 158–59.

41. Cone, 23.

42. Ibid., 63.

43. Virginia Writer's Program. *The Negro in Virginia.* New York: Arno Press, 1969. 109.

44. "In Song: Sounds of Slavery." NPR. January 7, 2008. Accessed October 18, 2015.

45. Baraka, 19.

46. Lawrence W. Levine. *The Unpredictable Past: Explorations in American Cultural History.* New York: Oxford University Press, 1993. 58.

47. Ibid., 54.

48. Cone, 12.

49. Levine, 52.

50. Ibid., 45.

51. Ibid., 50.

52. Thurman, 44.

53. Cone, 61.

54. Ibid., 17.

55. James Oliver Horton and Lois E. Horton. *Slavery and the Making of America.* Oxford: Oxford University Press, 2005. 45 and 125.

56. Official Site of the Negro Spirituals, Antique Gospel Music. Accessed August 16, 2015. http://www.negrospirituals.com.

57. Sterling A. Brown. "Negro Folk Expression: Spirituals, Seculars, Ballads and Work Songs." Modern American Poetry, Department of English, University of Illinois. Accessed August 16, 2015. http://www.english.illinois.edu/maps/poets/a_f/brown/folkexpression.htm.

58. "American Civil War." History.com. Accessed August 16, 2015. http://www.history.com/topics/american-civil-war.

59. "Today in History." Library of Congress. Accessed November 16, 2015. http://memory.loc.gov/ammem/today/apr14.html.

60. "Statistical Summary of America's Major Wars." Shotgun's Home of the American Civil War. Accessed August 16, 2015. http://www.civilwarhome.com/warstats.htm.

61. Ibid.

62. Richard Wormser. *The Rise & Fall of Jim Crow: The African-American Struggle against Discrimination, 1865–1954.* New York: Franklin Watts, 1999. 22.

63. "The Impeachment of Andrew Johnson." PBS. Accessed October 18, 2015. http://www.pbs.org/wgbh/americanexperience/features/general-article/grant-impeachment/.

64. "American Experience: Reconstruction [transcript]." PBS. Accessed August 16, 2015. http://www.pbs.org/wgbh/amex/reconstruction/players/ws1_10_b_tr_qry.html.

65. Vernon Lane Wharton. *The Negro in Mississippi: 1865–1890.* New York: Harper & Row, 1965. 60.

66. Oshinsky, 18.

67. Ibid., 14.

68. Ibid., 19.

69. John Hope Franklin and Alfred A. Moss. *From Slavery to Freedom: A History of African Americans.* 7th ed. New York: McGraw-Hill, 1994. 277.

70. "Capital and Moral Inheritance." *Squarely Rooted.* May 12, 2014. Accessed August 16, 2015. http://squarelyrooted.com/2014/05/12/1466/.

71. Franklin and Moss, 284–85.
72. Ibid., 281.
73. Ibid.
74. Gerald Early. "Jim Crow Era." PBS. Accessed November 12, 2015. http://www.pbs.org/jazz/time/time_jim_crow.htm.
75. Gunnar Myrdal. *An American Dilemma: The Negro Problem and Modern Democracy*. 20th anniversary ed. New York: Harper & Row, 1962. 561.
76. Wayne Flynt. *Poor But Proud: Alabama's Poor Whites*. Tuscaloosa: University of Alabama Press, 1989. 213.
77. Baraka, 52.
78. Kenneth F. Warren. *Encyclopedia of U.S. Campaigns, Elections, and Electoral Behavior*. Los Angeles: Sage, 2008. 17.
79. C. Vann Woodward. *The Strange Career of Jim Crow*. 3rd rev. ed. New York: Oxford University Press, 1974.
80. Baraka, 53.
81. "The Political Future of the South." *New York Times*. May 10, 1900. 6.
82. Franklin and Moss, 300.
83. U.S. Senate, *Congressional Record*, 56 Cong., I Sess., March 23, 1900, 3223–24.
84. "Booker T. Washington Delivers the 1895 Atlanta Compromise Speech." History Matters. Accessed October 18, 2015.
85. J.R. Pole. "Of Mr. Booker T. Washington and Others." *Historical Journal* (1974). 883.
86. W.E.B. Du Bois. "Of Mr. Booker T. Washington and Others." In *The Souls of Black Folk*. Charlottesville: University of Virginia Library, 1996. 25–36.
87. Randall Kennedy. *Nigger: The Strange Career of a Troublesome Word*. New York: Pantheon Books, 2002. 8.
88. Jesse J. Holland. "Blacks and the White House." *CBS News*. December 8, 2008. Accessed October 18, 2015. http://www.cbsnews.com/news/blacks-and-the-white-house/.

Chapter 5

1. Ken Burns, dir. *Jazz: A Film by Ken Burns*. PBS Home Video, 2004. DVD.
2. Max Jones. "On Blues." Our Blues. Accessed November 15, 2015. https://ourblues.files.wordpress.com/2011/11/jonepl46.pdf.
3. Giles Oakley. *The Devil's Music: A History of the Blues*. New York: Taplinger, 1977. 28.
4. Baraka, 25.
5. Jean Ferris. *America's Musical Landscape*. 4th ed. Boston: McGraw-Hill, 2002. 229.
6. Howard T. Weiner and N.J. Newark. *Early Twentieth-Century Brass Idioms: Art, Jazz, and Other Popular Traditions*. Lanham, Md.: Scarecrow Press, 2009. 134.
7. W.C. Handy and Arna Wendell Bontemps. *Father of the Blues: An Autobiography*. New York: Collier Books, 1941. 76–77.
8. Ibid.
9. Ibid.
10. Ibid., 87.
11. Ibid., 76–77.
12. "Early American Blues." Allmusic.com. Accessed August 16, 2015. http://www.allmusic.com/style/early-american-blues-ma0000011898.
13. "Blues." MSN Encarta. Accessed August 16, 2015. https://web.archive.org/web/20091028081817/http://encarta.msn.com/encyclopedia_761561248/Blues.html.
14. Reebee Garofalo. *Rockin' Out: Popular Music in the USA*. Boston: Allyn and Bacon, 1997. 44–47.
15. Baraka, 41.
16. "Blues," MSN Encarta.
17. "Down Hearted Blues Lyrics" (from Bessie Smith). Metro Lyrics. Accessed October 25, 2015. http://www.metrolyrics.com/down-hearted-blues-lyrics-bessie-smith.html.
18. "Blues," MSN Encarta.
19. Handy and Bontemps, 120.
20. Rob Bowman. "Crawdaddy Number Issue 23, Elvis Presley and the Impulse Towards Transculturation." Archive.is. 2000. Accessed August 16, 2015. https://archive.is/2ulWV.
21. Daniel E. Beaumont. *Preachin' the Blues: The Life and Times of Son House*. New York: Oxford University Press, 2011. 67.
22. "Classic Female Blues." Allmusic.com. Accessed October 18, 2015. http://www.allmusic.com/style/classic-female-blues-ma0000004403.
23. Paul Slade. "How Sex Turned the Blues Red Hot." *Telegraph*. September 13, 2007. Accessed October 18, 2015.

24. B.B. King and David Ritz. *Blues All Around Me: The Autobiography of B.B. King*. New York: Avon Books, 1996. 23.
25. Burns, *Jazz*.
26. Cone, 109.
27. Lomax, 106–11.
28. Cone, 109.
29. Cobb, 286.
30. Cone, 114.
31. Lomax, 121–25.
32. Cone, 102.
33. Ibid., 114.
34. Ibid., 100.
35. Ed Ward and Geoffrey Stokes. *Rock of Ages: The Rolling Stone History of Rock & Roll*. New York: Rolling Stone Press, 1986. 20.
36. Dr. Lewis Porter. "The Origins of the Word 'Jazz.'" WBGO. April 14, 2011. Accessed August 16, 2015. http://www.wbgo.org/blog/origins-word-jazz.
37. Ward and Stokes, 21.
38. "Jim Crow Era." PBS. Accessed August 17, 2015. http://www.pbs.org/jazz/time/time_jim_crow.htm.
39. Scott Yanow. "Jelly Roll Morton." Allmusic.com. Accessed August 17, 2015. http://www.allmusic.com/artist/jelly-roll-morton-mn0000317290/biography.
40. Cornel West. "Horace Pippin's Challenge to Art Criticism." In *Race-ing Art History: Critical Readings in Race and Art History*, edited by Kymberly N. Pinder. New York: Routledge, 2002.
41. Anne Shaw Faulkner. "Does Jazz Put the Sin in Syncopation?" *Ladies Home Journal* 38, no. 8 (August 1921). 34.
42. "Roarin' Twenties" (excerpted from *Jazz: A History of America's Music*). PBS. Accessed August 19, 2015. http://www.pbs.org/jazz/time/time_roaring.htm.
43. "Louis Armstrong Biography." Biography.com. Accessed August 17, 2015. http://www.biography.com/people/louis-armstrong-9188912.
44. Ibid.
45. "Bing and Louis: A Pocketful of Dreams with Gary Giddins." Riverwalk Jazz, Stanford University Libraries. Accessed August 19, 2015. http://riverwalkjazz.stanford.edu/program/bing-and-louis-pocketful-dreams-gary-giddins.
46. Perry A. Hall. "African-American Music: Dynamics of Appropriation and Innovation." In *Borrowed Power: Essays on Cultural Appropriation*, edited by Bruce H. Ziff. New Brunswick, N.J.: Rutgers University Press, 1997. 38.
47. Ibid., 37.
48. "Benny Goodman." *Encyclopedia Britannica Online*. Accessed August 28, 2015. http://www.britannica.com/biography/Benny-Goodman.
49. Pat Hentoff. "How Jazz Helped Hasten the Civil-Rights Movement." *Wall Street Journal*. January 15, 2009. Accessed August 28, 2015. http://www.wsj.com/articles/SB123197292128083217.
50. Ford, 163.
51. "What Louis Armstrong Really Thinks." *New Yorker*. February 25, 2014. Accessed November 15, 2015. http://www.newyorker.com/books/page-turner/what-louis-armstrong-really-thinks.
52. "Louis Armstrong, Barring Soviet Tour, Denounces Eisenhower and Gov. Faubus." *New York Times*. September 19, 1957. Retrieved August 30, 2007.
53. Hentoff.
54. Ibid.
55. Ward and Stokes, 23.
56. Lisa Tidd. *The Greenwood Encyclopedia of Rock History*. Volume I: *The Early Years, 1951–1959*. Westport, Conn.: Greenwood Press, 2006. 48.
57. "Louis Armstrong Biography." Rock and Roll Hall of Fame. Accessed September 12, 2015.

Chapter 6

1. "Jim Crow Stories: Ida B. Wells Forced Out of Memphis (1892)." PBS. http://www.pbs.org/wnet/jimcrow/stories_events_wells.html.
2. E.M. Beck and S.E. Tolnay, "The Killing Fields of the Deep South: The Market for Cotton and the Lynching of Blacks, 1882–1930." *American Sociological Review* (1990). 526.
3. Cobb, 164.
4. Ibid., 6, fn19.
5. Ibid., 147.
6. Ibid., 131.
7. William Alexander Percy and Carl

H. Pforzheimer. *Lanterns on the Levee: Recollections of a Planter's Son*. New York: Knopf, 1941. 20.

8. Lomax, 6, 20 and 97.
9. McMillen, 134.
10. Ibid., 30.
11. Cobb, 156.
12. Ralph Ellison. *Shadow and Act*. New York: Random House, 1964. 89–90.
13. McMillen, 118.
14. Cobb, 172.
15. Ibid., 173.
16. Ellison, 89–90.
17. McMillen, 90.
18. Ibid., 73.
19. Ibid., 8, fn34.
20. Cobb, 159.
21. Wormser, 57.
22. Ibid., 54.
23. Ibid., 55 and 57.
24. Ibid., 57.
25. Cobb, 117.
26. John Neal Phillips. *Running with Bonnie and Clyde: The Ten Fast Years of Ralph Fults*. Norman: University of Oklahoma, 1996. 369, fn49.
27. Bukka White, "Parchman Farm Blues Lyrics." Metro Lyrics. http://www.metrolyrics.com/parchman-farm-blues-lyrics-bukka-white.html.
28. Chad Williams. "African Americans and World War I." Africana Age. Accessed October 18, 2015. http://exhibitions.nypl.org/africanaage/essay-world-war-i.html.
29. "For Action on Race Riot Peril." *New York Times*. October 5, 1919. Accessed January 20, 2010.
30. David M. Kennedy. *Over Here: The First World War and American Society*. New York: Oxford University Press, 1980. 279, 281–82.
31. "For Action on Race Riot Peril."
32. Francis Davis. *The History of the Blues*. New York: Hyperion, 1995. 135.
33. Robert A. Gobson. "The Negro Holocaust: Lynching and Race Riots in the United States, 1880–1950." Yale–New Haven Teachers Institute. Accessed October 18, 2015. http://www.yale.edu/ynhti/curriculum/units/1979/2/79.02.04.x.html.
34. Anne Wallace Sharp. *A Dream Deferred: The Jim Crow Era*. Detroit: Lucent Books, 2005. 60.
35. Ibid., 70.
36. Cobb, 115.
37. Sharp, 70.
38. Ibid., 58.
39. Ibid.
40. David R. Colburn. "Rosewood and America in the Early Twentieth Century." *Florida Historical Quarterly* 76, no. 2 (Fall 1997). 175–92.
41. Franklin and Moss, 388.
42. Cobb, 130.
43. Lomax, 233.
44. Ibid., 97.
45. Davis, 47.
46. Lomax, prologue.
47. Cobb, 108–9.
48. Richard Wright. *Black Boy: A Record of Childhood and Youth*. New York: Harper & Bros., 1945. 227.
49. Cobb, 115. See also Gregory Wood. "Kansas Exodusters." In *Race and Racism in the United States: An Encyclopedia of the American Mosaic*, edited by Charles A. Gallagher and Cameron D. Lippard. Santa Barbara, Calif.: Greenwood, 2014.
50. Cobb, 170.
51. Ibid.
52. Ibid., 295.
53. Ibid., 168.
54. Cecil Brown. "Godfather of Gangsta." *The Guardian*. May 8, 2003. Accessed September 7, 2015. http://www.guardian.co.uk/music/2003/may/09/artsfeatures.
55. David L. Cohn. *Where I Was Born and Raised*. Notre Dame: University of Notre Dame Press, 1967. 71.
56. Oshinsky, 222.
57. Cohn, 71.
58. Ibid.
59. Ibid., 72.
60. Ibid., 74.
61. Ibid.
62. Charles S. Johnson, *Growing Up in the Black Belt*. Washington, D.C.: American Council on Education, 1941; New York: Schocken Books, 1967. 76.
63. Robert Palmer. *Deep Blues*. New York: Viking Press, 1981. 17.
64. Cobb, 282.
65. Gioia, 49.
66. James Miller. "The Origins of the Mississippi Delta Blues." Historical Text Archive. May 20, 2002. Accessed October

3, 2015. http://historicaltextarchive.com/sections.php?action=read&artid=410.

67. Davis, 100.

68. Cub Koda. "Charley Patton." Allmusic.com. Accessed September 4, 2015. http://www.allmusic.com/artist/charley-patton-mn0000166058/biography.

69. Koda, "Charley Patton."

70. Davis, 103.

71. Koda, "Charley Patton."

72. Ibid.

73. Palmer, *Deep Blues*, 58–61.

74. Koda, "Charley Patton."

75. Palmer, *Deep Blues*, 89.

76. Davis, 106–9.

77. Gioia, 109.

78. Cub Koda. "Son House." Allmusic.com. http://www.allmusic.com/artist/son-house-mn0000753094/biography.

79. Pearson and McCulloch, 9.

80. Elijah Wald, 107.

81. Ibid., 108.

82. Pearson and McCulloch, 7.

83. Ibid.

84. Ibid., 94.

85. Elijah Wald, 119.

86. Ibid., 7–9.

87. Lomax, 58.

88. Pearson and McCulloch, 221.

89. Andrew Buncombe. "The Grandfather of Rock'n'Roll: The Devil's Instrument." *The Independent*. July 26, 2006. Accessed October 18, 2015.

90. Pearson and McCulloch, 41.

91. Cobb, 292.

92. Elijah Wald, 122–23.

93. Ibid., 123.

94. G. Wayne Dowdy. *A Brief History of Memphis*. Charleston, S.C.: History Press, 2011. 23 and 25.

95. "Memphis & Charleston Railroad." Confederate Railroads. Accessed October 4, 2015. http://www.csa-railroads.com/Memphis_and_Charleston.htm.

96. Dowdy, 28–30.

97. Larry Nager. *Memphis Beat: The Lives and Times of America's Musical Crossroads*. New York: St. Martin's Press, 1998. 18.

98. Thomas J. Hennessey. *From Jazz to Swing: African-American Jazz Musicians and Their Music, 1890–1935*. Detroit: Wayne State University Press, 1994. 51–52.

99. John Wright, ed. *The New York Times 2002 Almanac*. New York: Penguin Putnam, 2001. 221.

100. William Barlow. "Looking Up at Down." In *Looking Up at Down: The Emergence of Blues Culture*. Philadelphia: Temple University Press, 1989. 208.

101. "Historic Beale Street." Beale Street. Accessed September 5, 2015. http://www.bealestreet.com/history.html.

102. Palmer, *Deep Blues*, 152.

103. James Dickerson. *Goin' Back to Memphis: A Century of Blues, Rock 'n' Roll, and Glorious Soul*. New York: Schirmer Books, 1996. 19.

104. Nager, 28.

105. Handy and Bontemps, x.

106. Nager, 145.

107. Dickerson, 51.

108. Ibid., 40.

109. Ibid., 82.

110. Louis Cantor. *Dewey and Elvis: The Life and Times of a Rock 'n' Roll Deejay*. Urbana: University of Illinois Press, 2005. 48–49.

111. King and Ritz, 91.

112. Ibid., 32.

113. Ibid.

114. Ibid., 33.

115. Ibid., 32.

116. Ibid., 36.

117. Ibid., 60.

118. Ibid., 36.

119. "B.B. King Interview (page: 2 / 7)." B.B. King Interview. Accessed April 10, 2016. http://www.achievement.org/autodoc/page/kin2int-2.

120. King and Ritz, 33.

121. Quincy Troupe. "B.B. King." Jazz and Blues Masters. Accessed September 5, 2015. http://www.jazzandbluesmasters.com/bbking.htm.

122. King and Ritz, 130.

123. Ibid., 23.

124. Ibid., 78.

125. Ibid., 41.

126. B.B. King Concert, Keswick Theater, Glenside, PA. July 5, 2010. Author attended.

127. Elaine Lipworth. "B.B. King: In the Court of the King." *The Independent*. March 29, 2006. Accessed September 5, 2015. http://www.independent.co.uk/arts-entertainment/music/features/bb-king-in-the-court-of-the-king-6105280.html.

128. King and Ritz, 122; Colin Escott and Martin Hawkins. *Good Rockin' Tonight: Sun Records and the Birth of Rock 'n' Roll*. New York: St. Martin's Press, 1991. 22.

129. Bill Dahl. "B.B. King." Allmusic.com. Accessed September 5, 2015. http://www.allmusic.com/artist/bb-king-mn0000059156.

130. Edward M. Komara. *Encyclopedia of the Blues*. New York: Routledge, 2006. 385.

131. Stephen Thomas Erlewine. "U2 Rattle and Hum—Review." Allmusic.com. Accessed October 19, 2015. http://www.allmusic.com/album/rattle-and-hum-mw0000375268; and "Christina Aguilera and B.B. King—'Merry Christmas Baby', 1999." YouTube. November 3, 2014. Accessed October 19, 2015.

132. King and Ritz, 284–85; and Kevin Carter and W. Speers. "B.B. King's Gift to the Pope: His Guitar 'Lucille.'" *Philly-archives*. December 19, 1997. Accessed October 19, 2015.

Chapter 7

1. Tocqueville, 184.
2. Ibid., 488.
3. Pattison, 51.
4. "Rob Roy." *Encyclopedia Britannica*. Accessed September 7, 2015. http://www.britannica.com/biography/Rob-Roy.
5. Charlotte Higgins. "Scotland's Image-Maker Sir Walter Scott 'Invented English Legends.'" *The Guardian*. August 16, 2010. Retrieved April 4, 2011.
6. Richard Wormser. "Ku Klux Klan." PBS. Accessed October 19, 2015. http://www.pbs.org/wnet/jimcrow/stories_org_kkk.html.
7. Bill C. Malone. *Country Music U.S.A.: A Fifty-Year History*. Austin: Published for the American Folklore Society by the University of Texas Press, 1968. 1.
8. Ibid.
9. Ibid., 11–12.
10. Ibid., 24.
11. Ibid., 17 and 18.
12. Ibid., 13.
13. Ibid., 15 and 23. See also Mark Zwonitzer and Charles Hirshberg. *Will You Miss Me When I'm Gone? The Carter Family and Their Legacy in American Music*. New York: Simon & Schuster, 2002. 102.
14. Cecelia Tichi. *High Lonesome: The American Culture of Country Music*. Chapel Hill: University of North Carolina Press, 1994. 64.
15. Ibid., 24.
16. Laura Ingalls Wilder. *Little House on the Prairie*. New York: Harper Trophy, 2007. 149.
17. Tichi, 39.
18. Ibid., 65.
19. Walt Whitman. "Song of the Open Road." *Leaves of Grass* (1900). Bartleby. Accessed November 15, 2015. http://www.bartleby.com/142/82.html.
20. Ibid.
21. Anthony Harkins. *Hillbilly: A Cultural History of an American Icon*. New York: Oxford University Press, 2004. 9.
22. Ibid., 47.
23. Ibid., 72.
24. Ibid., 16.
25. Ibid., 27.
26. Ibid., 19.
27. Ibid., 16–17.
28. Ibid., 17.
29. Ibid., 15.
30. Ibid., 15 and 4.
31. Ibid., 17.
32. Ibid., 16.
33. Ibid., 34.
34. Richard B. Drake. *A History of Appalachia*. Lexington: University Press of Kentucky, 2001. 200–210.
35. Jaime Joyce. *Moonshine: A Cultural History of America's Infamous Liquor*. Minneapolis: Zenith, 2014. 8–14.
36. John Alexander Williams. *Appalachia: A History*. Chapel Hill: University of North Carolina Press, 2002. 187.
37. Harkins, 34.
38. Ibid., 17.
39. Ibid.
40. Ibid., 34.
41. Percy and Pforzheimer, 20.
42. Harkins, 34.
43. Malone, 9.
44. Ibid., 31.
45. Pierro Scaruffi. "Country Music." A History of Country Music. Accessed October 5, 2015. http://www.scaruffi.com/history/country.html.

46. Chad Berry. *The Hayloft Gang: The Story of the National Barn Dance*. Urbana: University of Illinois Press, 2008. 154.
47. Malone, 97–98, 200.
48. Berry, 60.
49. Scaruffi, "Country Music."
50. Ibid.
51. Malone, 61.
52. Ibid., 52.
53. Ibid., 51–54.
54. "A.P. Carter—Early Life." Biography.com. Accessed November 15, 2015. http://www.biography.com/people/ap-carter-17188972#early-life.
55. Zwonitzer and Hirshberg, 62.
56. "A.P. Carter—Early Life," Biography.com.
57. Zwonitzer and Hirshberg, 93.
58. Ibid., 71.
59. Malone, 66.
60. Zwonitzer and Hirshberg, 71.
61. Ibid., 180–81.
62. Ibid., 245.
63. Ibid., 250.
64. Ibid., 361.
65. Malone, 78.
66. Ibid.
67. Ibid., 86.
68. Scaruffi, "Country Music."
69. Malone, 91.
70. "Howlin' Wolf Biography." Biography.com. Accessed November 16, 2015. http://www.biography.com/people/howlin-wolf-9345565#revered-by-rock-acts.
71. Malone, 2.
72. Scaruffi, "Country Music."
73. Ibid.
74. Scaruffi, "Country Music"; Dave Oliphant. *Texan Jazz*. Austin: University of Texas Press, 1996. 23.
75. Malone, 70.
76. Ibid.
77. Ibid., 72.
78. Ibid.
79. Ibid., 74.
80. Ibid., 75.
81. David C. Morton and Charles K. Wolfe. *DeFord Bailey: A Black Star in Early Country Music*. Knoxville: University of Tennessee Press, 1991. 39 and 16.
82. Palmer, *Deep Blues*, 17.
83. John George. "Imagining Tee-Tot: Blues, Race, and the Legend of Hank Williams." In *The Hank Williams Reader*, edited by Patrick Huber, Steve Goodson, and David Anderson. New York: Oxford University Press, 2014. 303.
84. Morton and Wolfe, 34.
85. Ibid., 39.
86. Ibid., 2.
87. Ibid.
88. Ibid., 113.
89. Palmer, *Deep Blues*, 103.
90. Morton and Wolfe, 114–18.
91. Ibid., 114.
92. Ibid.
93. Ibid., 111.
94. Ibid., 111 and 113.
95. Peter Guralnick. *Lost Highway: Journeys & Arrivals of American Musicians*. New York: Little, Brown, 2012. 21.
96. "Deford Bailey: A Legend Lost." PBS. Accessed November 16, 2015. http://www.pbs.org/deford/biography/opry4.html.
97. Ibid.
98. Stephen Thomas Erlewine. "Roy Acuff." Allmusic.com. http://www.allmusic.com/artist/roy-acuff-mn0000848784/biography.
99. Scaruffi, "Country Music."
100. Bill Williams. "A Crucial Decision for the World of Music." *Billboard*. February 3, 1968. A-43.
101. Davis, 10.
102. Ibid., 168.
103. Harkins, 94.
104. Caspar Llewellyn Smith. "Gene Autry Becomes Cinema's First Singing Cowboy." *The Guardian*. June 5, 2011. Accessed October 5, 2015. http://www.theguardian.com/music/2011/jun/16/gene-autry-first-singing-cowboy.
105. Scaruffi, "Country Music."
106. Ibid.
107. Charles R. Townsend. *San Antonio Rose: The Life and Music of Bob Wills*. Urbana: University of Illinois Press, 1976. 4. See also Denize Springer. "'Ahhhh-HA!' Discovering Bob Wills." *SF State News* (San Francisco State University). February 23, 2005. Retrieved May 2, 2010.
108. Guralnick, *Lost Highway*, 26; and Bob Dylan. "Excerpt from *Chronicles, Volume One* (2004)." In *The Hank Williams Reader*, edited by Patrick Huber, Steve Goodson, and David Anderson. New York: Oxford University Press, 2014. 299.

109. Scaruffi, "Country Music."
110. "Woody Guthrie's Biography." Official Woody Guthrie Website. Accessed November 16, 2015. http://www.woodyguthrie.org/biography/biography1.htm.
111. Malone, 130.

Chapter 8

1. Bruce Pegg. *Brown Eyed Handsome Man: The Life and Hard Times of Chuck Berry: An Unauthorized Biography.* New York: Routledge, 2002. 27.
2. Altschuler, 15.
3. Anthony DeCurtis. *The Rolling Stone Illustrated History of Rock & Roll: The Definitive History of the Most Important Artists and Their Music.* 3rd ed. New York: Random House, 1992. 3.
4. Preston Lauterbach. *The Chitlin' Circuit: And the Road to Rock 'n' Roll.* New York: W. W. Norton, 2011. 12.
5. Ibid.
6. Charlie Gillett. *The Sound of the City: The Rise of Rock and Roll.* New York: Outerbridge & Dienstfrey, 1970. 245.
7. Altschuler, 11, fn18.
8. Bill Dahl. "Louis Jordan." Allmusic.com. Accessed November 16, 2015. http://www.allmusic.com/artist/louis-jordan-mn0000287604.
9. Bruce Weber. "Jerry Wexler, a Behind-the-Scenes Force in Black Music, Is Dead at 91." *New York Times.* August 15, 2008. Accessed October 30, 2015. http://www.nytimes.com/2008/08/16/arts/music/16wexler.html?hp=&pagewanted=all&_r=0.
10. Robert Gordon. *Can't Be Satisfied: The Life and Times of Muddy Waters.* Boston: Little, Brown, 2002. 75.
11. Lomax, 412.
12. "Muddy Waters?" Bob Margolin. Accessed October 29, 2015. http://bobmargolin.com/327-2/.
13. Mark Deming. "Muddy Waters." Allmusic.com. Accessed October 30, 2015. http://www.allmusic.com/artist/muddy-waters-mn0000608701/biography.
14. Lomax, 417–18.
15. "Muddy Waters Biography." Rock and Roll Hall of Fame. Accessed November 15, 2015. http://rockhall.com/inductees/muddy-waters/bio/.
16. Nadine Cohodas. *Spinning Blues Into Gold: The Chess Brothers and the Legendary Chess Records.* New York: St. Martin's Press, 2000. 35.
17. Norm Cohen and David Cohen. *Long Steel Rail: The Railroad in American Folksong.* 2nd ed. Urbana: University of Illinois Press, 2000. 31.
18. Colin Escott and George Merritt. *Hank Williams: The Biography.* Boston: Little, Brown, 1994. 5–6, 12.
19. George, 305.
20. Ibid., 302–3.
21. Stephen Thomas Erlewine. "Hank WIlliams." Allmusic.com. Accessed November 15, 2015. http://www.allmusic.com/artist/hank-williams-mn0000549797.
22. Michael Bane. "Excerpt from *The Outlaws: Revolution in Country Music* (1978)." In *The Hank Williams Reader*, edited by Patrick Huber, Steve Goodson, and David Anderson. New York: Oxford University Press, 2014. 178
23. Minnie Pearl (with Joan Dew). "Excerpt from *Minnie Pearl: An Autobiography* (1980)." In *The Hank Williams Reader*, edited by Patrick Huber, Steve Goodson, and David Anderson. New York: Oxford University Press, 2014. 191.
24. David Halberstram. "Hank Williams Remembered (1971)." In *The Hank Williams Reader*, edited by Patrick Huber, Steve Goodson, and David Anderson. New York: Oxford University Press, 2014. 145.
25. "Hank Williams." Grand Ole Opry. October 16, 2014. Accessed October 11, 2015.
26. Halberstram, "Hank Williams Remembered," 146.
27. "About Pee Wee King." CMT Artists. Accessed November 15, 2015. http://www.cmt.com/artists/az/king_pee_wee/bio.jhtml.
28. Townsend, 252.
29. Daviod Vinopal. "Flatt & Scruggs." Allmusic.com. Accessed November 16, 2015. http://www.allmusic.com/artist/flatt-scruggs-mn0000227527/biography.
30. "Leo Fender Biography." Rock and Roll Hall of Fame. Accessed October 20, 2015. https://rockhall.com/inductees/leo-fender/bio/.
31. Richard S. Ginell. "Les Paul." Allmu-

sic.com. Accessed October 23, 2015. http://www.allmusic.com/artist/les-paul-mn0000818559/biography.

Chapter 9

1. "Mahalia Jackson: Inducted in 1997." Rock and Roll Hall of Fame. Accessed October 11, 2015.
2. Gayle Wald, 3 and 27.
3. Ibid., 19.
4. Ibid., 10.
5. Cox, 6.
6. Ibid., 91.
7. Gayle Wald, 10.
8. Cox, 15.
9. Acts 2:19, *The Holy Bible*, King James Version.
10. Ibid.
11. Morton T. Kelsey. *Tongue Speaking: An Experiment in Spiritual Experience*. Garden City, N.Y.: Doubleday, 1964. 46.
12. Allan Anderson. *An Introduction to Pentecostalism: Global Charismatic Christianity*. Cambridge: Cambridge University Press, 2004. 23.
13. Ibid.
14. Ibid., 23.
15. Ibid., 35.
16. Ibid., 33.
17. Ibid., 62.
18. Ibid., 40.
19. Grant Wacker. *Heaven Below: Early Pentecostals and American Culture*. Cambridge, Mass.: Harvard University Press, 2003. 232.
20. Anderson, 35.
21. Ibid., 34.
22. Cox, 49.
23. Anderson, 39.
24. Cox, 24.
25. Anderson, 39.
26. Cox, 24.
27. Anderson, 40.
28. Cox, 46.
29. Anderson, 40.
30. Cox, 57.
31. David W. Faupel, *Everlasting Gospel: The Significance of Eschatology in the Development of Pentecostal Thought*. Sheffield, U.K.: Sheffield Academic Press, 1996. 194–97, 200–202.
32. Cox, 48.
33. Ibid., 59.
34. Cecilia Rasmussen. "Vision of a Colorblind Faith Gave Birth to Pentecostalism." *Los Angeles Times*. June 14, 1998. Accessed October 11, 2015. http://articles.latimes.com/1998/jun/14/local/me-59833.
35. Peter Steinfels. "Speaking in Tongues, Performing Miracles: A Look at Pentecostalism from a Former Insider." *New York Times*. July 7, 2001. A9(L). Accessed June 15, 2010. http://www.nytimes.com/2001/07/07/us/beliefs-speaking-tongues-performing-miracles-look-pentecostalism-former-insider.html.
36. Anderson, 61.
37. Ibid.
38. Ibid., 42.
39. "The Founder & Church History." Church of God in Christ. Accessed October 29, 2015. http://www.cogic.org/our-foundation/the-founder-church-history/.
40. Kevin Sack. "A History of the Pentecostal Church in America." *New York Times On the Web*. June 4, 2000. Accessed November 16, 2015. https://partners.nytimes.com/library/national/race/060400sack-churchside.html.
41. Gayle Wald, 9.
42. Ibid., 19.
43. Ibid., 22.
44. Ibid., 53.
45. Ibid., 47.
46. Ibid., 38.
47. Cox, 79.
48. Gayle Wald, 116.
49. Ibid., 131.
50. Ibid., 127–28.
51. *Loving v. Virginia*, 388 U.S. 1, 11, fn15 (1967).
52. Ibid., 129–33.

Chapter 10

1. Cantor, 67.
2. Ibid.
3. Ibid.
4. Ibid.
5. Altschuler, 13.
6. Paula Froelich, with Bill Hoffmann and Corynne Steindler. "Blood Alcohol." *New York Post*. November 18, 2008. http://pagesix.com/2008/11/18/blood-alcohol/.

7. Susan Merrill Squier. *Communities of the Air: Radio Century, Radio Culture.* Durham, N.C.: Duke University Press, 2003. 119.
8. Cantor, 67.
9. Ibid., 68.
10. Ibid., 43–44.
11. Ibid., 40.
12. Ibid., 43–44.
13. Ibid., 51.
14. Ibid., 54.
15. Ibid., 53.
16. Ibid., 49.
17. Ibid., 32.
18. Ibid., 140.
19. Nager, 129.
20. Cantor, 7.
21. Ibid., 16.
22. Dewey Phillips. *Red Hot & Blue (Live Radio Broadcasts from 1952–1964).* Memphis, Tenn.: Memphis Archives, 1995.
23. Cantor, 93.
24. Ibid., 77.
25. Nager, 129.
26. Ibid.
27. Ibid.
28. Bertrand, 120, fn36.
29. Cantor, 120.
30. Escott and Hawkins, 1.
31. Ibid., 14.
32. Ibid., 26–27.
33. Jerry Naylor and Steve Halliday. *The Rockabilly Legends: They Called It Rockabilly Long Before They Called It Rock and Roll.* Milwaukee, Wis.: Hal Leonard, 2007.
34. Escott and Hawkins, 19.
35. Dave Laing. "Sam Phillips." *The Guardian.* July 31, 2003. Accessed September 7, 2015. http://www.theguardian.com/news/2003/aug/01/guardianobituaries.artsobituaries.
36. Marcus, *Mystery Train*, 12.
37. Guralnick, *Lost Highway*, 334–35.
38. Escott and Hawkins, 45–46.
39. Ibid., 21 and 23.
40. David McGee. *B.B. King: There Is Always One More Time.* San Francisco: Backbeat Books, 2005. 73.
41. Guralnick, *Lost Highway*, 330.
42. Sun Video, Bruce Sinofsky's *Good Rockin' Tonight* (2002).
43. Guralnick, *Lost Highway*, 331.
44. Marc Levin, dir. *Godfathers and Sons.* Sony Music Entertainment, 2003. DVD.
45. Ibid.
46. Michael Campbell. *Popular Music in America: The Beat Goes On.* 2nd ed. Belmont, Calif.: Wadsworth/Thomson Learning, 2005. 164.
47. Escott and Hawkins, 24–25.
48. Ibid., 26–27.
49. Ibid., 30.
50. Ibid., 31.
51. Koda, "Howlin' Wolf."
52. Ibid.
53. Milton Subotsky, dir. *Rock, Rock, Rock!* Passport Video, 2003. DVD ("rock and roll is a river of music that has absorbed many streams: rhythm and blues, jazz, rag time, cowboy songs, country songs, folk songs. All have contributed to the big beat").
54. Palmer, *Rock & Roll*, 199.
55. Holger Petersen. *Talking Music Blues Radio and Roots Music.* London: Insomniac Press, 2014. 156.
56. Bertrand, 175.
57. Anthony DeCurtis. *Present Tense: Rock & Roll and Culture.* Durham, NC: Duke University Press, 1992, 20.
58. Altschuler, 23.
59. "Alan Freed Biography." Rock and Roll Hall of Fame. Accessed November 17, 2015. http://rockhall.com/inductees/alan-freed/bio/.
60. John A. Jackson. *Big Beat Heat: Alan Freed and the Early Years of Rock & Roll.* New York: Schirmer Books, 1991. 35.
61. Ibid., 78 and 81.
62. "Rock and Roll." Encyclopedia of Cleveland History. Last viewed January 2, 2011. http://ech.cwru.edu/cgi/article.pl?id=RR.
63. Joel Whitburn. *Top R&B/Hip Hop Singles: 1942–2004.* Menomonee Falls, WI: Record Research, 2004. 168.
64. Ibid., 46.
65. Jude Sheerin, "How the World's First Rock Concert Ended in Chaos." *BBC News.* Retrieved November 11, 2012. http://www.bbc.co.uk/news/magazine-17440514.
66. Jackson, 47–48.
67. "Alan Freed Biography," Rock and Roll Hall of Fame.
68. Jackson, 84.
69. See http://www.cleveland.com/pop

music/index.ssf/2010/08/rock_and_roll_hall_of_fame_and_4.html.

70. Leon Bibb. "Did You Know: Wacky Radio Guys Pushed Hard for Cleveland to Get Rock Hall of Fame in 90s." News Net 5. April 14, 2015. Accessed October 9, 2015. http://www.newsnet5.com/news/local-news/recalling-a-couple-of-wacky-radio-guys-who-pushed-hard-for-cleveland-to-get-rock-hall-of-fame-in-90s. See also http://www.cleveland.com/popmusic/index.ssf/2010/08/rock_and_roll_hall_of_fame_and_4.html.

71. Jackson, 195.

72. Ibid., 326.

73. Gillett.

74. Palmer, *Rock & Roll*, 20.

75. Joe McGasko. "The Rolling Stones: Their Rogue Journey to Rock 'n' Roll." Biography.com. April 16, 2014. Accessed October 8, 2015.

76. Richie Unterberger. "Fats Domino." Allmusic.com. Accessed October 9, 2015.

77. Jason Blasco. "Soul Legend Al Green Merges Classic and Modern Sounds on His Album, *Lay It Down*." Singer Universe. http://www.singeruniverse.com/algreen123.htm.

78. Guralnick, *Lost Highway*, 335.

79. Dave Marsh. *Louie Louie: The History and Mythology of the World's Most Famous Rock 'n' Roll Song.* Ann Arbor: University of Michigan Press, 2004.

80. Ibid., 31.

81. Jim Dawson and Steve Propes, *What Was the First Rock and Roll Record?* Boston: Faber & and Faber, 1992.

82. Unterberger, "Fats Domino."

83. Marcus, *Mystery Train*, 9.

84. Bertrand, 105.

85. Damien Cave, Matt Diehl, Gavin Edwards, Jenny Eliscu, David Fricke, Lauren Gitlin, Matt Henrickson, Kirk Miller, Austin Scaggs, and Rob Sheffield. "Truck Driver Invents Rock." *Rolling Stone*. June 24, 2004. 84–85.

86. Otto Fuchs. *Bill Haley: The Father of Rock & Roll*. Gelnhausen, Germany: Wagner, 2011. 83.

87. Susan King. "'Blackboard' Still Rocks at 50." *Los Angeles Times*. March 24, 2005. Accessed October 24, 2015. http://articles.latimes.com/2005/mar/24/news/wk-blackboard24.

88. Altschuler, 33.

89. Fuchs, 453.

Chapter 11

1. Pamela Clarke Keough. *Elvis Presley: The Man, the Life, the Legend*. New York: Simon & Schuster, 2004.

2. Peter Guralnick. *Careless Love: The Unmaking of Elvis Presley*. Boston: Little, Brown, 1999. 658.

3. Ibid., 13.

4. Peter Guralnick. *Last Train to Memphis: The Rise of Elvis Presley*. Boston: Little, Brown, 1994. 13.

5. Ibid., 15. See also Vernon Presley. "Elvis by His Father Vernon Presley." As told to Nancy Anderson. *Good Housekeeping*. January 1978. 156.

6. Guralnick, *Last Train to Memphis*, 37.

7. Elaine Dundy. *Elvis and Gladys*. New York: Macmillan, 1985. 81.

8. David Leafe. "The King's Troubling Obsession." *Daily Mail*. March 29, 2010. http://www.dailymail.co.uk/news/article-1261082/The-Kings-troubling-obsession-Elvis-woman-So-able-form-relationships-virginal-girls.html.

9. Guralnick, *Last Train to Memphis*, 36.

10. Ibid., 14.

11. Bertrand, 153.

12. Guralnick, *Last Train to Memphis*, 17.

13. Guralnick, *Careless Love*, 24.

14. Ibid., 27.

15. Bertrand, 103.

16. Guralnick, *Last Train to Memphis*, 105.

17. Ibid., 129.

18. Ibid., 28.

19. Altschuler, 245.

20. Marcus, *Mystery Train*, 129.

21. Guralnick, *Careless Love*, 33.

22. Guralnick, *Last Train to Memphis*, 26.

23. Guralnick, *Careless Love*, 50.

24. LeRoy Ashby. *With Amusement for All: A History of American Popular Culture since 1830*. Lexington: University Press of Kentucky, 2006. 361.

25. Guralnick, *Careless Love*, 95.

26. Guralnick, *Last Train to Memphis*, 75.

27. "Sam Phillips." Memphis Music Hall

of Fame. Accessed October 10, 2015. http://memphismusichalloffame.com/inductee/samphillips/.

28. Guralnick, *Careless Love*, 95.
29. Ibid.
30. Escott and Hawkins, 15.
31. Dickerson, 96.
32. Bruce Sinofsky, dir. *Good Rockin' Tonight: The Legacy of Sun Records*. Image Entertainment, 2002. DVD.
33. See http://www.elvisinfonet.com/blues.html.
34. Altschuler, 50.
35. Cantor, 148.
36. Ibid., 149.
37. Ibid.
38. Ibid., 150.
39. Ibid., 149.
40. Ibid., 151.
41. Bertrand, 103¬¬.
42. Guralnick, *Careless Love*, 47–48.
43. Ashby, 361.
44. "Sam Phillips." Sun Records. Accessed October 5, 2015. http://www.sunrecords.com/artists/sam-phillips.
45. Ace Collins. *Untold Gold: The Stories Behind Elvis's #1 Hits*. Chicago: Chicago Review Press, 2005. 10–18.
46. Altschuler, 89.
47. See "Elvis Presley—Hound Dog (1956) HD 0815007." YouTube. Accessed October 5, 2015. https://www.youtube.com/watch?v=MMmljYkdr-w.
48. Altschuler, 67.
49. Ibid., 108.
50. Dan Coates. *Rolling Stone Sheet Music Classics*. Volume 1: *1950s–1960s*. Van Nuys, Calif.: Alfred Pub., 2008. 11.
51. Altschuler, 91.
52. Ibid.
53. Guralnick, *Lost Highway*, 30.
54. "Heartbreak, Hound Dogs Put Sales Zip Into Presley Products." *Wall Street Journal*. December 31, 1956. A-1.
55. Bertrand, 199.
56. Ibid., 103.
57. Ibid., 198.
58. Peter Guralnick. "How Did Elvis Get Turned Into a Racist?" *New York Times*. August 10, 2007. Accessed October 25, 2015. http://www.nytimes.com/2007/08/11/opinion/11guralnick.html?pagewanted=all&_r=0.
59. Bertrand, 218.
60. Guralnick, "How Did Elvis Get Turned Into a Racist?"
61. Robert Hilburn. "From the Man Who Would Be King." *Los Angeles Times*. February 6, 2005. Accessed November 16, 2015. http://articles.latimes.com/2005/feb/06/entertainment/ca-presley6.
62. Tony Douglas. *Jackie Wilson: Lonely Teardrops*. New York: Routledge, 2005. 49.
63. Bertrand, 108.
64. See http://m.imdb.com/name/nm0113768/quotes.
65. Guralnick, *Last Train to Memphis*.
66. Bertrand, 204.
67. Margaret McKee and Fred Chisenhall. *Beale Black & Blue: Life and Music on Black America's Main Street*. Baton Rouge: Louisiana State University Press, 1981. 36–37.
68. Guralnick, *Careless Love*, 474–78.
69. Benjamin D. Garber. "Parental Alienation and the Dynamics of the Enmeshed Parent-Child Dyad: Adultification, Parentification, and Infantilization." *Family Court Review* 49, issue 2 (April 2011). 322–35.
70. Peter Guralnick and Ernst Jorgensen. *Elvis Day by Day*. New York: Ballantine Books, 1999. 123–24.
71. Guralnick, *Careless Love*, 475.
72. Ibid.
73. Ibid.
74. Ibid.
75. Bertrand, 219, fn168.
76. Guralnick, *Careless Love*, 448.
77. Ibid., 82.
78. Jerry Leiber and Mike Stoller, with David Ritz. *Hound Dog: The Leiber and Stoller Autobiography*. New York: Simon & Schuster, 2009.
79. Ibid., 111.
80. Bob Greene, "The King Is Dead, Long Live the King." *New York Times*. July 6, 2009. http://www.nytimes.com/2009/07/07/opinion/07greene.html.
81. Guralnick, *Careless Love*, 653.
82. Ibid., 56.
83. Ibid., 29.
84. Ibid., 103.
85. Ibid., 98.
86. Fred L. Worth and Steve D. Tamerius. *Elvis: His Life from A to Z*. Chicago: Contemporary Books, 1988. 149.

87. Camille Wells. "Graceland." Tennessee Encyclopedia. December 25, 2009. http://tennesseeencyclopedia.net/entry.php?rec=564.

88. Ibid.

89. Greil Marcus. *Dead Elvis: A Chronicle of a Cultural Obsession*. New York: Doubleday, 1991. 71.

90. Andrew Ballantyne. "The Nest and the Pillar of Fire." In *What Is Architecture?* London: Routledge, 2002. 24.

91. Wells, "Graceland."

92. Guralnick, *Careless Love*, 194–98, 440 and 498.

93. Ibid., 155.

94. Roger Ebert. "*A Hard Day's Night* Movie Review (1964)." RogerEbert.com. October 27, 1996. Accessed November 16, 2015. http://www.rogerebert.com/reviews/great-movie-a-hard-days-night-1964.

95. Guralnick, *Careless Love*, 185 and 217.

96. Ibid., 436.

97. Leafe, "The King's Troubling Obsession."

98. Guralnick, *Careless Love*, 128.

99. Ibid., 289.

100. Ibid., 183.

101. Ibid., 144.

102. Ibid., 139.

103. Ibid., 323.

104. Harvey Kubernick. *The Complete '68 Comeback Special*. CD Booklet RCA/BMG. 26.

105. Ernst Jorgensen. *Elvis Presley: A Life in Music: The Complete Recording Sessions*. New York: St. Martin's Press, 1998. 287.

106. Guralnick, *Careless Love*, 349.

107. David E. James. *Rock 'n' Film: Cinema's Dance with Popular Music*. Oxford: Oxford University Press, 2016. 411.

108. Marcus, *Mystery Train*. 170.

109. Randy Lewis. "Ernst Jorgensen Remasters Elvis Presley's Legacy." *Los Angeles Times*. December 24, 2010. http://articles.latimes.com/2010/dec/24/entertainment/la-et-elvis-presley-box-20101224.

110. "Kentucky Rain." World Public Library. Accessed October 7, 2015. http://www.worldlibrary.org/articles/Kentucky_Rain.

111. Guralnick, *Careless Love*, 349.

112. Ibid., 435.

113. Ibid., 452.

114. Ibid., 447.

115. Ibid., 651.

116. Ibid., 652–53.

117. Ibid., 652.

118. Ibid.

119. Alan Higginbotham. "Doctor Feelgood." *The Guardian*. August 11, 2002 [cited December 29, 2009]. http://www.guardian.co.uk/theobserver/2002/aug/11/features.magazine27.

120. Ibid.

121. "Tabloid Nation." *The Daily Beast*. Accessed November 15, 2015. http://www.thedailybeast.com/newsweek/galleries/2008/09/10/photo-gallery-a-history-of-the-national-enquirer.html#slide1.

122. Iain Calder. *The Untold Story: My 20 Years Running the National Enquirer*. New York: Hyperion, 2004. 153.

123. Sara Pendergast and Tom Pendergast. *St. James Encyclopedia of Popular Culture*. 4th ed. Detroit: St. James Press, 2000. 108.

124. Scott Brown. "Elvis Presley: It's a Hound Dig." *Entertainment Weekly*. October 6, 2000.

125. "Tabloid Nation." *The Daily Beast*. Accessed November 15, 2015.

126. Guralnick, *Careless Love*, 660.

127. David J. Jefferson. "Elvis Lives." *Newsweek* 140, issue 8 (August 19, 2002). 54.

128. Cathryn Stout. "Viewpoint: Graceland and Its Whitehaven Neighbors May Be Finding Common Ground." *Commercial Appeal*. August 15, 2010. Last viewed January 21, 2011. http://www.commercialappeal.com/news/2010/aug/15/opening the gates of graceland all in this/.

129. Lindsay Lowe. "How Many People Visit Graceland Every Year?" *Parade*. August 16, 2014. Accessed October 24, 2015. http://parade.com/327562/linzlowe/how-many-people-visit-graceland-every-year/; and Thomas Bailey Jr., James Dowd, and Ted Evanoff. "Crowds Kick Off Promising Start for Memphis' Summer Tourism Industry." *Commercial Appeal*. May 24, 2013. Accessed October 24, 2015. http://www.commercialappeal.com/business/crowds-kick-off-promising-start-for-memphis-summer-tourism-industry-ep-361736153-323744291.html.

130. "King of Rock 'n' Roll Express Elvis Train Collection." Boutique Junction. Accessed November 15, 2015. http://www.boutiquejunction.com/King-Of-Rock-N-Roll-Express-Elvis-Train-Collection.html; and "Elvis Presley Signature Shot in Pink Classic Car Base." Graceland. Accessed November 15, 2015. http://shop.graceland.com/elvis-presley-signature-shot-in-pink-classic-car-base.html.

131. Leah Goldman and David M. Ewalt. "Top-Earning Dead Celebrities." *Forbes*. October 29, 2007. Accessed November 15, 2015. http://www.forbes.com/2007/10/29/dead-celebrity-earning-biz-media-deadcelebs07_cz_lg_1029celeb_land.html.

132. Erika Doss. *Elvis Culture: Fans, Faith, & Image*. Lawrence: University Press of Kansas, 1999. 72–73.

133. "How Big Was the King?" *CBS News*. August 7, 2002. Accessed November 15, 2015. http://www.cbsnews.com/news/how-big-was-the-king/.

134. Lee Siegel. "Long Live the King." *Time*. August 12, 2002. 70.

135. Doss, 52.

136. Craig Seymour. "False Rumor Fueled 'Racist' Label for Presley." *Seattle Post-Intelligencer*. August 12, 2002. Accessed September 7, 2015. http://www.seattlepi.com/ae/music/article/False-rumor-fueled-racist-label-for-Presley-1093361.php.

137. See http://www.mjblige.com/forum/default.aspx?cid'523&tid'252982 (last viewed February 7, 2011).

138. Lloyd Shearer, "Elvis Presley: How He Changed His Public Image." *Parade*. November 1962.

139. Bertrand, 426.

140. Ibid., 226.

141. Yusuf Jah. *Fight the Power: Rap, Race, and Reality*. New York: Dell, 1997. 196.

142. Bertrand, 221.

143. Ibid., 221–22.

144. Laing, "Sam Phillips."

145. William Bradford Huie. "The Shocking Story of Approved Killing in Mississippi." PBS (American Masters). Reprint of *Look* magazine article. Accessed November 15, 2015. http://www.pbs.org/wgbh/amex/till/sfeature/sf_look_confession.html.

146. Stephen J. Whitfield. *A Death in the Delta: The Story of Emmett Till*. New York: Free Press, 1988. 23.

147. Ibid.

148. Huie, "The Shocking Story of Approved Killing in Mississippi."

149. Huie, "The Shocking Story of Approved Killing in Mississippi."

150. Paul Schmitz. "How Change Happens: The Real Story of Mrs. Rosa Parks & the Montgomery Bus Boycott." *Huffington Post*. Accessed October 7, 2015.

151. "THE NATION: Retreat from Newport." *Time*. September 23, 1957. Accessed November 15, 2015. http://content.time.com/time/magazine/article/0,9171,893684,00.html.

152. Gillett, 18.

153. Andrew Michael Manis. *A Fire You Can't Put Out: The Civil Rights Life of Birmingham's Reverend Fred Shuttlesworth*. Tuscaloosa: University of Alabama Press, 1999. 152.

Chapter 12

1. John Collis. *Chuck Berry: The Biography*. London: Aurum, 2002. 158.

2. Ibid., 48–53.

3. Pegg, 26.

4. Ibid., 27 and 32.

5. Collis, 98–100.

6. "Chuck Berry, 'Maybellene'—500 Greatest Songs of All Time." *Rolling Stone*. Accessed September 7, 2015.

7. "Rock Hall Announces Full Week of American Music Masters Events Honoring Chuck Berry." Rock and Roll Hall of Fame. October 12, 2012. Accessed November 15, 2015. https://rockhall.com/pressroom/announcements/rock-hall-announces-full-week-of-amm-2012-events/.

8. Collis, 158.

9. Jack Kerouac. *On the Road*. New York: Viking, 1997. 179.

10. Bertrand, 175.

11. Ibid., 182.

12. Ibid., 114.

13. Altschuler, 266, fn84.

14. Lisa Jo Sagolla. *Rock 'n' Roll Dances of the 1950s*. Santa Barbara, Calif.: Greenwood, 2011. 74. See also Matthew F. Delmont. *The Nicest Kids in Town: American Bandstand, Rock 'n' Roll, and the Struggle for Civil Rights in 1950s Philadelphia*. Berke-

ley: University of California Press, 2012. 180–82.

15. Bertrand., 180–81.

16. Ibid., 182.

17. Ibid.

18. Ibid., 186.

19. Ibid.

20. Ibid., 179.

21. Ibid., 105.

22. Joe Bonomo. *Jerry Lee Lewis: Lost and Found*. New York: Continuum, 2009. 22.

23. Bertrand, 180–81.

24. Ibid., 175.

25. Pegg, 111–12.

26. Victor Malarek. *The Johns: Sex for Sale and the Men Who Buy It*. New York: Arcade, 2009. 4.

27. Jon Pareles. "Film: Documentary On Al Green, Singer." *New York Times*. September 8, 1987. Accessed October 24, 2015. http://www.nytimes.com/1987/09/09/movies/film-documentary-on-al-green-singer.html.

28. Altschuler, 97.

29. David Kirby. *Little Richard: The Birth of Rock 'n' Roll*. New York: Continuum International Publishing Group, 2009. 169.

30. Ibid., 37.

31. Ibid., 45.

32. Ibid.

33. Ibid., 101.

34. Ibid., 78.

35. Ibid., 83.

36. White, *The Life and Times of Little Richard*, 49.

37. Andrew Male. "Little Richard: Lou Reed's Rock'n'Roll Hero." *MOJO*. November 26, 2013. Accessed October 24, 2015. http://www.mojo4music.com/9539/lou-reeds-love-letter-little-richard/; and Matt Diehl. "The SPIN Interview: Lemmy." *Spin*. April 1, 2009. Accessed October 24, 2015. http://www.spin.com/2009/04/spin-interview-lemmy/.

38. Kirby, 83.

39. J.D. Davis. *Unconquered: The Saga of Cousins Jerry Lee Lewis, Jimmy Swaggart, and Mickey Gilley*. Dallas, Tex.: Brown Books, 2012. 30.

40. Ibid., 80–81.

41. Ibid., 16.

42. Ibid., 63.

43. Ibid., 62.

44. Ibid., 59.

45. Ibid., 141.

46. Acts 2:19, *The Holy Bible*, King James Version.

47. Davis, *Unconquered*, 319–21, 366–67.

48. Ibid., 79.

49. Ibid.

50. Ibid., 72.

51. Acts 2:19, *The Holy Bible*, King James Version.

52. Davis, 102 [second marriage and bigamy], 105 [stolen gun] and 106 [dropout].

53. Ibid., 145.

54. Altschuler, 164.

55. Gillett, 26.

56. Rick Coleman. *Blue Monday: Fats Domino and the Lost Dawn of Rock 'n' Roll*. Boston: Da Capo Press, 2006. 26–28.

57. "Fats Domino Biography." Rock and Roll Hall of Fame. http://rockhall.com/inductees/fats-domino/bio/.

58. "Fats Domino Discography." Allmusic.com. Accessed September 7, 2015. http://www.allmusic.com/artist/fats-domino-mn0000137494/awards.

59. Unterberger, "Fats Domino."

60. "Inside Rock Legend Fats Domino's World: Crawfish, Cards, Boogie-Woogie." Rolling Stone. 2016. Accessed April 09, 2016. http://www.rollingstone.com/music/news/inside-rock-legend-fats-dominos-world-crawfish-cards-boogie-woogie-20160226.

61. http://www.rollingstone.com/music/artists/bo-diddley/biography#ixzz3R89w2nPY.

62. Richie Unterberger. "Bo Diddley." Allmusic.com. http://www.allmusic.com/artist/bo-diddley-mn0000055128/biography.

63. "Bo Diddley Biography." *Rolling Stone*. Accessed October 15, 2015.

64. "Bo Diddley Biography." Rock and Roll Hall of Fame. https://rockhall.com/inductees/bo-diddley/bio/.

65. Ibid.

66. Cub Koda. "Carl Perkins." Allmusic.com. Accessed October 15, 2015.

67. Carl Perkins and David McGee. *Go, Cat, Go!* New York: Hyperion Press, 1996. 8–9.

68. Ibid., 13–14.

69. Ibid., 32, 70–71.

70. "Eddie Cochran." Rolling Stone. Accessed April 09, 2016. http://www.rolling

stone.com/music/artists/eddie-cochran#ixzz3R8B04EqC.

71. Ibid.

72. See http://www.rollingstone.com/music/artists/eddie-cochran#ixzz3R8B04EqC.

73. Ibid.

74. Richie Unterberger. "Gene Vincent." Allmusic.com. Accessed October 25, 2015. http://www.allmusic.com/artist/gene-vincent-mn0000803720/biography.

75. "C'mon Everybody," words and music by Eddie Cochran and Jerry Capehart. © 1958 (renewed) Warner-Tamerlane Publishing Corp. and EMI UNART Catalog Inc. All rights outside the U.S. controlled and administered by EMI UNART Catalog Inc. (publishing) and Alfred Music (print). All rights reserved.

76. "Sex Pistols | Features." Sexpistolsofficial.com. Retrieved 15 February 2010.

77. Legs McNeil and Gillian McCain. *Please Kill Me: The Uncensored Oral History of Punk*. New York: Penguin Books, 1997. 232.

78. Richie Unterberger. "The Everly Brothers." Allmusic.com. http://www.allmusic.com/artist/the-everly-brothers-mn0000046699/biography.

79. Patrick Doyle. "The Everly Brothers: 12 Essential Tracks." *Rolling Stone*. http://www.rollingstone.com/music/pictures/the-everly-brothers-12-essential-tracks-20140104.

80. Cub Koda, Biography, http://www.allmusic.com/artist/link-wray-mn0000240311/biography.

81. Vladimir Bogdanov, Chris Woodstra, and Stephen Thomas Erlewine. *All Music Guide to the Blues: The Definitive Guide to the Blues*. San Francisco: Backbeat Books, 2003. 226.

82. Komara, 415.

83. Ibid.

84. http://www.npr.org/sections/monkeysee/2011/01/27/133253953/censors-and-sensibility-rip-comics-code-authority-seal-1954–2011.

85. Jeremy Simmonds. *Encyclopedia of Dead Rock Stars: Heroin, Handguns, and Ham Sandwiches*. Rev. ed. Chicago: Chicago Review Press, 2008. 427–28.

86. Phillip Norman. *Rave On: The Biography of Buddy Holly*. New York: Simon & Schuster, 1996. 60.

87. Ibid., 138.

88. Bruce Eder. "Buddy Holly." Allmusic.com. Accessed September 20, 2015. http://www.allmusic.com/artist/buddy-holly-mn0000538677/biography.

89. Norman, 240 and 264.

90. Janet Brown. *Ray Charles*. New York: Chelsea House, 2008. 7.

91. Ibid., 71.

92. "Ray Charles Biography." Biography.com. Accessed September 22, 2015. http://www.biography.com/people/ray-charles-9245001.

93. "Ray Charles Biography." Rock and Roll Hall of Fame. http://rockhall.com/inductees/ray-charles/bio/.

94. Richie Unterberger. "Ray Charles." Allmusic.com. Accessed September 20, 2015. http://www.allmusic.com/artist/ray-charles-mn0000046861.

95. August 8, 1994, *Cincinnati Enquirer*, 27.

96. Bill Dahl. "Ray Charles: What'd I Say." Allmusic.com. Accessed September 20, 2015. http://www.allmusic.com/song/whatd-i-say-mt0040698692.

97. The Beatles. *The Beatles Anthology*. San Francisco: Chronicle Books, 2000. 49.

98. "Ray Charles Biography," Biography.com.

99. Richie Unterberger. 'Ray Charles.' Allmusic.com. Accessed September 20, 2015. http://www.allmusic.com/artist/ray-charles-mn0000046861/biography.

100. "James Brown Biography." Biography.com. http://www.biography.com/people/james-brown-9228350.

101. Ibid.

102. Don Rhodes. *Say It Loud! The Life of James Brown, Soul Brother No. 1*. Guilford, Conn.: Lyons Press, 2014. 25.

103. "James Brown Biography." Rock and Roll Hall of Fame. Accessed September 20, 2015. https://rockhall.com/inductees/james-brown/bio/.

104. "James Brown Biography," Biography.com.

105. "James Brown Biography," Rock and Roll Hall of Fame.

106. "James Brown Biography," Biography.com.

107. "James Brown Biography," Rock and Roll Hall of Fame.

Chapter 13

1. Pattison, 187.
2. Bertrand, 163.
3. Altschuler, 6.
4. Ibid.
5. Kevin J.H. Dettmar. *Is Rock Dead?* New York: Routledge, 2006. 67.
6. Todd Leopold. "The 50-Year-Old Song That Started It All." CNN. July 8, 2005. Accessed October 16, 2015.
7. Bertrand, 51.
8. Altschuler, 34.
9. Ibid., 101, fn5, and 103.
10. David Hajdu. *The Ten-Cent Plague: The Great Comic-Book Scare and How It Changed America*. New York: Farrar, Straus and Giroux, 2008. 128, 148.
11. Dettmar, 47.
12. Altschuler, 75–76.
13. Ibid., 109.
14. Bertrand, 51.
15. Ward and Stokes, 130.
16. Bertrand, 16.
17. Dettmar, 49.
18. Altschuler, 170.
19. Dr. Martin Luther King Jr. "Advice for Living." *Ebony* 104. April 1958. Retrieved on February 19, 2012. http://mlk-kpp01.stanford.edu/primarydocuments/Vol4/Apr-1958_AdviceForLiving.pdf.
20. Bertrand, 133, quoting Dwight Macdonald's "A Theory of Mass Culture." In *Mass Culture: The Popular Arts in America*, edited by Bernard Rosenberg and David Manning White. Glencoe, Ill.: Free Press, 1957.
21. Tocqueville, 182.
22. Altschuler, 5.
23. Ward and Stokes, 131.
24. Altschuler, 70.
25. Alexandra Nikolchev. "A Brief History of the Birth Control Pill." PBS. May 7, 2010. Accessed October 16, 2015.
26. Altschuler, 67–68.
27. Ibid., 69.
28. Ibid., 75–76.
29. John J. O'Connor. "Television Review: Rock's Story as Told by Rockers." *New York Times*. March 8, 1995. C20.
30. Richard Harrington. "'A Wopbopaloobop'; and 'Alopbamboom', as Little Richard Himself Would Be (and Was) First to Admit." *Washington Post*. November 12, 1984. C1.
31. Altschuler, 176–77.
32. Ibid., 77.
33. Ibid., 131, fn1.
34. Bruce Weber. "TV Emperor of Rock 'n' Roll and New Year's Eve Dies at 82." *New York Times*. April 18, 2012. Accessed October 16, 2015.
35. James Sullivan. "The Legacy of Dick Clark, 'The Fastest Follower in the Business.'" *Rolling Stone*. April 18, 2012. Accessed October 16, 2015.
36. Weber, "TV Emperor of Rock 'n' Roll and New Year's Eve Dies at 82."
37. Sullivan, "The Legacy of Dick Clark.'"
38. Ibid.
39. Altschuler, 136.
40. Ibid., 135–36.
41. Katie Venanzi. "An Examination of Television Quiz Show Scandals of the 1950s." 1997. Accessed October 17, 2015. http://www.plosin.com/BeatBegins/projects/venanzi.html.
42. Mitchell K. Hall. *The Emergence of Rock and Roll: Music and the Rise of American Youth Culture*. New York: Routledge, 2014. 31.
43. Altschuler, 31.
44. Kerry Segrave. *Payola in the Music Industry: A History, 1880–1991*. Jefferson, N.C.: McFarland, 2013. 21.
45. Linda Martin and Kerry Segrave. *Anti-rock: The Opposition to Rock 'n' Roll*. Boston: Da Capo, 1993. 85–86.
46. Ibid., 99.
47. Jason Ankeny. "Pat Boone." Allmusic.com. http://www.allmusic.com/artist/pat-boone-mn0000131681/biography.
48. Pat Boone. *'Twixt Twelve and Twenty*. Englewood Cliffs, N.J.: Prentice-Hall, 1958.
49. Altschuler, 114.
50. Jeremy Arnold. "April Love." Turner Classic Movies. Accessed November 14, 2015. http://www.tcm.com/this-month/article.html?isPreview=&id=628646|637799&name=April-Love.
51. Coleman.
52. Deena Weinstein. *Rock'n America: A Social and Cultural History*. Toronto: University of Toronto Press, 2015. 68.

53. Elizabeth Barfoot Christian. *Rock Brands: Selling Sound in a Media Saturated Culture*. Lanham, Md.: Lexington Books, 2010. 306

54. "1959: Buddy Holly Killed in Air Crash." BBC. February 3, 1959. Retrieved November 2, 2008. http://news.bbc.co.uk/onthisday/hi/dates/stories/february/3/newsid_2802000/2802541.stm.

55. "Rock and Roll May Be the Great Unifying Force!" *Cash Box*. March 17, 1956; Altschuler, 34.

56. Weinstein, 87.

Conclusion

1. David Fricke. Liner notes to *Peel Slowly and See*. Velvet Underground, Polydor, Label number, CD. 1995.

2. Richard Delgado. *Critical White Studies: Looking Behind the Mirror*. Philadelphia: Temple University Press, 1997. 273.

3. Steve Huey. "Vernon Reid." Allmusic.com. Accessed October 21, 2015. http://www.allmusic.com/artist/vernon-reid-mn0000268762/biography.

4. Luke Dick. *The Rolling Stones and Philosophy: It's Just a Thought Away*. Chicago: Open Court, 2011. 252.

5. Kevin Chong. *Neil Young Nation: A Quest, an Obsession, and a True Story*. Vancouver, B.C.: Greystone Books, 2005. 128–32.

6. "Rick James." BET.com. Accessed September 19, 2015. http://www.bet.com/topics/r/rick-james.html.

7. Ben Sisario. "Rick James, Rebel Rocker of 'Punk-Funk,' Is Dead at 56." *New York Times*. August 6, 2004. Accessed September 19, 2015. http://www.nytimes.com/2004/08/07/arts/rick-james-rebel-rocker-of-punk-funk-is-dead-at-56.html.

Bibliography

Books/Articles

Alcoholics Anonymous: The Story of How Many Thousands of Men and Women Have Recovered from Alcoholism. 3rd ed. New York: Alcoholics Anonymous World Services, 1976.

Altschuler, Glenn C. *All Shook Up: How Rock 'n' Roll Changed America*. Oxford: Oxford University Press, 2003.

Anderson, Allan. *An Introduction to Pentecostalism: Global Charismatic Christianity*. Cambridge: Cambridge University Press, 2004.

Appleby, R. Scott. *Catholics in the American Century: Recasting Narratives of U.S. History*. Ithaca, N.Y.: Cornell University Press, 2012.

Ashby, LeRoy. *With Amusement for All: A History of American Popular Culture since 1830*. Lexington: University Press of Kentucky, 2006.

Auden, W.H. *The Age of Anxiety: A Baroque Eclogue*. New York: Random House, 1947.

Ballantyne, Andrew. "The Nest and the Pillar of Fire." In *What Is Architecture?* London: Routledge, 2002.

Bane, Michael. "Excerpt from *The Outlaws: Revolution in Country Music* (1978)." In *The Hank Williams Reader*, edited by Patrick Huber, Steve Goodson, and David Anderson. New York: Oxford University Press, 2014.

Baraka, Amiri. *Blues People: Negro Music in White America*. New York: W. Morrow, 1963.

Barlow, William. "Looking Up at Down." In *Looking Up at Down: The Emergence of Blues Culture*. Philadelphia: Temple University Press, 1989.

Barrett, William. *Irrational Man: A Study in Existential Philosophy*. New York: Doubleday, 1958.

Battersby, Paul, and Joseph M. Siracusa. *Globalization and Human Security*. Lanham, Md.: Rowman & Littlefield, 2009.

The Beatles. *The Beatles Anthology*. San Francisco: Chronicle Books, 2000.

Beaumont, Daniel E. *Preachin' the Blues: The Life and Times of Son House*. New York: Oxford University Press, 2011.

Beck, E.M., and S.E. Tolnay. "The Killing Fields of the Deep South: The Market for Cotton and the Lynching of Blacks, 1882–1930." *American Sociological Review* (1990).

Berry, Chad. *The Hayloft Gang: The Story of the National Barn Dance*. Urbana: University of Illinois Press, 2008.

Bertrand, Michael T. *Race, Rock, and Elvis*. Urbana: University of Illinois Press, 2000.

Billias, George Athan. *American Constitutionalism Heard Round the World, 1776–1989: A Global Perspective*. New York: New York University Press, 2009.

Bjornsgaard, Kirk. *The Encyclopedia of Christian Literature*. Edited by George Thomas Kurian and James D. Smith III. Lanham, Md.: Scarecrow Press, 2010.

Bogdanov, Vladimir, Chris Woodstra, and Stephen Thomas Erlewine. *All Music Guide to the Blues: The Definitive Guide to the Blues*. San Francisco: Backbeat Books, 2003.

Bonomo, Joe. *Jerry Lee Lewis: Lost and Found*. New York: Continuum, 2009.

Boone, Pat. *'Twixt Twelve and Twenty*. Englewood Cliffs, N.J.: Prentice-Hall, 1958.

Brown, Janet. *Ray Charles*. New York: Chelsea House, 2008.

Brown, Scott. "Elvis Presley: It's a Hound Dig." *Entertainment Weekly*. October 6, 2000.

Brown, Sterling A. "Negro Folk Expression: Spirituals, Seculars, Ballads and Work Songs." Modern American Poetry, Department of English, University of Illinois.

Calder, Iain. *The Untold Story: My 20 Years Running the National Enquirer*. New York: Hyperion, 2004.

Campbell, Michael. *Popular Music in America: The Beat Goes On*. 2nd ed. Belmont, Calif.: Wadsworth/Thomson Learning, 2005.

Cantor, Louis. *Dewey and Elvis: The Life and Times of a Rock 'n' Roll Deejay*. Urbana: University of Illinois Press, 2005.

Cartwright, Samuel A. "Diseases and Peculiarities of the Negro Race." In *The Cause of the South: Selections from De Bow's Review, 1846–1867*, edited by Paul F. Paskoff, 26–43. Baton Rouge: Louisiana State University Press, 1982.

Cheseborough, Steve. *Blues Traveling: The Holy Sites of Delta Blues*. 3rd ed. Jackson: University Press of Mississippi, 2009.

Chong, Kevin. *Neil Young Nation: A Quest, an Obsession, and a True Story*. Vancouver, B.C.: Greystone Books, 2005.

Christian, Elizabeth Barfoot. *Rock Brands: Selling Sound in a Media Saturated Culture*. Lanham, Md.: Lexington Books, 2010.

Coates, Dan. *Rolling Stone Sheet Music Classics*. Volume 1: *1950s–1960s*. Van Nuys, Calif.: Alfred Pub., 2008.

Cobb, James C. *The Most Southern Place on Earth: The Mississippi Delta and the Roots of Regional Identity*. New York: Oxford University Press, 1992.

Cohen, Norm, and David Cohen. *Long Steel Rail: The Railroad in American Folksong*. 2nd ed. Urbana: University of Illinois Press, 2000.

Cohn, David L. *Where I Was Born and Raised*. Notre Dame: University of Notre Dame Press, 1967.

Cohodas, Nadine. *Spinning Blues Into Gold: The Chess Brothers and the Legendary Chess Records*. New York: St. Martin's Press, 2000.

Colburn, David R. "Rosewood and America in the Early Twentieth Century." *Florida Historical Quarterly* 76, no. 2 (Fall 1997): 175–92.

Coleman, Rick. *Blue Monday: Fats Domino and the Lost Dawn of Rock 'n' Roll*. Boston: Da Capo Press, 2006.

Collins, Ace. *Untold Gold: The Stories Behind Elvis's #1 Hits*. Chicago: Chicago Review Press, 2005.

Collis, John. *Chuck Berry: The Biography*. London: Aurum, 2002.

Cone, James H. *The Spirituals and the Blues: An Interpretation*. New York: Seabury Press, 1972.

Conrad, Peter, and Joseph W. Schneider. *Deviance and Medicalization: From Badness to Sickness*. St. Louis: Mosby, 1980.

Cox, Harvey. *Fire from Heaven: The Rise of Pentecostal Spirituality and the Reshaping of Religion in the 21st Century*. Cambridge, Mass.: Da Capo Press, 2009.

Davis, Francis. *The History of the Blues*. New York: Hyperion, 1995.

Davis, J.D. *Unconquered: The Saga of Cousins Jerry Lee Lewis, Jimmy Swaggart, and Mickey Gilley*. Dallas, Tex.: Brown Books, 2012.

Dawson, Jim, and Steve Propes. *What Was the First Rock and Roll Record?* Boston: Faber & and Faber, 1992.

Deburg, William L. *Slavery & Race in American Popular Culture*. Madison: University of Wisconsin Press, 1984.

DeCurtis, Anthony. *The Rolling Stone Illustrated History of Rock & Roll: The Definitive History of the Most Important Artists and Their Music*. 3rd ed. New York: Random House, 1992.

Delgado, Richard. *Critical White Studies: Looking Behind the Mirror*. Philadelphia: Temple University Press, 1997.

Delmont, Matthew F. *The Nicest Kids in Town: American Bandstand, Rock 'n' Roll, and the Struggle for Civil Rights in 1950s Philadelphia*. Berkeley: University of California Press, 2012.

Dettmar, Kevin J. H. *Is Rock Dead?* New York: Routledge, 2006.

Dickerson, James. *Goin' Back to Memphis: A Century of Blues, Rock 'n' Roll, and Glorious Soul*. New York: Schirmer Books, 1996.

Doss, Erika. *Elvis Culture: Fans, Faith, & Image*. Lawrence: University Press of Kansas, 1999.

Douglas, Tony. *Jackie Wilson: Lonely Teardrops*. New York: Routledge, 2005.

Dick, Luke. *The Rolling Stones and Philosophy: It's Just a Thought Away*. Chicago: Open Court, 2011.

Dowdy, G. Wayne. *A Brief History of Memphis*. Charleston, S.C.: History Press, 2011.

Drake, Richard B. *A History of Appalachia*. Lexington: University Press of Kentucky, 2001.

Du Bois, W. E. B. "Of Mr. Booker T. Washington and Others." In *The Souls of Black Folk*. Charlottesville: University of Virginia Library, 1996.

Dundy, Elaine. *Elvis and Gladys*. New York: Macmillan, 1985.

Dylan, Bob. "Excerpt from *Chronicles, Volume One* (2004)." In *The Hank Williams Reader*, edited by Patrick Huber, Steve Goodson, and David Anderson. New York: Oxford University Press, 2014.

Ellison, Ralph. *Shadow and Act*. New York: Random House, 1964.

Escott, Colin, and Martin Hawkins. *Good Rockin' Tonight: Sun Records and the Birth of Rock 'n' Roll*. New York: St. Martin's Press, 1991.

Escott, Colin, and George Merritt. *Hank Williams: The Biography*. Boston: Little, Brown, 1994.

Faulkner, Anne Shaw. "Does Jazz Put the Sin in Syncopation?" *Ladies Home Journal* 38, no. 8 (August 1921).

Faupel, David W. *Everlasting Gospel: The Significance of Eschatology in the Development of Pentecostal Thought*. Sheffield, U.K.: Sheffield Academic Press, 1996.

Ferris, Jean. *America's Musical Landscape*. 4th ed. Boston: McGraw-Hill, 2002.

Flynt, Wayne. *Poor But Proud: Alabama's Poor Whites*. Tuscaloosa: University of Alabama Press, 1989.

Franklin, John Hope. *From Slavery to Freedom: A History of Negro Americans*. 3rd ed. New York: Knopf, 1967.

______, and Alfred A. Moss. *From Slavery to Freedom: A History of African Americans*. 7th ed. New York: McGraw-Hill, 1994.

Ford, Henry, Sr. *The International Jew: Being an Abridged Version of a Series of Articles*. Johannesburg: Global Publishers, 1997.

Fredrickson, George M., and Christopher Lasch. "Resistance to Slavery." *Civil War History* 13, no. 4 (1967): 315–29.

Freye, E. *Pharmacology and Abuse of Cocaine, Amphetamines, Ecstasy and Related Designer Drugs: A Comprehensive Review on Their Mode of Action, Treatment of Abuse and Intoxication*. Dordrecht: Springer, 2009.

Fricke, David. Liner notes to *Peel Slowly and See*. Velvet Underground, Polydor, Label number, CD. 1995.

Fuchs, Otto. *Bill Haley: The Father of Rock & Roll*. Gelnhausen, Germany: Wagner, 2011.

Garber, Benjamin D. "Parental Alienation and the Dynamics of the Enmeshed Parent-Child Dyad: Adultification, Parentification, and Infantilization." *Family Court Review* 49, issue 2 (April 2011): 322–35.

Garofalo, Reebee. *Rockin' Out: Popular Music in the USA*. Boston: Allyn and Bacon, 1997.

George, John R. "Imagining Tee-Tot: Blues, Race, and the Legend of Hank Williams." In *The Hank Williams Reader*, edited by Patrick Huber, Steve Goodson, and David Anderson. New York: Oxford University Press, 2014.

Gillett, Charlie. *The Sound of the City: The Rise of Rock and Roll*. New York: Outerbridge & Dienstfrey, 1970.

Gioia, Ted. *Delta Blues: The Life and Times of the Mississippi Masters Who Revolutionized American Music*. New York: W.W. Norton, 2008.

Gitlin, Todd. *The Sixties: Years of Hope, Days of Rage*. Toronto: Bantam Books, 1987.

Goldman, Eric Frederick. *The Crucial Decade: America, 1945–1955*. New York: Knopf, 1956.

Gordon, Robert. *Can't Be Satisfied: The Life and Times of Muddy Waters*. Boston: Little, Brown, 2002.

______. *It Came From Memphis*. Boston: Faber and Faber, 1994.

Greco Larson, Stephanie. *Media & Minorities: The Politics of Race in News and Entertainment*. Lanham, Md.: Rowman & Littlefield, 2006.

Green, Michael S., and Scott L. Stabler. *Ideas and Movements That Shaped America:*

From the Bill of Rights to "Occupy Wall Street." 3 vols. Santa Barbara, Calif.: ABC-CLIO, 2015.

Guralnick, Peter. *Careless Love: The Unmaking of Elvis Presley*. Boston: Little, Brown, 1999.

_____. *Last Train to Memphis: The Rise of Elvis Presley*. Boston: Little, Brown, 1994.

_____. *Lost Highway: Journeys & Arrivals of American Musicians*. New York: Little, Brown, 2012.

_____, and Ernst Jorgensen. *Elvis Day by Day*. New York: Ballantine Books, 1999.

Hajdu, David. *The Ten-Cent Plague: The Great Comic-Book Scare and How It Changed America*. New York: Farrar, Straus and Giroux, 2008.

Halberstam, David. *The Fifties*. Reprint ed. New York: Ballantine Books, 1994.

_____. "Hank Williams Remembered (1971)." In *The Hank Williams Reader*, edited by Patrick Huber, Steve Goodson, and David Anderson. New York: Oxford University Press, 2014.

Hall, Mitchell K. *The Emergence of Rock and Roll: Music and the Rise of American Youth Culture*. New York: Routledge, 2014.

Hall, Perry A. "African-American Music: Dynamics of Appropriation and Innovation." In *Borrowed Power: Essays on Cultural Appropriation*, edited by Bruce H. Ziff. New Brunswick, N.J.: Rutgers University Press, 1997.

Handy, W. C., and Arna Wendell Bontemps. *Father of the Blues: An Autobiography*. New York: Collier Books, 1941.

Harkins, Anthony. *Hillbilly: A Cultural History of an American Icon*. New York: Oxford University Press, 2004.

Hennessey, Thomas J. *From Jazz to Swing: African-American Jazz Musicians and Their Music, 1890–1935*. Detroit: Wayne State University Press, 1994.

Herman, Arthur. *Joseph McCarthy: Reexamining the Life and Legacy of America's Most Hated Senator*. New York: Free Press, 2000.

Horton, James Oliver, and Lois E. Horton. *Slavery and the Making of America*. Oxford: Oxford University Press, 2005.

Jackson, John A. *Big Beat Heat: Alan Freed and the Early Years of Rock & Roll*. New York: Schirmer Books, 1991.

Jackson, Kenneth T. *Crabgrass Frontier: The Suburbanization of the United States*. New York: Oxford University Press, 1985.

Jah, Yusuf. *Fight the Power: Rap, Race, and Reality*. New York: Dell, 1997.

James, David E. *Rock 'n' Film: Cinema's Dance with Popular Music*. Oxford: Oxford University Press, 2016.

Johnson, Charles S. *Growing Up in the Black Belt*. Washington, D.C.: American Council on Education, 1941; New York: Schocken Books, 1967.

Jones, Beverly. *The Negro in Virginia*. New York: Arno Press, 1969.

Jorgensen, Ernst. *Elvis Presley: A Life in Music: The Complete Recording Sessions*. New York: St. Martin's Press, 1998.

Joyce, Jaime. *Moonshine: A Cultural History of America's Infamous Liquor*. Minneapolis: Zenith, 2014.

Keats, John. *The Crack in the Picture Window*. Boston: Houghton Mifflin, 1957.

Kelsey, Morton T. *Tongue Speaking: An Experiment in Spiritual Experience*. Garden City, N.Y.: Doubleday, 1964.

Kennedy, David M. *Over Here: The First World War and American Society*. New York: Oxford University Press, 1980.

Kennedy, Randall. *Nigger: The Strange Career of a Troublesome Word*. New York: Pantheon Books, 2002.

Keough, Pamela Clarke. *Elvis Presley: The Man, the Life, the Legend*. New York: Simon & Schuster, 2004.

Kerouac, Jack. *On the Road*. New York: Viking, 1997.

Keyes, Ralph. *The Quote Verifier: Who Said What, Where, and When*. New York: St. Martin's Press, 2006.

Kimmel, Michael S. *Manhood in America: A Cultural History*. New York: Free Press, 1996.

King, B. B., and David Ritz. *Blues All Around Me: The Autobiography of B.B. King*. New York: Avon Books, 1996.

Kirby, David. *Little Richard: The Birth of Rock 'n' Roll*. New York: Continuum International Publishing Group, 2009.

Komara, Edward M. *Encyclopedia of the Blues*. New York: Routledge, 2006.

Kubernick, Harvey. *The Complete '68 Comeback Special*. CD Booklet RCA/BMG.

Lahr, Angela M. *Millennial Dreams and*

Apocalyptic Nightmares: The Cold War Origins of Political Evangelicalism. New York: Oxford University Press, 2007.

Larson, Stephanie Greco. *Media & Minorities: The Politics of Race in News and Entertainment*. Lanham, Md.: Rowman & Littlefield, 2006.

Lauterbach, Preston. *The Chitlin' Circuit: And the Road to Rock 'n' Roll*. New York: W. W. Norton, 2011.

Leiber, Jerry, and Mike Stoller, with David Ritz. *Hound Dog: The Leiber and Stoller Autobiography*. New York: Simon & Schuster, 2009.

Lester, Julius, and Tom Feelings. *To Be a Slave*. New York: Dial Press, 1968.

Leuchtenburg, William E. *A Troubled Feast: American Society since 1945*. Boston: Little, Brown, 1973.

Levine, Lawrence W. *The Unpredictable Past: Explorations in American Cultural History*. New York: Oxford University Press, 1993.

Lomax, Alan. *The Land Where the Blues Began*. New York: Pantheon Books, 1993.

Malarek, Victor. *The Johns: Sex for Sale and the Men Who Buy It*. New York: Arcade, 2009.

Malone, Bill C. *Country Music U.S.A.: A Fifty-Year History*. Austin: Published for the American Folklore Society by the University of Texas Press, 1968.

Manis, Andrew Michael. *A Fire You Can't Put Out: The Civil Rights Life of Birmingham's Reverend Fred Shuttlesworth*. Tuscaloosa: University of Alabama Press, 1999.

Marcus, Greil. *Dead Elvis: A Chronicle of a Cultural Obsession*. New York: Doubleday, 1991.

_____. *Mystery Train: Images of America in Rock 'n' Roll Music*. New York: E.P. Dutton, 1975.

Marsh, Dave. *Louie Louie: The History and Mythology of the World's Most Famous Rock 'n' Roll Song*. Ann Arbor: University of Michigan Press, 2004.

Martin, Linda, and Kerry Segrave. *Anti-rock: The Opposition to Rock 'n' Roll*. Boston: Da Capo, 1993.

McFedries, Paul. *Word Spy: The Word Lover's Guide to Modern Culture*. New York: Broadway Books, 2004.

McGee, David. *B.B. King: There Is Always One More Time*. San Francisco: Backbeat Books, 2005.

McKee, Margaret, and Fred Chisenhall. *Beale Black & Blue: Life and Music on Black America's Main Street*. Baton Rouge: Louisiana State University Press, 1981.

McKenna, Michael. *Real People and the Rise of Reality Television*. Lanham, Md.: Rowman & Littlefield, 2015.

McMillen, Neil R. *Dark Journey: Black Mississippians in the Age of Jim Crow*. Urbana: University of Illinois Press, 1989.

McNeil, Legs, and Gillian McCain. *Please Kill Me: The Uncensored Oral History of Punk*. New York: Penguin Books, 1997.

Morton, David C., and Charles K. Wolfe. *DeFord Bailey: A Black Star in Early Country Music*. Knoxville: University of Tennessee Press, 1991.

Myrdal, Gunnar. *An American Dilemma: The Negro Problem and Modern Democracy*. 20th anniversary ed. New York: Harper & Row, 1962.

Nager, Larry. *Memphis Beat: The Lives and Times of America's Musical Crossroads*. New York: St. Martin's Press, 1998.

Naylor, Jerry, and Steve Halliday. *The Rockabilly Legends: They Called It Rockabilly Long Before They Called It Rock and Roll*. Milwaukee, Wis.: Hal Leonard, 2007.

Norman, Philip. *Rave On: The Biography of Buddy Holly*. New York: Simon & Schuster, 1996.

Oakley, Giles. *The Devil's Music: A History of the Blues*. New York: Taplinger, 1977.

Oliphant, Dave. *Texan Jazz*. Austin: University of Texas Press, 1996.

Oshinsky, David M. *Worse than Slavery: Parchman Farm and the Ordeal of Jim Crow Justice*. New York: Free Press, 1997.

Palmer, Robert. *Deep Blues*. New York: Viking Press, 1981.

_____. *Rock & Roll: An Unruly History*. New York: Harmony Books, 1995.

Paris, Peter J. *The Spirituality of African Peoples: The Search for a Common Moral Discourse*. Minneapolis: Fortress Press, 1995.

Patterson, James T. *Grand Expectations: The United States, 1945–1974*. New York: Oxford University Press, 1996.

Pattison, Robert. *The Triumph of Vulgarity:*

Rock Music in the Mirror of Romanticism. New York: Oxford University Press, 1987.

Peale, Norman Vincent. *The Power of Positive Thinking*. New York: Prentice-Hall, 1952.

Pearl, Minnie (with Joan Dew). "Excerpt from *Minnie Pearl: An Autobiography* (1980)." In *The Hank Williams Reader*, edited by Patrick Huber, Steve Goodson, and David Anderson. New York: Oxford University Press, 2014.

Pearson, Barry Lee, and Bill McCulloch. *Robert Johnson: Lost and Found*. Urbana: University of Illinois Press, 2003.

Pegg, Bruce. *Brown Eyed Handsome Man: The Life and Hard Times of Chuck Berry: An Unauthorized Biography*. New York: Routledge, 2002.

Pendergast, Sara, and Tom Pendergast. *St. James Encyclopedia of Popular Culture*. 4th ed. Detroit: St. James Press, 2000.

Percy, William Alexander, and Carl H. Pforzheimer. *Lanterns on the Levee: Recollections of a Planter's Son*. New York: Knopf, 1941.

Perkins, Carl, and David McGee. *Go, Cat, Go!* New York: Hyperion Press, 1996.

Petersen, Holger. *Talking Music Blues Radio and Roots Music*. London: Insomniac Press, 2014.

Phillips, Dewey. *Red Hot & Blue (Live Radio Broadcasts from 1952–1964)*. Memphis, Tenn.: Memphis Archives, 1995.

Phillips, John Neal. *Running with Bonnie and Clyde: The Ten Fast Years of Ralph Fults*. Norman: University of Oklahoma, 1996.

Phillips, Ulrich Bonnell. *American Negro Slavery: A Survey of the Supply, Employment and Control of Negro Labor as Determined by the Plantation Regime*. Baton Rouge: Louisiana State University Press, 1966.

_____. *Life and Labor in the Old South*. Boston: Little, Brown, 1929.

Rhodes, Don. *Say It Loud! The Life of James Brown, Soul Brother No. 1*. Guilford, Conn.: Lyons Press, 2014.

Riesman, David, and Nathan Glazer. *The Lonely Crowd: A Study of the Changing American Character*. Abridged and rev. ed. New Haven, Conn.: Yale University Press, 2001.

"Rock and Roll May Be the Great Unifying Force!" *Cash Box*. March 17, 1956.

Sagolla, Lisa Jo. *Rock 'n' Roll Dances of the 1950s*. Santa Barbara, Calif.: Greenwood, 2011.

Salinger, J. D. *The Catcher in the Rye*. New York: Little, Brown, 2001.

Stark, Steven D. *Glued to the Set: The 60 Television Shows and Events That Made Us Who We Are Today*. New York: Free Press, 1997.

Segrave, Kerry. *Payola in the Music Industry: A History, 1880–1991*. Jefferson, N.C.: McFarland, 2013.

Sharp, Anne Wallace. *A Dream Deferred: The Jim Crow Era*. Detroit: Lucent Books, 2005.

Simmonds, Jeremy. *Encyclopedia of Dead Rock Stars: Heroin, Handguns, and Ham Sandwiches*. Rev. ed. Chicago: Chicago Review Press, 2008.

Sollors, Werner. *Interracialism: Black-White Intermarriage in American History, Literature, and Law*. Oxford: Oxford University Press, 2000.

Sondhaus, Lawrence. *World War I: The Global Revolution*. Cambridge: Cambridge University Press, 2011.

Springer, Denize. "'Ahhhh-HA!' Discovering Bob Wills." *SF State News* (San Francisco State University). February 23, 2005.

Squier, Susan Merrill. *Communities of the Air: Radio Century, Radio Culture*. Durham, N.C.: Duke University Press, 2003.

Stampp, Kenneth M. *The Peculiar Institution: Slavery in the Ante-bellum South*. New York: Knopf, 1956.

Thurman, Howard. *Deep River and the Negro Spiritual Speaks of Life and Death*. Richmond, Ind.: Friends United Press, 1975.

Tichi, Cecelia. *High Lonesome: The American Culture of Country Music*. Chapel Hill: University of North Carolina Press, 1994.

Tidd, Lisa. *The Greenwood Encyclopedia of Rock History*. Volume I: *The Early Years, 1951–1959*. Westport, Conn.: Greenwood Press, 2006.

Tocqueville, Alexis de, and Harvey Claflin Mansfield. *Democracy in America*. Chicago: University of Chicago Press, 2000.

Tolstoy, Leo. *The Kingdom of God Is Within You. What Is Art? What Is Religion?* New York: T.Y. Crowell, 1899.

Townsend, Charles R. *San Antonio Rose: The Life and Music of Bob Wills*. Urbana: University of Illinois Press, 1976.

Virginia Writer's Program. *The Negro in Virginia*. New York: Arno Press, 1969.

Voorst, Robert E. "Ritual." In *Anthology of World Scriptures*. 6th ed. Australia: Thomson Wadsworth, 2008.

Wacker, Grant. *Heaven Below: Early Pentecostals and American Culture*. Cambridge, Mass.: Harvard University Press, 2003.

Wald, Elijah. *Escaping the Delta: Robert Johnson and the Invention of the Blues*. New York: Amistad, 2004.

Wald, Gayle. *Shout, Sister, Shout! The Untold Story of Rock-and-Roll Trailblazer Sister Rosetta Tharpe*. Boston: Beacon Press, 2007.

Walton, Jonathan L. *Watch This! The Ethics and Aesthetics of Black Televangelism*. New York: New York University Press, 2009.

Ward, Ed, and Geoffrey Stokes. *Rock of Ages: The Rolling Stone History of Rock & Roll*. New York: Rolling Stone Press, 1986.

Warren, Kenneth F. *Encyclopedia of U.S. Campaigns, Elections, and Electoral Behavior*. Los Angeles: Sage, 2008.

Watts, Steven. *Mr. Playboy: Hugh Hefner and the American Dream*. Hoboken, N.J.: Wiley, 2008.

Weiner, Howard T., and N.J. Newark. *Early Twentieth-Century Brass Idioms: Art, Jazz, and Other Popular Traditions*. Lanham, Md.: Scarecrow Press, 2009.

Weinstein, Deena. *Rock'n America: A Social and Cultural History*. Toronto: University of Toronto Press, 2015.

Wellmann, Molly. *Handcrafted Cocktails: The Mixologist's Guide to Classic Drinks for Morning, Noon & Night*. Cincinnati: F+W Media, 2013.

West, Cornel. "Horace Pippin's Challenge to Art Criticism." In *Race-ing Art History: Critical Readings in Race and Art History*, edited by Kymberly N. Pinder. New York: Routledge, 2002.

Whalin, Terry. *Billy Graham: A Biography of America's Greatest Evangelist*. New York: Morgan James, 2015.

Wharton, Vernon Lane. *The Negro in Mississippi: 1865–1890*. New York: Harper & Row, 1965.

Whitburn, Joel. *Top R&B/Hip Hop Singles: 1942–2004*. Menomonee Falls, WI: Record Research, 2004.

White, Charles. *The Life and Times of Little Richard: The Authorised Biography*. 3rd ed. London: Omnibus Press, 2003.

White, Forrest. *Fender: The Inside Story*. San Francisco: GPI Books, 1994.

Whitfield, Stephen J. *A Death in the Delta: The Story of Emmett Till*. New York: Free Press, 1988.

Whyte, William Hollingsworth. *The Organization Man*. New York: Simon & Schuster, 1956.

Wilder, Laura Ingalls. *Little House on the Prairie*. New York: Harper Trophy, 2007.

Williams, Bill. "A Crucial Decision for the World of Music." *Billboard*. February 3, 1968.

Williams, John Alexander. *Appalachia: A History*. Chapel Hill: University of North Carolina Press, 2002.

Wilson, Sloan. *The Man in the Grey Flannel Suit*. New York: Simon & Schuster, 1955.

Wood, Gregory. "Kansas Exodusters." In *Race and Racism in the United States: An Encyclopedia of the American Mosaic*, edited by Charles A. Gallagher and Cameron D. Lippard. Santa Barbara, Calif.: Greenwood, 2014.

Woodward, C. Vann. *The Strange Career of Jim Crow*. 3rd rev. ed. New York: Oxford University Press, 1974.

Wormser, Richard. *The Rise & Fall of Jim Crow: The African-American Struggle against Discrimination, 1865–1954*. New York: Franklin Watts, 1999.

Worth, Fred L., and Steve D. Tamerius. *Elvis: His Life from A to Z*. Chicago: Contemporary Books, 1988.

Wright, John, ed. *The New York Times 2002 Almanac*. New York: Penguin Putnam, 2001.

Wright, Richard. *Black Boy: A Record of Childhood and Youth*. New York: Harper & Bros., 1945.

Zwonitzer, Mark, and Charles Hirshberg. *Will You Miss Me When I'm Gone? The Carter Family and Their Legacy in American Music*. New York: Simon & Schuster, 2002.

Websites

Africana Age, http://exhibitions.nypl.org/africanaage/index2.html
Allmusic.com, www.allmusic.com
American Presidency Project, http://www.presidency.ucsb.edu
Archive.is, https://archive.is/2ulWV
The Atlantic, http://www.theatlantic.com
Bartleby, http://www.bartleby.com
Beale Street, http://www.bealestreet.com/history.html
BET.com, http://www.bet.com
Biography.com, http://www.biography.com
Bob Margolin, http://bobmargolin.com
Boutique Junction, https://www.boutiquejunction.com
British Broadcasting Corporation (BBC), http://www.bbc.co.uk
Cable News Network (CNN), https://cnn.com
CBS News, http://www.cbsnews.com
Chicago Tribune, http://www.chicagotribune.com
Church of God in Christ, http://www.cogic.org
CMT Artists, http://www.cmt.com/music
Confederate Railroads, http://www.csa-railroads.com
Crawdad Archive, https://archive.is/2ulWV
The Daily Beast, http://thedailybeast.com
Daily Mail, http://www.dailymail.co.uk
Encyclopedia Britannica Online, http://www.britannica.com
Encyclopedia of Cleveland History, http://ech.cwru.edu
Fortune Archives, http://archive.fortune.com
Graceland, http://www.graceland.com
The Guardian, http://theguardian.com
Historical Text Archive, http://historical-textarchive.com
History.com, http://www.history.com
History Matters, http://historymatters.gmu.edu
A History of Country Music, http://www.scaruffi.com
Huffington Post, http://www.huffingtonpost.com
The Independent, http://www.independent.co.uk
Jazz.com, http://www.jazz.com
Jazz and Blues Masters, http://www.jazzandbluesmasters.com
Library of Congress, http://.loc.gov
Liverpool Museums, http://www.liverpoolmuseums.org.uk
Los Angeles Times, http://latimes.com
Louisiana State University, http://www.cwc.lsu.edu
Mary J. Blige, http://www.mjblige.com
Memphis Music Hall of Fame, http://memphismusichalloffame.com
Merriam-Webster, http://www.merriam-webster.com
Metro Lyrics, http://www.metrolyrics.com
MSN Encarta, http://encarta.msn.com
National Humanities Center, http://nationalhumanitiescenter.org
National Public Radio (NPR), https://npr.org
News Net 5, http://www.newsnet5.com
New Yorker, http://www.newyorker.com
New York Post, http://pagesix.com
New York Times, http://www.nytimes.com
Official Site of the Negro Spirituals, Antique Gospel Music, http://www.negrospirituals.com
Official Woody Guthrie Website, http://www.woodyguthrie.org
Our Blues, https://ourblues.files.wordpress.com
Oxford Biblical Studies Online, http://www.oxfordbiblicalstudies.com
Parade, http://www.parade.com
Philly.com, http://philly.com
PR Newswire, http://www.prnewswire.com
PRWatch.org, http://www.prwatch.org
Public Broadcasting Service (PBS), http://www.pbs.org
Riverwalk Jazz, Stanford University Libraries, http://riverwalkjazz.stanford.edu
Rock and Roll Hall of Fame, http://www.rockhall.com
RogerEbert.com, http://www.rogerebert.com
Rolling Stone, https://rollingstone.com
Schomburg-Mellon Humanities Summer Institute, http://exhibitions.nypl.org
Seattle Post-Intelligencer, http://www.seattlepi.com
Shotgun's Home of the American Civil War, http://www.civilwarhome.com
Singer Universe, http://www.singeruniverse.com

Spin, http://www.spin.com
Squarely Rooted, http://squarelyrooted.com
Sun Records, http://www.sunrecords.com
Telegraph, http://www.telegraph.co.uk
Tennessee Encyclopedia, http://tennesseeencyclopedia.net
Texas Monthly, www.texasmonthly.com
Time, http://time.com
Tobacco BBS, http://tobacco.org
Turner Classic Movies, http://www.tcm.com
Vanity Fair, http://www.vantiyfair.com
Vice, http://www.vice.com
Wall Street Journal, http://www.wsj.com
Washington Post, http://www.washingtonpost.com
Washington Times, http://www.washingtontimes.com
WBGO, http://www.wbgo.org
Wiley [*Forbes* magazine archive], http://www.wiley.com
World Public Library, http://www.worldlibrary.org
Yale–New Haven Teachers Institute, http://www.yale.edu/ynhti

Youtube Videos

"Elvis Presley—Hound Dog (1956) HD 0815007." YouTube. Accessed October 5, 2015. https://www.youtube.com/watch?v=MMmljYkdr-w.
"Sister Rosetta Tharpe—Up Above My Head." YouTube. Accessed October 5, 2015. https://www.youtube.com/watch?v=JeaBNAXfHfQ.

Periodicals

Commercial Appeal (2013)
Historical Journal
Los Angeles Times (2005)
MOJO (2013)
Newsweek
U.S. Senate, *Congressional Record* (1900)
Weekly Compilation of Presidential Documents, Volume 29, Issue 52 (Monday, January 3, 1994)

Television and Film

Burns, Ken, dir. *Jazz: A Film by Ken Burns*. PBS Home Video, 2004. DVD.
Haefeli, Mark, dir. *Paul McCartney in Red Square*. A&E Home Video, 2003. DVD.
Jarmusch, Jim, dir. *Mystery Train*. Kinowelt Home Entertainment, 2005. DVD.
Levin, Marc, dir. *Godfathers and Sons*. Sony Music Entertainment, 2003. DVD.
Rafferty, Kevin, dir. *The Atomic Cafe*. Docurama, 2003. DVD.
Sinofsky, Bruce, dir. *Good Rockin' Tonight: The Legacy of Sun Records*. Image Entertainment, 2002. DVD.
Stevens, George, Jr., writer. "Xmas In Washington (1999)." Directed by Glenn Weiss. Turner Network Television. December 12, 1999.
Subotsky, Milton, dir. *Rock, Rock, Rock!* Passport Video, 2003. DVD.

Index

Numbers in ***bold italics*** refer to pages with photographs.